THE **FUTURE** IN THE **BALANCE**

ESSAYS ON GLOBALIZATION AND RESISTANCE

WALDEN BELLO

EDITED WITH A PREFACE
BY ANURADHA MITTAL

FOOD FIRST BOOKS
OAKLAND, CALIFORNIA

CO-PUBLISHED WITH
FOCUS ON THE GLOBAL SOUTH

TEXT AND COVER DESIGN BY COLORED HORSE STUDIOS
    TYPESET IN ADOBE GARAMOND WITH ADOBE JENSON HEADINGS,
    KINESIS AND ENGRAVER'S GOTHIC TITLING
INDEX BY KEN DELLAPENTA

Food First Books
398 60th Street
Oakland, California 94618
www.foodfirst.org

Library of Congress Cataloguing-in-Publication Data

Bello, Walden F.
    The future in the balance : essays on globalization and resistance/Walden Bello ; edited with a preface by Anuradha Mittal.
        p. cm.
    Includes bibliographical references and index.
    ISBN 0-935028-84-4
    1. International economic relations. 2. International business enterprises. 3. Globalization. 4. International trade 5. International finance. I. Mittal, Anuradha, 1967– II. Title.

HF1359 .B4325 2001
337—dc21   2002023940

Food First Books are distributed by:
    LPC Group
    1436 West Randolph Street
    Chicago, IL 60607
    (800) 243-0138
    www.coolbooks.com

10 9 8 7 6 5 4 3 2 1

ACKNOWLEDGMENTS AND DEDICATION

Discussions and debates with many colleagues, friends, and fellow activists sparked many of the ideas developed in this book. Anuradha Mittal of Food First/Institute for Food and Development Policy and Nicola Bullard of Focus on the Global South must be singled out for being such wonderful intellectual and political partners over the last few years. My greatest debt, of course, is to Marilen Abesamis, who has borne the most of the costs of the political engagements reflected in this book. To her I dedicate this book as an expression of gratitude and love, and as a token of profound apology.

WFB, Bangkok, March 15, 2001

Preface by Anuradha Mittal, co-director of Food First vii

Introduction. xi

PART I: THE BRETTON WOODS SYSTEM IN CRISIS

1. The Iron Cage: The WTO, the Bretton Woods Institutions,
   and the South 1

2. Why Reform of the WTO is the Wrong Agenda 35

3. Jurassic Fund: Should Developing Countries Push to
   Decommission the IMF? 49

4. Meltzer Report Builds the Case for Abolition of
   Bretton Woods Twins 60

PART II: SPECULATIVE CAPITAL AND THE ASIAN FINANCIAL CRISIS

5. Asian Financial Crisis: The Movie 66

6. Fast Track Capitalism, Geoeconomic Competition, and the
   Sustainable Development Challenge. 79

7. East Asia: On the Eve of the Great Transformation? 98

8. Notes on the Ascendancy and Regulation of Global Finance 123

9. Breaking with the Faith 156

10. Power, Timidity, and Irresponsibility in Global Finance. 160

PART III: THE US: GLOBALIZATION, GEOPOLITICS, AND UNILATERALISM

11. US Economic Expansion: Boon or Bane for Asia? 164

12. The Shrimp-Turtle Controversy and the
    Rise of Green Unilateralism 170

13. Dangerous Liaisons: Progressives, the Right, and the
    Anti-China Trade Campaign 177

14. Why Land Reform is No Longer Possible without Revolution 194

15. Washington and the Demise of the Third Wave of Democratization . . 203

PART IV: THE STRUGGLE FOR THE FUTURE

16. Prague 2000: Toward a De-globalized World 209

17. Global Civil Society: Promise and Pitfalls. 227

18. 2000: The Year of Global Protest Against Globalization 231

19. Washington's Political Transition Threatens Bretton Woods Twins 237

20. When Davos Meets Porto Alegre: A Memoir 243

Index. 247

PREFACE

Anuradha Mittal, co-director of Food First

On January 27, 2001, peaceful Switzerland bared its teeth. In the biggest security alert the Alpine nation had ever seen, riot police sealed off all approaches to Davos, the genteel ski resort that hosts the annual network-a-thon of CEOs, heads of state, finance ministers, and other VIPs, known as the World Economic Forum.

Activists had promised to stop the meeting in the same way they had halted the millennium round of trade talks at the Seattle WTO meeting in late 1999. The authorities took this threat seriously. Declaring any demonstration illegal, they transformed the ski resort into an armed camp with security personnel touting guns, turning back hundreds of protestors at Swiss borders, and responding with rubber pellets, tear gas, and water cannons when some got too near the forum site. It once again took the imposition of restrictions on the political rights of global citizens to protect the corporate interest.

Some 6,700 miles away, around 12,000 protestors gathered in Porto Alegre in southern Brazil for a formal anti-Davos gathering, called the World Social Forum. The Forum was a space for dialogue between delegates working to define planetary citizenship and on how to bridge the growing chasm between the rich and poor, and come up with alternatives for sustainable human development.

The world has changed since the WTO meeting in Seattle at the end of 1999. Back then the gurus of economic globalization were preaching their mantra of free trade, free markets, and even larger corporate mergers. Soaring markets seemed to prove them right and there was much talk of permanent growth. But the collapse of the talks in Seattle painted a different picture. Then came the Nasdaq crash, followed by the slowdown of the US economy. Countries all over the world worried that the downturn in the world's largest economy would soon spread. Crises like Kosovo combined with global warming, mad-cow disease, and genetically engineered food panic only exacerbated the sinking feeling that markets could not solve it all.

This shift was apparent in Davos where under the conference title "Bridging the Digital Divide," even the corporate leaders were discussing problems like poverty and disease. Ministers from the Third World countries like Brazil, India, and Thailand pointed out the impact of the industrialized world on the world's poor.

Derrick Jensen in his book, *A Language Older Than Words*, says: "In order for us to maintain our way of living, we must, in a broad sense, tell lies to each other, and especially to ourselves. It is not necessary that the lies be particularly believable. The lies act as barriers to truth. These barriers to truth are necessary because without them many deplorable acts would become impossibilities. Truth must at all costs be avoided. When we do allow self-evident truths to percolate past our defenses and into our consciousness, they are treated like so many hand grenades rolling across the dance floor of an improbably macabre party. We try to stay out of harm's way, afraid they will go off, shatter our delusions, and leave us exposed to what we have done to the world and to ourselves, exposed as the hollow people we have become. And so we avoid these truths, these self-evident truths, and continue the dance of world destruction." Davos was about this world of make-believe.

The uplifting speeches and promises made in Davos will not mollify the civil society as long as the corporate deal-making goes on behind closed doors. Despite the water cannons, tear gas, and the rubber pellets, the protestors are not going away.

Despite the controversy surrounding the international financial institutions, the World Bank, the International Monetary Fund (IMF) and the WTO continue to forge ahead with their agenda of economic globalization. They claim that this is their duty in assisting the Third World nations to work their way out of poverty. They quote the help they have provided to rescue their partners in Asia and Mexico at the time of financial crisis. The corporate-owned media has celebrated these efforts and held incompetent and dysfunctional governments, corruption, and cronyism responsible for the financial meltdown. The bailouts by the IMF have been declared acts of charity towards "developing" nations who are still learning the rules of the casino economy.

Rarely have the true causes of the financial crisis—the American,

European, and Japanese financial institutions that advocated free market economies based on the principles of liberalization, deregulation, and privatization—and the power of the Wall Street traders on the lives of working poor been clearly and eloquently spelled out. The essays in *The Future in the Balance* fill this need and show how a world has been created where the poor are left to meet their needs in a skyrocketing free market and protectionism and cronyism exists for banks and corporations. These essays also lay bare the role of the currency speculators in the Asian crisis. With the new technology networks, these speculators can move over a trillion dollars from one part of the globe to another in a day, leaving behind destabilized economies, currencies, and communities.

As the ecological, social, and economic fabric of the world unravels around us, it is time that we begin to speak of the unspeakable, and to listen to what we have not wanted to hear. For the last twenty-five years, Food First's mandate has been to expose the true causes of injustices that prevent us from ending global hunger and poverty. We hope that this collection of essays by Walden Bello, one of the most astute and ardent critics of the international financial institutions from the Third World, will help break the mindset that sees economic globalization a boon for the Third World, and offer new opportunities for the possibility of another world based on fairness and justice.

These essays also reflect Walden Bello's long history of activism on issues ranging from democracy in the Philippines to challenging the Washington consensus that colonizes the Third World countries and prevents them from embarking on the path of true development based on the sovereign will of its people. Spanning a period over a decade, these essays tell us the truth about the international financial structure of the World Bank, IMF, and the WTO and their grip on humanity that lives on the peripheries of the corporate state. They shatter the myths of development as prescribed by these institutions and put forward an agenda by the Third World for taking control of its own destiny. They rekindle our hope as they chart out a way for the future which will be paved by the struggle of the landless, the peasants, and the working poor around the world and offers an alternative for a more and just world for all.

Meir Berliner, who died fighting the SS at Trebilinka, said that "when oppressors give me two choices, I always take the third." The third choice was not the "third way" as articulated by British prime minister Tony Blair at the World Economic Forum in Davos, which supports wealth creation for the few at the expense of the bent backs of the poor. As we reflect on the meaningless talk of shuffling numbers on free trade ledgers, and see the real world effects of decisions made by the elites in corporate board rooms, our choice is clear: we need to make a different choice. This book offers that choice. This was one of many compelling reasons for Food First to publish this collection of essays.

It is not possible to work in isolation. If we, as a movement, wish to stop the atrocities, we need merely step away from the isolation. There is a whole world waiting for us to bridge the gap between the North and the South, between labor and environmentalists and others. As Porto Alegre pointed out, we can build another world.

INTRODUCTION
The Future in the Balance

The essays in this book are about the exercise of power in international relations, and the way this generates inequities, crisis, and, ultimately, resistance. They are, for the most part, about the exercise of power by the United States: about the different expressions or modalities of US power, about its impact on the global economy and on global politics, and about the responses it has evoked from other societies, peoples, and communities.

These essays focus on developments in the last decade of the twentieth century and the first year of the twenty-first century. These years were marked by the seemingly unassailable hegemony of American economic and military power, a phenomenon that was, paradoxically enough, accompanied by its increasing loss of legitimacy.

The last decade of the twentieth century began with the resounding collapse of the socialist economies of Eastern Europe and a lot of triumphalist talk about the genesis of a new market-driven global economy that rendered all borders obsolete and rode on the advances of information technology. The key agents of the new global economy were the transnational corporations (TNCs), which were depicted as the supreme incarnation of market freedom owing to their superior ability to bring about the most efficient mix of land, labor, capital, and technology.

Midway in the decade was born the World Trade Organization (WTO), which was painted by partisans of globalization as providing the legal and institutional scaffolding for the new global economy. By creating a rule-based global system based on the primordial principle of freer trade, the WTO would serve as the catalyst of an economic process that would bring about the greatest good for the greatest number. It was the third pillar of a holy trinity that would serve as the guardian of the new economic order, the other two being the International Monetary Fund (IMF), which promoted ever freer global capital flows, and the World Bank, which would supervise the transformation of developing countries along free market lines and manage their integration into the new world economy.

US CORPORATIONS AND GLOBALIZATION

Yet even as the prophets of globalization talked about the increasing obsolescence of the nation-state and the growing irrelevance of national interests, the main beneficiaries of the new global order were US transnational corporations. Supposedly an agent of free trade, the WTO's most important agreements promoted monopoly for US firms: the Trade Related Intellectual Property Rights Agreement consolidated the hold over high tech innovations by US corporations like Intel and Microsoft, while the Agreement on Agriculture institutionalized a system of monopolistic competition for third-country markets between the agribusiness interests of the United States and the European Union.

When the Asian financial crisis engulfed countries that had been seen by many in the US business and political elites as America's most formidable competitors, Washington did not try to save the Asian economies by promoting expansionary policies, Instead, it used the IMF to dismantle the structures of state-assisted Asian capitalism that had been regarded as formidable barriers to the entry of goods and investments from US transnationals that had been clamoring vociferously for years to get their piece of the "Asian miracle." It was less the belief in spreading the alleged benefits of free trade than maximizing geoeconomic and geostrategic advantage that lay behind US support for the policies of the IMF, the World Bank, and the WTO. As Chalmers Johnson has noted, a good case can be made that Washington's opportunistic behavior during the Asian financial crisis reflected the fact that "having defeated the fascists and the communists, the United States now sought to defeat its last remaining rivals for global dominance: the nations of East Asia that had used the conditions of the Cold War to enrich themselves."[1]

The increasingly brazen employment of the global multilateral system to serve the interests of the United States was one of the causes of the crisis that gripped the system at the end of decade. "Hegemonic leadership," in short, was giving way to direct control—a reality that was underlined by wry jokes from European and Japanese technocrats that during the Asian financial crisis, the IMF managing director Michel Camdessus was micromanaged by US Treasury secretary Robert Rubin and his key aide, Larry Summers.

THE MULTILATERAL SYSTEM IN CRISIS

Equally important as a source of de-legitimization was the spreading realization that the system could not deliver on its promise. That the system could not create prosperity for all but only the illusion of it was something that many observers had known for sometime. However, the realities of growing global poverty and inequality were neutralized by the high growth rates and the prosperity of a few enclaves of the world economy, like East Asia in the 1980s, which were (mistakenly) painted as paragons of market-led development. However, when the Asian economies collapsed in 1997, the follies of neoliberal economics were brought to the fore. All talk about the Asian financial crisis being caused by crony capitalism could not obscure the fact that it had been the liberation of speculative capital from the constraints of regulation, largely on account of pressure from the International Monetary Fund (IMF), that brought about Asia's collapse. The IMF also came under severe public scrutiny for imposing draconian programs on the Asian economies in the wake of the crisis—policies that merely accelerated economic contraction, saved foreign banks and speculative investors, and restructured economies along "American lines."

The IMF's role in East Asia triggered a fresh reexamination of its role in imposing structural adjustment programs in much of Africa, South Asia, and Latin America in the 1980s, and the fact that these programs had, as they did in Asia, exacerbated stagnation, widened inequalities, and deepened poverty now became widely realized—so much so that the IMF, in a desperate effort to exorcise its record, felt compelled to change the name of the extended structural adjustment fund facility (ESAF) into the poverty reduction and growth facility prior to the World Bank-IMF annual meeting in Washington in September 1999.

The Asian financial crisis triggered the unraveling of the legitimacy of the IMF. In the case of the WTO, the situation was even more dramatic. In the last five years of the decade, growing numbers of people and communities began to realize that in signing on to the WTO, they had signed on to a charter for corporate rule that enshrined what consumer advocate Ralph Nader called the principle of "trade *uber alles*," or corporate trade above equity, justice, environment, and most everything else we hold dear. Many developing countries discovered that in signing on to the WTO, they had signed away their rights to development. The many streams of discontent and opposition converged in the streets of Seattle and the meeting rooms of the Seattle Convention Center in December 1999 to bring down the third ministerial of the WTO and trigger a severe institutional crisis from which the organization has yet to recover.

The World Bank, under the leadership of Australian-turned-American James Wolfensohn, appeared to be charting a course that would allow it to escape the damage inflicted on its sister institutions, until it was subjected to fire in early 2000 from an unexpected quarter: the Meltzer Commission. Ever since he took over as chief of the institution in the mid-1990s Australian-American James Wolfensohn had managed to defuse criticism through very skilled public relations work and co-optation of non-governmental organizations (NGOs). But when the same criticisms that had been made by people from the left were made by a commission created by the US Congress, the game was up. Headed by a conservative academic, Alan Meltzer, the commission concluded that the Bank's performance when it came to addressing its avowed goal of eliminating global poverty was miserable and that it would be better to devolve the task to regional bodies.

THE CRISIS OF THE CORPORATION

By the end of the last decade of the twentieth century, in short, the triumphalism that marked the beginning of the decade had evaporated and given way to a deep crisis of legitimacy of the multilateral order. The crisis of the multilateral system was, moreover, translating into a deepening unease globally with the prime actor of globalization: the corporation. Several factors came together to focus public attention on the corporation in the 1990s—the most egregious being the predatory practices of Microsoft, the environmental depredations of Shell, the irresponsibility of Monsanto and Novartis in promoting genetically modified organisms, Nike's systematic exploitation of dirt-cheap labor, and Mitsubishi, Ford, and Firestone's concealment from consumers of serious product defects. A sense of environmental emergency was also spreading by the beginning of the 21st century, and to increasing numbers of people, the rapid melting of the polar ice caps could be traced to Big Oil and the automobile giants' continuing promotion of an environmentally destabilizing petroleum civilization, and, more generally, to the process of uncontrolled growth driven by the transnational corporations.

Ironically, in the United States, it was during the apogee of the New Economy that the distrust of the corporation was also at its highest in decades. According to *Business Week* survey, "72 per cent of Americans say business has too much power over their lives."[2] And the magazine warned: "Corporate America, ignore these trends at your peril."[3]

Some of the more enlightened members of the global elite took such warnings seriously, and their annual meeting in Davos, Switzerland, became the venue to elaborate a response that would go beyond the bankrupt strategy of denying that corporate-driven globalization was creating tremendous problems to promote a vision of "globalization with compassion." Yet, the task was formidable, for it became increasingly clear that in an unregulated global market, it was even more difficult to reconcile the demands of social responsibility with the demands of profitability. The best that "globalization with a conscience" could offer was, as C. Fred Bergsten, a noted pro-globalization advocate, admitted, a system of "transitional safety nets…to help the adjustment to dislocation" and "enable people to take advantage of the phenomenon [of globalization] and roll with it rather than oppose it."[4]

STRATEGIC POWER AND CORPORATE POWER

Corporate power is one dimension of US power. But there is, equally of consequence, the strategic power of the US state, a dimension that is explored in the third part of the book. Strategic power cannot be reduced, as in orthodox Marxism to simply being driven by the dynamics of corporate control. The US state cannot be reduced simply to being a servant of US capital. The Pentagon has its own dynamics, and one cannot understand the US role in the Balkans or its changing posture towards China as simply determined by the interests of US corporations. Indeed, in Asia, it has been strategic extension, not corporate expansionism, that has been the mainspring of US policy, at least until the mid-1980s. And, in the case of China, US capital's desire to exploit the China market has increasingly found itself in opposition to the Pentagon's definition of China as the Enemy, which must be headed off at the pass instead of being assisted by western investment to become a full-blown threat. In many instances, indeed, corporate power and state power may not be in synch.

Having said this, a primordial aim of the US transnational garrison state that is ensconced deeply in East Asia, the Middle East, and Europe and projects power to the rest of the globe, is the maintenance of a global order that secures the primacy of US economic interests. With the growing illegitimacy of corporate-driven globalization and the growing divide between a prosperous minority and an increasingly marginalized majority, military intervention to maintain the global status will become a constant feature of international relations, whether this is justified in terms of fighting drugs, fighting terrorism, containing "rogue states," opposing "Islamic fundamentalism," or containing China.

One cannot say, however, that the military structure of US hegemony is suffering as profound a crisis of legitimacy as that which has gripped the processes and institutions of corporate globalization. The US military structure remains solidly rooted in both Europe and Asia, and the reason it remains so is to be found at the level of the ideological: the deep-seated fear of both European and Asian elites that without the US to serve as a "benevolent hegemon," they would not be able to create by themselves benign regional orders that would ensure the peace among themselves.

THE CRISIS OF LIBERAL DEMOCRACY

It is not, however, corporate power or military power that is the US's strongest asset but its ideological power. This "soft power" of the hegemon is explored in the fourth part of this book.

The US is a Lockean democracy, and its ability to project its mission as the extension of systems centered on free elections to choose governments devoted to promoting liberal rights and freedoms continues to be a strong fountain of legitimacy in many parts of the world. The trend away from authoritarian regimes and toward formal democracies in the Third World happened in spite of rather than because of the United States. Yet, especially under the Clinton administration, Washington was able to skillfully jibe to catch the democratic winds, in the process reconstructing its image from being a supporter of repressive regimes to being an opponent of dictatorships.

In the last few years, however, Washington or Westminster-style democracies with their focus on formal rights and formal elections and their bias against economic equality achieved through such measures as asset and income redistribution has led to increasingly stagnant and polarized political systems, such as those in the Philippines, Brazil, and Pakistan. This stagnation of Third World liberal democratic systems has been paralleled by the realization of increasing numbers of Americans that their liberal democracy has been so thoroughly corrupted by corporate money politics that it deserves being designated a plutocracy. Liberal democracy Washington-style is, in other words, entering into crisis everywhere.

THE CRISIS OF LEGITIMACY

The crisis of liberal democracy is paralleled by a massive crisis of legitimacy of the institutions of global economic governance. It was this massive crisis of legitimacy that propelled thousands of people from both the North and the South to engage in militant protest civil disobedience in Seattle during the WTO ministerial in December 1999, in Washington during the World Bank-IMF spring meeting in April 2000, in Chiang Mai, Thailand, during the Asian Development Bank annual meeting in May 2000, in Melbourne during the World Economic Forum gathering in early September 2000, and in Prague during the World Bank-IMF annual meeting in late September 2000. These mass actions, in turn, further eroded the credibility of the institutions of globalization, despite the effort of television and mass media to portray the protesters as either uninformed critics or anarchists. The structures of the system may appear to still be firm, but when legitimacy or consensus goes, it may only be a matter of time before the structures themselves begin to unravel.

THE CHALLENGE

Yet the crisis of the system does not necessarily result in its replacement by a much more benign system of international relations. As Rosa Luxemburg so presciently pointed out before the rise of fascism in crisis-ridden Europe, the outcome may be "barbarism," where the ideals and themes of the progressive opposition are hijacked and perverted by demagogic forces that are hostile to freedom, equality, and democracy. Which is why the articulation of an alternative order, which is the concern of the final part of this book, is so critical at this point in time. Creating this alternative vision and program centered on a participatory process to build the institutions that would again subordinate the market to society, promote genuine equality across gender and color lines and within and among countries, and establish a benign relationship between human community and the biosphere remains the great challenge of the opponents of corporate-driven globalization.

On the success of this enterprise depends our future.

NOTES

1. Johnson, Chalmers. *Blowback: the Costs and Consequences of American Empire* (New York: Henry Holt and Company, 2000), pg. 206.
2. "Too Much Corporate Power," *Business Week,* September 11, 2000, pg. 53.
3. "New Economy, New Social Contract," *Business Week,* September 11, 2000, pg. 80.
4. Bergsten, C. Fred. "The Backlash against Globalization," speech delivered at 2000 meeting of the Trilateral Commission, Tokyo, April 2000 (downloaded from Internet).

PART ONE

The Bretton Woods System in Crisis

I

THE IRON CAGE: THE WTO, THE BRETTON WOODS INSTITUTIONS, AND THE SOUTH

From *Views from the South* (Oakland, CA: Food First Books, 2000)

The World Trade Organization (WTO) is a multilateral body that elicits fear, anger, and exasperation throughout the South. This, despite the oft-repeated claim by WTO apologists that by providing a set of rules and dispute settlement mechanisms for global trade, the organization protects the weaker and poorer countries from unilateralist actions by the stronger ones. This Southern view stems from a strong sense that the WTO is essentially an institution that is deeply biased against the development of the South. This attitude was epitomized for many by the resistance of key Northern countries led by the United States to the appointment of Thai deputy prime minister Supachai Panitchpakdi as director general of the organization.

The Southern attitude toward the WTO can best be appreciated if the emergence of the institution is placed in the context of the South's struggle for development over the last 50 years. Situated in this broad historical canvas, the Uruguay Round Agreement of 1994 emerges not so much as the triumph of enlightened free trade over benighted protectionism, but as the culminating point of a campaign of global economic containment of the legitimate aspirations to development on the part of Third World countries.

Earlier milestones in this process were the reorientation of the World Bank toward managing development in the South in the late 1950s, the IMF being turned into the watchdog of the external economic relations of Third World countries in the 1970s, the universalization of structural adjustment in the 1980s, and the unilateralist trade campaign waged against the Asian "tiger economies" by Washington beginning in the early 1980s.

This is not to say that the struggle between advanced industrial countries, which revolved around the issue of free trade or protection, was not a central driving force for the establishment of the WTO. It definitely was. It is to assert that containing the South was an equally key dynamic that intersected crucially with the fight for markets among the developed countries.

EMERGENCE OF THE SOUTHERN AGENDA

The place to begin this analysis is the period of de-colonization in the 1950s and 1960s. The emergence of scores of newly independent states took place in the politically charged atmosphere of the Cold War. Although they were often split between East and West in their political alliances, Third World countries gravitated towards an economic agenda that had two underlying thrusts: rapid development and a global redistribution of wealth.

While the more radical expression of this agenda in the shape of the Leninist theory of imperialism drew much attention and, needless to say, condemnation in some quarters, it was the more moderate version that was most influential in drawing otherwise politically diverse Third World governments into a common front. This was the vision, analysis, and program of action forged by Raul Prebisch, an Argentine economist, who from his base at the United Economic Commission for Latin America (CEPAL) won a global following with his numerous writings.

Developed in the late 1950s and early 1960s, Prebisch's theory centered on the worsening terms of trade between industrialized and non-industrialized countries, an equation which posited that more of the South's raw materials and agricultural products were needed to purchase fewer of the North's manufactured products. Moreover, the trading relationship was likely to get worse since Northern producers were developing substitutes for raw materials from the South, and Northern consumers would spend a decreasing proportion of their income on agricultural products from the South.[1]

Known in development circles as "structuralism," Prebisch's theory of "bloodless but inexorable exploitation," as one writer described it,[2] served as the inspiration for Third World organizations, formations, and programs that sprang up in the 1960s and 1970s. These including the Non-Aligned Movement, Group of 77, Organization of Petroleum Exporting Countries (OPEC), and the New International Economic Order (NIEO). It was also central to the establishment of the UN Conference on Trade and Development (UNCTAD) in 1964, which became over the next decade the principal vehicle used by the Third World countries in their effort to restructure the world economy.

With Prebisch as its first secretary general, UNCTAD advanced a global reform strategy with three main prongs. The first was commodity price stabilization through the negotiation of price floors below which commodity prices would not be allowed to fall. The second was a scheme of preferential tariffs, or allowing Third World exports of manufactures, in the name of development, to enter First World markets at lower tariff rates than those applied to exports from other industrialized countries. The third was an expansion and acceleration of foreign assistance, which, in UNCTAD's view, was not charity but "compensation, a rebate to the Third World for the years of declining commodity purchasing power."[3] UNCTAD also sought to gain legitimacy for the Southern countries' use of protectionist trade policy as a mechanism for industrialization and demanded accelerated transfer of technology to the South.

To a greater or lesser degree, the structuralist critique came to be reflected in the approaches of other key economic agencies of the United Nations secretariat, such as the Economic and Social Council (ECOSOC) and the United Nations Development Program (UNDP), and became the dominant viewpoint among the majority at the General Assembly.

The response of the leading countries of the North to the challenge of economic de-colonization posed by the emerging countries was conditioned by several developments. Most important of these was the Cold War. The priority of the political enterprise of containing the Soviet Union and communism pushed the North, particularly the US government, to a less hard-line stance when it came to the question of whether the economic structures of its client countries conformed to free market principles. While the US upheld private enterprise and demanded access for its corporations, it was more tolerant when it came to protectionism, investment controls, and a strong role for government in managing the economy. It also veered away from a classic exploitative stance to promote at least the image of supporting limited global redistribution of wealth, this being accomplished mainly through foreign aid. As the emerging countries gravitated toward the UN system, the leading governments increasingly relied on the International Monetary Fund (IMF) and the International Bank for Reconstruction and Development (IBRD) to push their agenda.

The Bretton Woods institutions, founded in 1944, began with missions quite distinct from their latter-day involvement with North-South relations. The IMF was conceived by John Maynard Keynes and Harry Dexter White, the two pillars of the Bretton Woods meeting, as the guardian of global liquidity, a function that it was supposed to fulfill by monitoring member countries' maintenance of stable exchange rates and providing facilities on which they could periodically draw to overcome cyclical balance of payments difficulties. On the other hand, the IBRD was, as its name implied, set up to assist in the reconstruction of the war-torn economies, particularly those of Western Europe, by lending to them at manageable rates of interest.

By the early 1970s, however, President Nixon's taking the dollar off the gold standard had inaugurated a new era of floating exchange rates that made the IMF's original mission superfluous. Instead, the Fund was deeply involved in stabilizing Third World economies with balance of payments difficulties. As for the World Bank, it had evolved into the prime multilateral development agency for aid and development.

In the case of the World Bank, a turning point of sorts was the debate triggered by the 1951 report of a group of experts entitled

"Measures for the Economic Development of Under-Developed Countries," which proposed making grant aid available to Third World countries.4 Using this as a springboard, Third World countries at the General Assembly tried to push through resolutions that would establish the Special UN Fund for Economic Development (SUN-FED), which would be controlled not by the North but by the UN and whose criterion for providing loans would not be narrow banking rules but development need.

The North, led by the United States, strenuously resisted these efforts, resorting at first to delay and diversion, like proposing the creation of a $100 million fund to be used to finance an investment survey that the IBRD or some other Western agency would undertake.5 But when diversion and delay failed to derail the South's drive to set up SUNFED, the North came out with an alternative: an institution for making soft loans for development from capital subscribed by the North but one controlled by the North rather than the Third World majority at the United Nations. Thus came into being the International Development Association (IDA), which was attached to the World Bank as the latter's soft-loan window. As one analyst of this period has pointed out:

> Much of the impetus for IDA came from the Bank itself, increasingly worried over Southern demands for a competing UN fund. Eugene R. Black, the bank's shrewd president, said bluntly that "the International Development Association was really an idea to offset the urge for Sunfed." Black, like any other banker, had little use for soft loans. But if anybody would make them, he reasoned, it had better be the Bank. If new business was to be done, Black wanted to do it.6

The IDA was part of a compromise package that effectively killed the idea of a UN-controlled development fund. The other part of the package was the establishment of the UN Special Fund, later renamed the UN Development Program (UNDP), which served as the channel of much smaller quantities of mainly technical aid to Third World countries.7

The IDA–UNDP compromise derailed the demand for a UN-controlled agency, but it did not stop the escalation of Third World demands for a redistribution of global economic power. This process resulted in the establishment of UNCTAD in 1964, and attained dramatic results with the Organization of Petroleum Exporting Countries' (OPEC) ability to seize control of oil pricing in the early and mid-1970s, culminating with the adoption by the UN General Assembly Special Session of 1974 of the "new international economic order" program. The thrust of these moves was clearly reformist rather than revolutionary, expressing demands of Third World elites rather than Third World masses. Nevertheless, their prominence in the context of successful struggles waged by revolutionary movements in Vietnam and other Third World countries lent a note of urgency to Washington's search for an effective counter-strategy of managed reform.

THE SOUTHERN CHALLENGE IN THE 1970s

In the 1970s, the World Bank was to be the centerpiece of liberal Washington's response. Robert McNamara, who was appointed in 1968 as the World Bank's president after his troubled stint at the US Defense Department, became the point man in the expanded liberal approach. The McNamara approach had several elements. First was a massive escalation in the World Bank's resources, with McNamara raising World Bank lending from an average of $2.7 billion a year when he took office in 1968, to $8.7 billion in 1978 and $12 billion by the time he left office in 1981. Second was a global program aimed at ending poverty via a program that sought to sidestep the difficult problems associated with social reform by focusing aid on improving the "productivity of the poor." Third was an effort to split the South by picking a few countries as "countries of concentration" to which the flow of bank assistance would be higher than average for countries of similar size and income.

The rise of OPEC, however, made World Bank aid and foreign aid less critical to many of the leading countries in UNCTAD and the Group of 77 in the mid-1970s. These countries could gain access to massive quantities of loans that the commercial banks were only too happy to make available in their effort to turn a profit on the billions of dollars of deposits made to them by the OPEC countries.

Instead of aid, UNCTAD focused on changing the rules of international trade, and in this enterprise it registered some success. During the fourth conference of UNCTAD (UNCTAD IV) in Nairobi in 1976, agreement was reached, without dissent from the developed countries, on the Integrated Program for Commodities (IPC). The IPC stipulated that agreements for 18 specified commodities would be negotiated or renegotiated with the principal aim of avoiding excessive price fluctuations and stabilizing commodity prices at levels remunerative to the producers and equitable to consumers. It was also agreed that a common fund would be set up to regulate prices when they either fall below or climb too far above the negotiated price targets.

UNCTAD and Group of 77 pressure was also central to the IMF's establishing a new window, the Compensatory Financing Facility (CFF), to assist Third World countries in managing foreign exchange crises created by sharp falls in the prices of the primary commodities they exported. Another UNCTAD achievement was getting the industrialized countries to accept the principle of preferential tariffs for developing countries. Some 26 developed countries were involved in 16 separate "general system of preference" schemes by the early 1980s.

These concessions were, of course, limited. In the case of commodity price stabilization, it soon became apparent that the rich countries had replaced a strategy of confrontation with an evasive strategy of frustrating concrete agreements. A decade after UNCTAD IV, only one new commodity stabilization agreement, for natural rubber, had been negotiated; an existing agreement on cocoa was not operative; and agreements on tin and sugar had collapsed.[8]

RIGHT WING REACTION AND THE DEMONIZATION OF THE SOUTH

By the late 1970s, however, even such small concessions were viewed with alarm by increasingly influential sectors of the US establishment. Such concessions within the UN system were seen in the context of other developments in North-South relations. These appeared to show that the strategy of liberal containment spearheaded by the Bank in the area of economic relations had not produced what it promised to deliver: security for Western interests in the South through the co-optation of Third World elites.

While professing anti-communism, governing elites throughout the Third World, which were the backbone of the UNCTAD system, gave in to popular pressure, abetted by local industrial interests, to tighten up on foreign investment. Nowhere did this trend spark more apprehension among American business people than in two countries which were considered enormously strategic by US multinational firms. In Brazil, where foreign-owned firms accounted for half of total manufacturing sales,[9] the military-technocrat regime invoked national security considerations, and moved in the late 1970s to reserve the strategic information sector to local industries, provoking bitter denunciation from IBM and other US computer firms.[10] In Mexico, where foreign firms accounted for nearly 30 percent of manufacturing output,[11] legal actions and threats of pulling investments by the powerful US drug industry followed the government's program for the pharmaceutical industry. The industry proposed no-patent policies, promotion of generic medicines, local development of raw materials, price controls, discriminatory incentives for local firms, and controls on foreign investment.[12]

Disturbing though these concessions and actions were, they could not compare in their impact with OPEC's second "oil shock" in 1979. Despite the fact that Western oil companies were passing on the oil price increases to consumers in order to preserve their enormous profit margins, to many Americans OPEC became the symbol of the South: an irresponsible gang that was bent on using its near monopoly over a key resource in order to bring the West to its knees. Although OPEC was not dominated by communists or radical nationalists like Libya's Khadafy but by US allies such as Saudi Arabia, Kuwait, and Venezuela, its "oil weapon" evoked more apprehension than the nuclear arms of the Soviet Union. The oil cartel was feared as the precursor of a unified Southern bloc controlling most strategic commodities, and right wing propagandists pointed to the Algiers Declaration of the Non-Aligned

Movement in 1973 in their efforts to fan fear and loathing in the North:

> The heads of state or government recommend the establishment of effective solidarity organizations for the defense of the raw materials producing countries such as the Organization of Petroleum Export Countries...to recover natural resources and ensure increasingly substantial export earnings.[13]

TARGETING THE UN SYSTEM

The United Nations system was a central feature of the demonology of the South that right wing circles articulated in the late 1970s and early 1980s. In their view, the UN had become the main vehicle for the South's strategy to bring about the New International Economic Order (NIEO). As the right wing think tank Heritage Foundation saw it, the governments of the South devoted "enormous time and resources to spreading the NIEO ideology throughout the UN system and beyond. Virtually no UN agencies and bureaus have been spared."[14] The South's effort to redistribute global economic power via UN mechanisms was viewed as a concerted one: private business data flows are under attack internationally and by individual Third World countries; proposals for strict controls of the international pharmaceutical trade are pending before more than one UN body; other international agencies are drafting restrictive codes of conduct for multinational corporations; and UNESCO has proposed international restraints on the press.[15]

Especially threatening to the Foundation was the effort by the Third World to "redistribute natural resources" by bringing the seabed, space, and Antarctica under their control through Law of the Sea Treaty, the Agreement Governing Activities of States on the Moon and Other Celestial Bodies (called the Moon Treaty), and an ongoing UN study and debate over Antarctica. Malaysian prime minister Mahathir Bin Mohamad, the principal architect of the effort to get the UN to claim Antartica, told the General Assembly "all the unclaimed wealth of this earth" is the "common heritage of mankind," and therefore subject to the political control of the Third World.[16]

RESUBORDINATING THE SOUTH I: STRUCTURAL ADJUSTMENT

When the Reagan administration came to power in 1981, it was riding on what it considered a mandate not only to roll back communism, but also to discipline the Third World. What unfolded over the next four years was a two-pronged strategy aimed at dismantling the system of "state-assisted capitalism" that was seen as the domestic base for Southern national capitalist elites, and drastically weakening the United Nations system as a forum and instrument for the South's economic agenda.

The opportunity came none too soon in the form of the global debt crisis that erupted in the summer of 1982, which drastically weakened the capabilities of Southern governments in dealing with Northern states and corporations and Northern-dominated multilateral agencies. The instruments chosen for rolling back the South were the World Bank and the IMF. This was an interesting transformation for the World Bank, which had previously been vilified by *The Wall Street Journal* and the right wing as one of the villains behind the weakening of the North's global position by "promoting socialism" in the Third World via its loans to Southern governments. But the liberal McNamara, who was now faulted by the right wing for losing Vietnam and failing to contain the Southern challenge, was replaced by a more pliable successor, and ideological right-wingers seeking the closure of the Bank were restrained by pragmatic conservatives who wished to use the Bank instead as a disciplinary mechanism.

"Structural adjustment" referred to a new lending approach that had been formulated during McNamara's last years at the Bank. Unlike the traditional World Bank project loan, a structural adjustment loan was intended to push a program of "reform" that would cut across the whole economy or a whole sector of the economy. In the mid-1980s, IMF and World Bank-imposed structural adjustment became the vehicle for a program of free market liberalization that was applied across the board to Third World economies suffering major debt problems. Almost invariably, structural adjustment programs had the following elements:

Radically reducing government spending, ostensibly to control inflation and reduce the demand for capital inflows from abroad, a measure that in practice translated into cutting spending on health, education, and welfare.

Liberalizing imports and removing restrictions on foreign investment, ostensibly to make local industry more efficient by exposing them to foreign competition.

Privatizing state enterprises and embarking on radical deregulation in order to promote more efficient allocation and use of productive resources by relying on market mechanisms instead government decree.

Devaluing the currency in order to make exports more competitive, thus resulting in more dollars to service the foreign debt.

Cutting or constraining wages and eliminating or weakening mechanisms protecting labor like the minimum wage to remove what were seen as artificial barriers to the mobility of local and foreign capital.

By the late 1980s, with over 70 Third World countries submitting to IMF and World Bank programs, stabilization, structural adjustment, and shock therapy managed from distant Washington became the common condition of the South. While structural adjustment was justified as necessary to create the conditions that would enable Third World countries to repay their debts to Northern banks, there was a more strategic objective—to dismantle the system of state-assisted capitalism that served as the domestic base for the national capitalist elites. In 1988, a survey of structural adjustment programs (SAPs) carried out by the UN Commission for Africa concluded that the essence of SAPs was the "reduction/removal of direct state intervention in the productive and redistributive sectors of the economy."[17]

As for Latin America, one analyst noted that the US took advantage of "this period of financial strain to insist that debtor countries remove the government from the economy as the price of getting credit."[18] Similarly, a retrospective look at the decade of adjustment in a book published by the Inter-American Development Bank in 1992 identified the removal of the state from economic activity as the centerpiece of the ideological perspective that guided the structural reforms of the 1980s.

By the end of the 12-year-long Reagan-Bush era in 1992, the South had been transformed: from Argentina to Ghana, state participation in the economy had been drastically curtailed; government enterprises were passing into private hands in the name of efficiency; protectionist barriers to Northern imports were being radically reduced; and through export-first policies, the internal economy was more tightly integrated into the North-dominated capitalist world markets.

RE-SUBORDINATING THE SOUTH II: BRINGING THE NEWLY INDUSTRIALIZED COUNTRIES TO HEEL

There was one area of the South that was relatively untouched by the first phase of the Northern economic counterrevolution. That was East and Southeast Asia. Here practically all the economic systems displayed the same features of state-assisted capitalism found elsewhere in the South: an activist government intervening in key areas of the economy, a focus on industrialization in order to escape the fate of being simply agricultural or raw material producers, protection of the domestic market from foreign competition, and tight controls on foreign investment. Where the key East and Southeast Asian economies appeared to differ from other economies in the South was mainly in the presence of a fairly strong state that was able to discipline local elites, the greater internalization of a developmentalist direction by the state elite, and the pursuit of aggressive mercantilist policies aimed at gaining markets in First World countries, particularly the United States.

The frontline status in Asia of many of these so-called "newly industrializing countries" (NICs) during the Cold War ensured that Washington would turn a blind eye to many of their deviations from the free market ideal. But as the Cold War wound down from the mid-1980s, the US began to redefine its economic policy toward East Asia as the creation of a "level playing field" for its corporations via liberalization, deregulation, and more extensive privatization of Asian economies.

It was a goal that Washington pursued by various means in the late 1980s and early 1990s. However, Japanese capital was relocating many of its industrial operations to East and Southeast Asia to offset the loss of competitiveness in Japan owing to the rapid appreciation of the yen triggered by the Plaza Accord in 1985. Access to this capital allowed countries like South Korea, Thailand, and Indonesia to ignore the requirements of formal structural adjustment programs that were foisted on them by the World Bank and the IMF in the early 1980s when they were temporarily destabilized by the debt crisis. This left unilateralism in trade and financial diplomacy as the principal mechanism employed by the US to deal with the increasingly successful Asian "tigers."

Unilateralism was aggressively pursued, sometimes to the point of *de facto* trade war. Washington's mood was aptly captured by a senior US official who told a capital markets conference in San Francisco that "Although the NICs may be regarded as tigers because they are strong, ferocious traders, the analogy has a darker side. Tigers live in the jungle, and by the law of the jungle, they are a shrinking population."[19]

With some assistance from the IMF and the World Bank, unilateral pressure succeeded in getting key Asian countries to liberalize their capital accounts and to move to greater liberalization of their financial sectors. But when it came to trade liberalization, the results were meager, except perhaps in the case of Korea, whose trade surplus with the US had been turned into a trade deficit by the early 1980s. But even this development did not change the US trade representative's assessment of Korea as "one of the toughest places in the world to do business."[20] As for the Southeast Asian countries, Washington's assessment was that while they might have liberalized their capital accounts and financial sectors, they remained highly protected when it came to trade and were dangerously flirting with "trade distorting" exercises in industrial policy, like Malaysia's national car project, the Proton Saga, or Indonesia's drive to set up a passenger aircraft industry.

The indiscriminate financial liberalization demanded by Washington and the Bretton Woods institutions, coupled with the high interest rate and fixed currency regime favored by local financial authorities, brought in massive amounts of foreign capital into the region. But it also served as the wide highway through which $100 billion exited in 1997 in a massive stampede in response to dislocations caused by over-investment and unrestricted capital inflows, like the collapse of the real estate market and widening current account deficits.

A golden opportunity to push the US agenda opened up with the financial crisis, and Washington did not hesitate to exploit it to the hilt, advancing its interests behind the banner of free market reform. The rollback of protectionism and activist state intervention was incorporated into stabilization programs imposed by the IMF on the key crisis countries of Indonesia, Thailand, and South Korea.

In Thailand, local authorities agreed to remove all limitations on foreign ownership of Thai financial firms, accelerate the privatization of state enterprises, and revise bankruptcy laws along lines demanded by the country's foreign creditors. As the US trade representative told Congress, the Thai government's "commitments to restructure public enterprises and accelerate privatization of certain key sectors—including energy, transportation, utilities, and communications—which will enhance market-driven competition and deregulation—[are expected] to create new business opportunities for US firms."[21]

In Indonesia, the US trade representative emphasized that the IMF's conditions for granting a massive stabilization package addressed practices that have long been the subject of this [Clinton] Administration's bilateral trade policy... Most notable in this respect is the commitment by Indonesia to eliminate the tax, tariff, and credit privileges provided to the national car project. Additionally, the IMF program seeks broad reform of Indonesian trade and investment policy, like the aircraft project, monopolies and domestic trade restrictive practices, that stifle competition by limiting access for foreign goods and services.[22]

The national car project and the plan to set up a passenger jet aircraft industry were efforts at industrial policy that had elicited the strong disapproval of Detroit and Boeing, respectively.

In the case of Korea, the US Treasury and the IMF did not conceal their close working relationship, with the Fund clearly in a subordinate position. Not surprisingly, the concessions made by the Koreans—including raising the limit on foreign ownership of corporate stocks to 55 percent, permitting the establishment of foreign financial institutions, full liberalization of the financial and capital market, abolition of the car classification system, and agreement to end government-directed lending for industrial policy goals—had a one-to-one correspondence with US bilateral policy toward Korea before the crisis. As the US trade representative candidly told US congressmen:

Policy driven, rather than market-driven economic activity, meant that US industry encountered many specific structural barriers to trade, investment, and competition in Korea. For example, Korea maintained restrictions on foreign ownership and operations, and had a list of market access impediments...The Korea stabilization package, negotiated with the IMF in December 1997, should help open and expand competition in Korea by creating a more market-driven economy...[I]f it continues on the path to reform there will be important benefits not only for Korea but also the United States.[23]

Summing up Washington's strategic goal, Jeff Garten, undersecretary of commerce during President Bill Clinton's first term, said, "Most of these countries are going through a dark and deep tunnel...But on the other end there is going to be a significantly different Asia in which American firms have achieved a much deeper market penetration, much greater access."[24] By 1998, transnationals and US financial firms were buying up Asian assets from Seoul to Bangkok at fire sale prices.

RESUBORDINATING THE SOUTH IV:
DISMANTLING THE UN DEVELOPMENT SYSTEM

This assault on the NICs via the IMF stabilization programs and on the broader South via Bretton Woods-imposed structural adjustment was accompanied by a major effort to emasculate the United Nations as a vehicle for the Southern agenda. Wielding the power of the purse, the United States, whose contribution funds some 20–25 percent of the UN budget, moved to silence NIEO rhetoric in all the key UN institutions dealing with the North-South divide: the Economic and Social Council (ECOSOC), the UN Development Program, and the General Assembly. US pressure resulted as well in the effective dismantling of the UN Center on Transnational Corporations (TNCs), whose high quality work in tracking the activities of the TNCs in the South, had earned the ire of the TNCs. Also abolished was the post of director general for international economic cooperation and development, which "had been one of the few concrete outcomes, and certainly the most noteworthy, of the efforts of the developing countries during the NIEO negotiations to secure a stronger UN presence in support of international economic cooperation and development."[25]

But the focus of the Northern counteroffensive was the defanging, if not dismantling of UNCTAD. After giving in to the South during the UNCTAD IV negotiations in Nairobi in 1976 by agreeing to the creation of the commodity stabilization scheme known as the Integrated Program for Commodities, the North, during UNCTAD V in Belgrade, refused the South's program of debt cancellation and other measures intended to revive Third World economies and thus contribute to global recovery at a time of worldwide recession.[26] The northern offensive escalated during UNCTAD VIII, held in Cartagena in 1992. At this watershed meeting, the North successfully opposed all linkages of UNCTAD discussions with the Uruguay Round negotiations of the GATT and managed to erode UNCTAD's negotiation functions, thus calling its existence into question.[27] UNCTAD's main function would henceforth be limited to "analysis, consensus building on some trade-related issues, and technical assistance."[28]

This drastic curtailing of UNCTAD's scope was apparently not enough for certain Northern interests. For instance, the Geneva-based Independent Commission on Global Governance identified UNCTAD as one of agencies that could be abolished in order to streamline the UN system.[29] The Commission's views apparently coincided with that of Karl Theodor Paschke, head of the newly created UN Office of Internal Oversight Services, who was quoted by *Stern Magazine* as saying that UNCTAD had been made obsolete by the creation of the World Trade Organization.[30]

THE WORLD TRADE ORGANIZATION: SEALING THE DEFEAT OF THE SOUTH

UNCTAD continues to survive, but the truth of the matter is that it has been rendered impotent by the WTO, which came into being following the signing of the Marrakech Accord in April 1994, which put in force the agreements concluded during the eight-year Uruguay Round of the General Agreement on Tariffs and Trade (GATT). The WTO was 46 years late in coming into being, though it had initially been regarded by liberal internationalists in the US and Britain as the third pillar of the Bretton Woods system, doing for trade what the IMF did for finance and the World Bank for economic reconstruction. A global trading organization had initially been scheduled to come into existence as the International Trade Organization (ITO) in 1948, but the threat of non-ratification by unilaterialist forces in the US Senate led to it being shelved in favor of the much weaker GATT by the defensive Truman administration.

By the mid-1980s, trade rivalries with Europe and Japan, rising import penetration of the US market by Third World countries, frustration at the inability of US goods to enter Southern markets, and the rise of new competitors in the shape of the East Asian NICs made the US the leading advocate of a much expanded GATT with real coercive teeth. Central to the founding of the WTO were the twin drives of managing the trade rivalry among the leading industrial countries while containing the threat posed by the South to the prevailing global economic structure. In this sense, the WTO must be seen as a continuation or extension of the same Northern reaction that drove structural adjustment.

The WTO, with its enshrinement of the principle of free trade as the organizing principle of the global trading system, represents the defeat of everything that the South fought for in UNCTAD: getting fair prices for their commodities via commodity price agreements; the institutionalization of trade preferences for Southern goods owing to their underdeveloped status; preferential treatment for local investors; the use of trade policy as a legitimate instrument for industrialization; and more concerted technology transfer to the South.

Instead, the WTO institutionalizes free trade, the most favored nation principle, and national treatment as the pillars of the new world trading order. National treatment, which is institutionalized in the General Agreement on Trade in Services (GATS) of the Uruguay Round, is perhaps the most revolutionary of these principles and the most threatening to the South. It gives foreign service providers, from telecommunications companies to lawyers to educational agencies, the same rights and privileges as their domestic counterparts. Although the GATT-WTO Accord does recognize the "special and differential status" of the developing countries, it does not see this as a case of structurally determined differences but as one of the gaps that can be surmounted by giving developing countries a longer adjustment period than the developed countries.

While Northern environmental organizations are critical of the WTO owing to their fears that environmental standards in the North are being subordinated to free trade, the Southern countries have articulated their concerns about the GATT-WTO's anti-developmental thrust. In their view, GATT-WTO is inherently unsympathetic to industrialization, at the same time that it erodes the agricultural base of the developing societies.

THE WTO AND INDUSTRIALIZATION IN THE SOUTH

In signing on to the GATT, Third World countries, the critique goes, have agreed to ban all quantitative restrictions on imports, reduce tariffs on many industrial imports, and promise not to raise tariffs on all other imports. In so doing, they have effectively given up the use of trade policy to pursue industrialization objectives. The way that the newly industrializing countries made it to industrial status via the policy of import substitution, is now effectively removed as a route to industrialization.

The anti-industrialization thrust of the GATT-WTO Accord is even more manifest in the Agreement on Trade Related Investment Measures (TRIMs) and the Agreement on Trade Related Intellectual Property Rights (TRIPs). In their drive to industrialize, NICs like South Korea and Malaysia made use of many innovative mechanisms such as trade balancing requirements that tied the value of a foreign investor's imports of raw materials and components to the value of his or her exports of the finished commodity, or "local content" regulations which mandated that a certain percentage of the components that went into the making of a product was sourced locally.

These rules restricted the maneuvering space of foreign investors, but they were successfully employed by the NICs to marry foreign investment to national industrialization. They enabled the NICs to raise income from capital-intensive exports, develop support industries, bring in technology, while still protecting local entrepreneurs' preferential access to the domestic market. In Malaysia, for instance, the strategic use of local content policy enabled the Malaysians to build a "national car," in cooperation with Mitsubishi, that has now achieved about 80 percent local content and controls 70 percent of the Malaysian market. Thanks to the TRIMs accord, these mechanisms are now illegal.

Like the TRIMs agreement, the TRIPs regime is seen as effectively opposed to the industrialization efforts of Third World countries. This becomes clear from a survey of the economic history not only of the NICs but of almost all late-industrializing countries. A key factor in their industrial take-off was their relatively easy access to cutting-edge technology: The US industrialized, to a great extent by using but paying very little for British manufacturing innovations, as did the Germans. Japan industrialized by liberally borrowing US technological innovations, but barely compensating the Americans for this. And the Koreans industrialized by copying quite liberally US and Japanese product and process technologies and with little payment.

But what is "technological diffusion" from the perspective of the late industrializer is "piracy" from that of the industrial leader. The TRIPs regime takes the side of the latter and makes the process of industrialization by imitation much more difficult from now on. It represents what UNCTAD describes as "a premature strengthening of the intellectual property system...that favors monopolistically controlled innovation over broad-based diffusion."[31]

The TRIPs regime provides a generalized minimum patent protection of 20 years; increases the duration of the protection for semiconductors or computer chips; institutes draconian border regulations against products judged to be violating intellectual property rights; and places the burden of proof on the presumed violator of process patents.

The TRIPs accord is seen by the South a victory for the US high tech industry, which has long been lobbying for stronger controls over the diffusion of innovations. Innovation in the knowledge-intensive high tech sector—in electronic software and hardware, biotechnology, lasers, optic electronics, liquid crystal technology, to name a few—has become the central determinant of economic power in our time. And when any company in the NICs and Third World wishes to innovate, say in chip design, software programming, or computer assembly, it necessarily has to integrate several patented designs and processes, most of them from US electronic hardware and software giants like Microsoft, Intel, and Texas Instruments.[32] As the Koreans have bitterly learned, exorbitant multiple royalty payments to what has been called the American "high tech mafia" keeps one's profit margins very low while reducing incentives for local innovation. The likely outcome is for a Southern manufacturer simply to pay royalties for a technology rather than to innovate, perpetuating the technological dependence on Northern firms.

Thus, TRIPs enables the technological leader, in this case the United States, to greatly influence the pace of technological and industrial development in rival industrialized countries, the NICs, and the Third World.

TRIPs AND AGRICULTURE

These considerations do not exhaust the developing countries' concerns about TRIPs. The agreement is also of concern because of the threat it poses to the very existence of agrarian communities. Because it strengthens considerably the system of private patenting of intellectual property, TRIPs have opened the way for the privatization of products developed from genetic processes or communal technological innovation in the South. As one analyst puts it,

> Once modified, no matter how slightly, such genetic material can be patented by corporations or individuals who thus appropriate all financial benefits. As it stands now, an individual or company can collect a plant from a developing country, modify it or isolate a useful gene and patent a new plant variety or product that contains it, without having to make any payment whatever to the communities whose traditional knowledge enabled the plant to be identified in the first place.[33]

While the GATT-WTO accord does mention the possibility of a *sui generis* system for patenting agricultural products and process technologies, which could apply to those developed collectively by agrarian communities and indigenous peoples in the South, the emphasis of TRIPs is on the privatization of the nexus between natural processes and human intervention.

The threat posed by TRIPs to Third World agrarian communities is no longer one that is simply looming on the horizon. A US firm has patented "Jasmati" rice which is a cross of Thailand's jasmine rice and India's basmati rice. Monsanto is now enforcing its proprietary rights to the use of seeds from harvests produced by "Monsanto-improved" seeds purchased by farmers. W.R. Grace applied for and received a US patent for a process that extracts an active ingredient of the Neem tree, known for its wide variety of medical and other uses in India.[34] This patent created an international moral outrage, and was revoked in 2000 by the European patent office.

There are other less well-known examples of what some scholars from the South have labeled "biopiracy" in the guise of intellectual property rights. One US pharmaceutical company stands to make millions of dollars from two drugs, an anti-carcinogenic and anti-leukemia agent, whose source is Madagascar.[35] Merck, a leading western pharmaceutical firm, is also likely to profit from the anti-coagulant it is developing from the *tikluba* plant, which has long been used by indigenous peoples in the Amazon.[36] Some 11 patents have already been filed in the United States and Japan covering the extraction and use of *nata de coco* from coconut, a major cottage industry in the Philippines, and patents by foreign entities and individuals are reported to have been filed on *lagundi* and *banaba,* two Philippine plants with medicinal qualities.[37]

THE AGREEMENT ON AGRICULTURE

The TRIPs accord is an example to the South of the double standards in the GATT-WTO. While it pushes free trade on the South in some of its subsidiary agreements, it actually promotes monopoly for the North in others. This is true as well of the Agreement on Agriculture (AOA), which was opened up for new negotiations after the third ministerial in Seattle in late November 1999.

A close examination of the development and impact of the AOA would be useful. It illustrates how the dynamics of rivalry among the trade superpowers that is one of the driving forces of the GATT-WTO intersects with the equally dominant dynamic of subordinating the South to the North.

Prior to the Uruguay Round, agriculture was *de facto* outside GATT discipline, mainly because the US had sought in the 1950s a waiver from Article XI of GATT, which prohibited quantitative restrictions on imports. With the US threatening to leave the GATT unless it was allowed to maintain protective mechanisms for sugar, dairy products, and other agricultural commodities, Washington was given a "non-time-limited waiver" on agricultural products.[38] This led to the GATT's lax enforcement of Article XI on other agricultural producers for fear of being accused of having double standards.

The US and the other agricultural powers not only ignored Article XI but they also exploited Article XVI, which exempted agricultural products from the GATT's ban on subsidies. One effect of these moves was the transformation of the EU from being a net food importer into a net food exporter in the 1970s. By the beginning of the Uruguay Round in the mid-1980s, the EU's Common Agricultural Policy (CAP) had developed into what was described as "a complex web of price and sales guarantees, subsidies, and other support measures that largely insulated farmers' incomes from market forces."39

With domestic prices set considerably above world prices and no controls on production, European farmers expanded production. The mounting surpluses could only be disposed of through exports, sparking competition with the previously dominant subsidized US farmers for third country markets. The competition between the agricultural superpowers turned fierce, but it was not so much their subsidized farmers that suffered. The victims were largely farmers in the South, such as the small scale cattle growers of West Africa and South Africa, who were driven to ruin by low priced EU exports of subsidized beef.

With state subsidies mounting to support the bitter competition for third country markets, the EU and US gradually came to realize that continuing along the same path could only lead to a no-win situation for both. By the late 1980s, for instance, close to 80 percent of the EU's budget was going to support agricultural programs. The US had inaugurated a whole new set of expensive programs such as the Export Enhancement Program, to win back markets, such as the North African wheat market from the EU.40

This mutual realization of the need for rules in the struggle for third country markets is what led the EU and US to press for inclusion of agriculture in the Uruguay Round. Rather than seriously promoting a mechanism to advance free trade, the two superpowers resorted to the rhetoric of free trade to regulate a condition of monopolistic competition, with each seeking advantage at the margins.

The manner in which the agreement came into being lends support to this interpretation. The final agreement was essentially the Blair House Accord, which was negotiated only between the US and the EU in 1992 and 1993. The accord was then promptly tossed to other GATT members by the two superpowers in 1994 on a take-it-or-leave-it basis. Understandably, many of the other GATT members, and not only those from the South, felt that they were practically coerced into signing the agreement.

Here are the key provisions of the Agreement on Agriculture:

Domestic support, quantified into a common measure called the "aggregate measure of support (AMS)," would be reduced by 20 percent over a six year period; that is AMS would be 20 percent lower in 2001 than AMS in 1986–1988. However, certain domestic subsidies, including direct income payments for farmers (the so-called "green box" and "blue box" measures) were exempted from cuts.

Export subsidies would be reduced over a six-year-period by 21 percent in volume terms and by 36 percent in terms of total cash value, and members would not agree to expand subsidies beyond the level reached at the end of the six-year-period.

Import quotas would be transformed into tariffs (tariffication), and these tariffs would be reduced over a period of six year by an average of 31 percent, with a 15 percent minimum tariff line, again with the base being the "tariff equivalents" of these quotas in 1986–1988.

Countries would pledge "minimum access volume (MAV)" to agricultural imports that would start at three percent of 1986–1988 consumption and rise to five percent in 1999. Under the so-called "special differential status" treatment accorded to them under GATT, developing countries would be subject to only two-thirds of the cuts in tariffs, domestic support, and export subsidies applied to developed countries, and they would be given a grace period of ten years, instead of six years, to put these into effect.

By the time of the Seattle ministerial in late 1999, the Agreement had been in effect for nearly five years. So far it appears to have had little or no effect in terms of effectively reducing the protection and subsidization enjoyed by agriculture in developed countries. Several mechanisms have worked to produce these results.

First, for the aggregate measure of support, export subsidies, and tariffs, the 1986–1988 level at which the items were bound were quite high relative to the levels in 1995 when the Agreement took effect. This resulted in minimal actual reductions in subsidies and tariffs relative to 1995 levels. In the case of the US, for instance, between 1992 and 1996, the simple average tariffs for agriculture and livestock production rose from 5.7 percent to 8.5 percent, for food products from 6.6 to 10.0 percent, and for tobacco products from 14.6 to 104.4 percent.[41] Also the Uruguay Round's requirements that import quotas be transformed into tariffs has been abused by EU and the US, with the latter levying an *ad valorem* duty of 350 percent for above minimum access imports of tobacco products.[42]

Second, the rules for achieving the 36 percent average tariff reduction (on the very high 1986–1988 levels) were quite loose, so that countries could meet the GATT requirement through a combination of minimal tariff cuts on sensitive or valued product lines and deep cuts in non-sensitive products, and by "backloading" their already minimal tariff cuts on the valued products toward the end of the six-year-period.

Third, major subsidies to farmers in the North, such as direct income payments to make up for the vagaries of the market, have been exempted from cuts.

The exemption of direct income payments to farmers from GATT discipline was a major blow to the hopes of many countries that the Agreement on Agriculture would serve as a mechanism for freer international trade. Such payments were excluded on the specious grounds that they were "decoupled from production" and thus "non-trade distorting."

In the EU, these direct income payments are mainly based on output, the bulk of them via a "land set-aside program" which entitles each farmer to a subsidy when she or he withdraws 15 percent of his/her land from cultivation. The idea behind the set-aside program is to restrict output, thus raising prices. In the US farm bill, farmers get the same level of direct income subsidy in good and bad crop years.

Deficiency payments are projected to average US $5.1 billion a year between 1996 and 2002.[43]

But the truth is that direct payments to European and US farmers are anything but decoupled from production, since without them agriculture would scarcely remain profitable. Deficiency payments for instance, make up between one-fifth and one-third of US farm incomes.[44] By enshrining the notion of decoupled payments as untouchable subsidies in green box, the US and the EU were, as one analyst put it, "taking away direct support of markets and replacing it with direct subsidization of [Northern] farmers."[45]

The combination of minimal cuts in tariffs, export subsidies, and AMS, and the maintenance of direct income payments has had the predictable result of raising the total amount of agricultural subsidies in the Organization for Economic Cooperation and Development (OECD) countries since the Agreement came into force: from US $182 billion in 1995 to an astounding $280 billion in 1997, with the major share of this figured accounted for by the EU and the US. Over 40 percent of the total value of production in the OECD countries is now accounted for by different forms of producer subsidies.[46] In contrast to this massive subsidization in the OECD countries, farmers in many developing countries have not only had little financial support from the government but where some subsidization exists, this often does not reach the ten percent of the value of production allowed by the AOA. In fact, developing countries have been penalized by policies that have brought about the "negative subsidization" of their agricultural sector.[47]

One study estimates that for 18 developing countries, "taxation," or the transfer of value from agricultural production as subsidies to other sectors of the economy, amounted to an average of 30 percent of the value production. Yet it is the farmers of the countries of the South that will be forced to bear the burden of adjustment to the new agricultural regime. Their lack of subsidies is paralleled by their clear commitments to give greater market access to Northern farming interests, whose runaway subsidization continues to push them to create mountains of commodities seeking export outlets.

A 1997 report to the EU farm ministers projected the surplus of wheat to rise from 2.7 million metric tons to 45 million tons by 2005, and total cereal surplus to shoot up to 58 million metric tons. The solution to this condition of subsidized overproduction, said EU agriculture minister Franz Fischler, was intensified efforts to export grain.[48] Continuing subsidization has also deepened US agriculture's dependence on massive exporting. Admitting that "one out of every three farm acres in America is dedicated to exports," US trade representative Charlene Barshefsky has concluded that "given the limitations inherent in US demand-led growth, we must find new markets for American agriculture. We must open new markets to support the increasingly productive US agricultural sector."[49]

So the story continues: subsidized Northern producers that make a mockery of global free trade in agriculture fight for developing country markets, squeezing the non-subsidized farmers in the latter.

Undoubtedly, AOA does offer some concessions to the South in the form of the lifting of quotas and some reduction in tariffs on developing country exports of commercial crops like palm oil and coconut oil. But these are concessions that benefit mainly organized lobbies of cash crop exporters and processors, such as Malaysian palm oil plantations, big cocoa and coffee planters in Africa and Asia, and big sugar interests in the Caribbean. The vast majority of unorganized small farmers specializing in corn, rice, and other food crops are hurt by this trade off, for the *quid pro quo* is precisely the liberalization of their markets for staples and other basic foods.

In the case of Southeast Asia, for instance, limited gains for palm oil interests in Malaysia and coconut oil exporters in Manila stemming from the Uruguay Round has been outbalanced by the tremendous damage imposed by liberalization on rice farmers in Malaysia, Indonesia, and the Philippines. Thai rice farmers are hardly benefiting—it's the Bangkok-based middlemen that are profiting from increased Thai rice exports. Further liberalization in a new round of negotiations will simply drive the region's small farmers over the edge, as it will small farmers in other parts of the South.

The profound inequality institutionalized in the AOA was best summed up by the Philippines' Secretary of Trade and Industry in his speech at the Second Ministerial of the WTO in May 1998: "The agriculture agreement as it now stands... has perpetuated the unevenness of the playing field which the multilateral trading system has been seeking to correct. Moreover, this has placed the burden of adjustment on developing countries relative to countries who can afford to maintain high levels of domestic support and export subsidies."[50]

OLIGARCHIC DECISION MAKING

There are other inequalities structured into the WTO system. The system of decision making is perhaps among the most blatant of these. While pro-WTO propaganda has projected the agency as a one nation/one vote organization, where the United States has exactly one vote, like Rwanda or the Dominican Republic, in fact, it is quite undemocratic and actually run by an oligarchy of countries, much like the World Bank and the IMF. Were majority rule to prevail, then the WTO would, like the UN General Assembly, be structurally very responsive to the needs of the South. But, as it did at the World Bank and the IMF, the North evolved other mechanisms of control. While at the Bank and the Fund, the prime mechanism of control is the size of rich countries' capital subscriptions, which gives them enormous voting power vis-a-vis the mass of developing countries, at the WTO, Northern domination is achieved via what is euphemistically referred to as "consensus."

This process was described in the following manner before the US Congress by an influential WTO advocate: after noting that there had not been a vote taken in GATT, the WTO's predecessor, since 1959, economist C. Fred Bergsten underlined that the WTO "does not work by voting. It works by a consensus arrangement which, to tell the truth, is managed by four—the Quads: the United States, Japan, European Union, and Canada."[51] He continued: "Those countries have to agree if any major steps are going to be made, that is true. But no votes. I do not anticipate votes in the new institution."[52]

The way that the consensus rule assures the hegemony of the North was on display in the selection of the successor to Renato Ruggiero as director general. The US-led bloc that supported New Zealander Mike Moore refused a head count, as proposed by backers of Thailand's Supachai, on grounds that this would violate the WTO's consensus tradition. Indeed, so undemocratic is the WTO that decisions are arrived at informally, via caucuses convoked in the corridors of the ministerials by the big trading powers. The formal sessions are reserved for speeches. The key agreements to come out of the first and second ministerials of the WTO—the decision to liberalize information technology trade taken in Singapore in 1996 and the agreement to liberalize trade in electronic commerce arrived at in Geneva in 1998—were all decided in informal backroom sessions and simply presented to the full assembly as *fait accompli.*

STRATEGY FOR CHANGE

It is against this dismal background that we now to move to the question of reform. Here one does not feel like taking the path of those who, after indicting the Bretton Woods institutions, do a turnaround when asked for solutions and appeal to the Bretton Woods institutions and the WTO to become answerable to the UN and to reorient their policies to serve the interests of the world's poor majority since this would be "truly in the enlightened self-interest of people in the rich, industrialized countries, their children, and their children's children."[53] This is utopian thinking, especially at a time that the North has just completed a campaign of global rollback that has delivered the *coup de grace* to the Southern project of reform. Reform, not revolution, was what the NIEO, the Non-Aligned Movement, and UNCTAD was all about... and look where this already very limited enterprise—what one Northern observer described as "the present order, with extra helpings for the flag bearers of the South"[54]—got the Third World.

At this time, change means not spending or wasting time trying to enlarge areas of reform within the World Bank, IMF, and WTO. They are, to borrow a metaphor from Max Weber, an iron cage of three overlapping bureaucracies and mandates where Southern aspirations and interests are structurally constrained.

One prong of a possible counter-strategy for defending the interests of the South must be directed at containing the gutting of the UN system and preserving its legitimacy, at a time that its effectiveness as an instrument of development is hobbled by Northern hostility and lack of money. A little money can go a long way when funneled into the right instrument, as is shown by the example of the UNDP Human Development Report, which is now seen as the magisterial authority in both the North and the South on the social and economic state of the world, no matter what the whole arsenal of World Bank publications says. A very good candidate for doing in trade what the Human Development Report does for development is the UNCTAD Trade and Development Report, whose focus on global structures impeding the ascent of the South is a good antidote to the WTO publications' doctrinal assertions on the benefits of free trade.

Beyond this, the project of making the UN agencies the pillars of an alternative global order is not going to result in success for a long time. What then should Southern movements for global reform focus their energies on? The main thrust, in our view, is to overload the system, to make it non-functional by constantly pushing demands that cannot be met by the system. In the case of the IMF, governments of the South and non-governmental organizations (NGOs) should press for the following demands: more transparency in IMF decision making, more accountability of IMF staff, one country/one vote decision making arrangements, and end to structural adjustment programs, no new funding for extended structural adjustment programs (ESAP), no extension of IMF authority to governance issues, and subordination of structural adjustment programs to global environmental agreements.

When it comes to the WTO, among the key tactics that could be deployed to overload the system might be pressing for the replacement of consensus decision making with majority voting, creative use of anti-dumping mechanisms against import penetration, and exploiting loopholes in the sanitary and phyto-sanitary agreement to restrict agricultural imports. Developing country governments must approach WTO rules in the same way a good defense lawyer approaches criminal law, which is to exploit the ambiguities of the system for the client—in this case for Third World farmers, manufacturers, and other producers.

Of course, the success of a strategy of overloading the system depends greatly on creating global political alliances, including coalitions with anti-globalization social and political forces in the North.

There are examples to draw from: a global pressure campaign by NGOs from both the North and the South on OECD governments prevented the adoption of the multilateral agreement on investment (MAI) by that body in 1999. NGO pressure on the US Congress killed the granting of "fast track" authority to negotiated free trade agreements to the US executive in 1998, weakening the ability of the US to demand greater trade liberalization at the Seattle WTO ministerial.

Where structures are hopeless, the next best solution is to have non-functioning structures or no operative structures at all. It was, for instance, during a period where no bodies supervised aid and development—the WW II era and immediate post-war era—that the countries of Latin America were able to successfully engage in import substitution to build up industrial structures. And it was during the period from the 1960s up to late 1980s, before the establishment of the WTO, that the NICs of East and Southeast Asia were able to marry domestic protectionism to mercantilism, and move from underdevelopment to industrial status in one generation.

Multilateral structures entrench the power of the Northern superpowers under the guise of creating a set of global rules for all. This is the reason why, in promoting the WTO in the US Congress, former US trade representative Mickey Kantor characterized the WTO as a "sword" that can be used to pry open economies. This is the reason Washington's academic point man on trade, C. Fred Bergsten, could tell the US Senate that ratification of the Marrakech agreement would serve the interests of the US because in addition to unilateral action, "we can now use the full weight of the international machinery to go after those trade barriers, reduce them, get them eliminated."[55]

Though the threat of unilateral action by the powerful is ever present, on balance a global system where there are either no or ineffective multilateral structures works to the benefit of the South.

Of course, the ideologues of the North will shout that this is tantamount to "anarchy." But then it has always been the powerful that have stoked this fear. The image of international relations in a world marked by few international arrangements as "nasty" and "brutish" has always been a Hobbesian fallacy that has not corresponded to reality. For the principal objective of most multilateral or international arrangements in history has never been to assure law and order to protect the weak. These structures have been pushed by the strong mainly to reduce the tremendous cost of policing the system to ensure that the less powerful do not cease to respect the rules set by the more powerful or break away completely.

In short, a fluid international system, where there are multiple zones of ambiguity that the less powerful can exploit in order to protect their interests, may be the only realistic alternative to the current global multilateral order that would weaken the hold of the North. The main beneficiaries of clearly articulated structures are always the powerful and the rich. The fewer structures and the less clear the rules, the better for the South.

NOTES

1. See among other works, *Towards a New Trade Policy for Development* (New York: UNCTAD, 1964).
2. Nossiter, Bernard. *The Global Struggle for More* (New York: Harper and Row, 1987), pp. 42–43.
3. Ibid., pg. 45.
4. Adams, Nassau. "The UN's neglected brief—'the advancement of all peoples,'" in Erskine Childers, *Challenges to the UN* (New York: St. Martin's Press), pg. 31.
5. *The Global Struggle for More*, pg. 34.
6. Ibid., pg. 35.
7. "The UN's neglected brief," op. cit.
8. Maizels, Alfred. "Reforming the world commodity economy," in Michael Cutajar, ed., *UNCTAD and the North-South Dialogue* (New York: Pergamon Press, 1985, pg. 108; United Nations, *World Economic Survey* (New York: United Nations, 1988), pg. 42.
9. Lissakers, Karin. *Banks, Borrowers, and the Establishment: A Revisionist Account of the International Debt Crisis* (New York: Basic Books, 1991), pg. 56.
10. White, Eduardo. "The question of foreign investments and the economic crisis of Latin America," in Richard Feinberg and Ricardo Ffrench-Davis, eds., *Development and External Debt in Latin America: Bases for a New Consensus* (Notre Dame, IN: University of Notre Dame Press, 1988), pp. 157–158.
11. *Banks, Borrowers, and the Establishment*, pg. 56.
12. "The question of foreign investments," pg. 158.

13. Quoted in *The Global Struggle for More*, pg. 57.

14. Bandow, Doug. "The US role in promoting Third World development," in Heritage Foundation, *US Aid to the Developing World: A Free Market Agenda* (Washington, DC: Heritage Foundation, 1985), pg. xxii.

15. Ibid., pg. xxiv.

16. Ibid., pp. xxiii–xxiv.

17. Cited in Seamus Cleary, "Toward a new adjustment in Africa," in "Beyond adjustment," special issue of *African Environment*, Vol. 7, Nos. 1–4, pg. 357.

18. Sheahan, John. "Development dichotomies and economic development strategy," in Simon Teitel, ed., *Towards a New Development Strategy for Latin America* (Washington, DC: Inter-American Development Bank, 1992), pg. 33.

19. Mulford, David. "Remarks before the Asia-Pacific capital markets conference," San Francisco, November 17, 1987.

20. Testimony of ambassador Charlene Barshefsky, US trade representative, before the House Ways and Means Trade Subcommittee, US Congress, February 24, 1998.

21. Ibid.

22. Ibid.

23. Ibid.

24. Quoted in "Worsening financial flu lowers immunity to US business," *The New York Times,* February 1, 1998.

25. "The UN's neglected brief," pg. 43.

26. South Commission. *The Challenge to the South* (New York: Oxford University Press, 1991), pg. 217.

27. Van der Stichele, Myriam. "World trade—free trade for whom, fair for whom?," in Erskine Childers, *Challenges to the UN* (New York: St. Martin's Press), pg. 69.

28. Ibid.

29. "South decries moves to close UNCTAD, UNIDO," *Third World Resurgence,* No. 56, pg. 41.

30. Ibid.

31. UNCTAD. *Trade and Development Report 1991* (New York: United Nations, 1991), pg. 191.

32. See discussion of this in Walden Bello and Stephanie Rosenfeld, *Dragons in Distress: Asia's Miracle Economies in Crisis* (Oakland, CA: Food First Books, 1990), pg. 161.

33. Atkinson, Jeff. "GATT: What do the poor get?" *Background Report No. 5* (Melbourne, Australia: Community Aid Abroad, 1994), pg. 12.

34. Chatterjee, Pratap. "Riders of the apocalypse," *The New Internationalist,* July 1994, pg. 10.

35. "GATT: What do the poor get?"

36. Ibid.

37. Perlas, Nicarnor. "GATT, biotechnology, and the church," Paper presented at the Catholic Bishops Conference for the Philippines—Visaya Secretariat, November 16, 1994, pg. 5.

38. Trebilcock, Michael and Robert Howse. *The Regulation of International Trade* (London, UK: Routledge, 1995), pg. 193.

39. Ibid., pg. 201.

40. Ibid., pg. 202.

41. World Trade Organization. *Trade Policy Review: United States* (Geneva: WTO, 1996), pp. 116–117.

42. Ibid.

43. Zepezauer, M. and A. Naiman. *Take the Rich Off Welfare* (Tucson, AZ: Odonian Press, 1996).

44. Faeth, cited in A.P.G. Moor, *Perverse Incentives* (The Hague: Institute for Research on Public Expenditure, 1997).

45. Gardner, Brian. "EU dumping to continue," in *The GATT Agreement on Agriculture: Will It Help Developing Countries?* (London, UK: Catholic Institute of International Relations, 1994).

46. Moor, A.P.G. *Perverse Incentives* (The Hague: Institute for Research on Public Expenditure, 1997).

47. Ibid.

48. "Threats of food surplus for EU," *Bridges,* Vol. 1, No. 13, 1997.

49. US trade representative Charlene Barshefsky, remarks prepared for delivery at the US Department of Agriculture Agricultural Outlook Forum, Washington, DC, February 24, 1997.

50. Speech at the second ministerial of the World Trade Organization, May 18–20, 1998.

51. C. Fred Bergsten, director, Institute for International Economics, testimony before the US Senate Committee on Commerce, Science, and Technology, Washington, DC, October 13, 1994.

52. Ibid.

53. Jamal, Amir. "The IMF and World Bank—managing the planet's money," in Erskine Childers, *Challenges to the UN* (New York: St. Martin's Press),pp. 53–54.

54. *The Global Struggle for More*, op. cit.

55. C. Fred Bergsten, testimony.

2

WHY REFORM OF THE WTO
IS THE WRONG AGENDA

Food First Backgrounder, Summer 2000

In the wake of the collapse of the Seattle ministerial, there has emerged the opinion that reform of the World Trade Organization (WTO) is now the program that non-governmental organizations (NGOs), governments, and citizens must embrace. The collapse of the WTO ministerial is said to provide a unique window of opportunity for a reform agenda.

Cited by some as a positive sign is United States trade representative Charlene Barshefsky's comment, immediately after the collapse of the Seattle ministerial in late 1999, that "the WTO has outgrown the processes appropriate to an earlier time. An increasing and necessary view, generally shared among the members, was that we needed a process which had a greater degree of internal transparency and inclusion to accommodate a larger and more diverse membership."[1]

Also seen as an encouraging gesture was UK secretary of state for trade and industry Stephen Byers' statement to Commonwealth trade ministers in New Delhi in January 2000 that the "WTO will not be able to continue in its present form. There has to be fundamental and radical change in order for it to meet the needs and aspirations of all 134 of its members."[2]

These are, in our view, damage control statements and provide little indication of the seriousness about reform of the two governments that were, pre-Seattle, the strongest defenders of the inequalities built into the structure, dynamics, and objectives of the WTO. It is unfortunate that they are now being cited to convince developing countries and NGOs to take up an agenda of reform that could lead precisely to the strengthening of an organization that is very fundamentally flawed.

What civil society, North and South, should instead be doing at this point is radically cutting down the power of the institution, and reducing it to simply another institution in a pluralistic world trading system with multiple systems of governance.

DOES WORLD TRADE NEED
THE WORLD TRADE ORGANIZATION?

This is the fundamental question on which the question of reform hinges. World trade did not need the WTO to expand 17-fold between 1948 and 1997, from $124 billion to $10,772 billion.[3] This expansion took place under the flexible General Agreement on Trade and Tarrifs (GATT) trade regime. The founding of the WTO in 1995 did not respond to a collapse or crisis of world trade, such as happened in the 1930s. It was not necessary for global peace, since no world war or trade-related war had taken place during that period. In the seven major interstate wars that took place in that period—the Korean War of 1950–1953, the Vietnam War of 1945–1975, the Suez Crisis of 1956, the 1967 Arab-Israeli War, the 1973 Arab-Israeli War, the 1982 Falklands War, and the Gulf War of 1990—trade conflict did not figure even remotely as a cause.

GATT was, in fact, functioning reasonably well as a framework for liberalizing world trade. Its dispute settlement system was flexible, and its recognition of the "special and differential status" of developing countries provided the space in a global economy for Third World countries to use trade policy for development and industrialization.

Why was the WTO established following the Uruguay Round of 1986–1994? Of the major trading powers, Japan was very ambivalent, concerned as it was to protect its agriculture as well as its particular system of industrial production that, through formal and informal mechanisms, gave its local producers primary right to exploit the domestic market. The European Union (EU), well on the way of becoming a self-sufficient trading bloc, was likewise ambivalent, knowing that its highly subsidized system in agriculture would come under attack. Though demanding greater access to their manufactured and agricultural products in the Northern economies, the developing countries did not see this as being accomplished through a comprehensive agreement enforced by a powerful trade bureaucracy, but through discrete negotiations and agreements in the model of the integrated program for commodities (IPCs) and commodity stabilization fund agreed upon under the aegis of the UN Conference on Trade and Development (UNCTAD) in the late 1970s.

The founding of the WTO served primarily the interest of the United States. Just as it was the US which blocked the founding of the International Trade Organization (ITO) in 1948, when it felt that this would not serve its position of overwhelming economic dominance in the post-war world, so it was that the US became the dominant lobbyist for the comprehensive Uruguay Round and the founding of the WTO in late 1980s and early 1990s, when it felt that more competitive global conditions had created a situation where its corporate interests now demanded an opposite stance.

Just as it was the United State's threat in the 1950s to leave GATT if it was not allowed to maintain protective mechanisms for milk and other agricultural products that led to agricultural trade's exemption from GATT rules, it was US pressure that brought agriculture into the GATT-WTO system in 1995. And the reason for Washington's change of mind was articulated quite candidly by then US agriculture secretary John Block at the start of the Uruguay Round negotiations in 1986: "[The] idea that developing countries should feed themselves is an anachronism from a bygone era. They could better ensure their food security by relying on US agricultural products, which are available, in most cases at much lower cost."[4] Washington, of course, did not just have developing country markets in mind, but also Japan, South Korea, and the EU.

It was the US that mainly pushed to bring services under the WTO coverage, with its assessment that in the new burgeoning area of international services, and particularly in financial services, its corporations had a lead that needed to be preserved. It was also the US that pushed to expand WTO jurisdiction to the so-called "trade-related investment measures" (TRIMs) and "trade-related intellectual property rights (TRIPs)." The first sought to eliminate barriers to the system of internal cross-border trade of product components among TNC (transnational corporation) subsidiaries that had been imposed by developing countries in order to develop their industries; the second to consolidate the US advantage in the cutting edge knowledge-intensive industries.

It was the US that forced the creation of the WTO's formidable dispute-resolution and enforcement mechanism after being frustrated with what US trade officials considered weak GATT efforts to enforce rulings favorable to the US. As Washington's academic point man on trade, C. Fred Bergsten, head of the Institute of International Economics, told the US Senate, the strong WTO dispute settlement mechanism serves American interests because "we can now use the full weight of the international machinery to go after those trade barriers, reduce them, get them eliminated."[5]

In sum, it has been Washington's changing perception of the needs of its economic interest groups that have shaped and reshaped the international trading regime. It was not global necessity that gave birth to the WTO in 1995. It was the United State's assessment that the interests of its corporations were no longer served by a loose and flexible GATT but needed an all-powerful and wide-ranging WTO. From the free market paradigm that underpins it, to the rules and regulations set forth in the different agreements that make up the Uruguay Round, to its system of decision making and accountability, the WTO is a blueprint for the global hegemony of corporate America. It seeks to institutionalize the accumulated advantages of US corporations.

Is the WTO necessary? Yes, to the United States. But not to the rest of the world. The necessity of the WTO is one of the biggest lies of our time, and its acceptance is due to the same propaganda principle practiced by Joseph Goebbels: if you repeat a lie often enough, it will be taken as truth.

CAN THE WTO SERVE THE INTERESTS
OF THE DEVELOPING COUNTRIES?

What about the developing countries? Is the WTO a necessary structure—one that, whatever its flaws, brings more benefits than costs, and would therefore merit efforts at reform?

When the Uruguay Round was negotiated, there was considerable lack of enthusiasm for the process by the developing countries. After all, these countries had formed the backbone of UNCTAD. With its system of one-country/one-vote and majority voting, they felt was an international arena more congenial to their interests. They entered the Uruguay Round greatly resenting the large trading powers' policy of weakening and marginalizing UNCTAD in the late 1970s and early 1980s. Largely passive spectators, with a great number not even represented during the negotiations owing to resource constraints, the developing countries were dragged into unenthusiastic endorsement of the Marrakech accord of 1994 that sealed the Uruguay Round and established the WTO. True, there were some developing countries, most of them in the Cairns Group of developed and developing country agro-exporters, that actively promoted the WTO in the hope that they would gain greater market access to their exports, but they were a small minority.

To try to sell the WTO to the South, US propagandists evoked the fear that staying out of the WTO would result in a country's isolation from world trade ("like North Korea") and stoked the promise that a "rules-based system" of world trade would protect the weak countries from unilateral acts by the big trading powers.

With their economies dominated by the IMF and the World Bank, and the structural adjustment programs pushed by these agencies as a central element in radical trade liberalization, the developing countries were much weaker as a bloc owing to the debt crisis compared to the 1970s, the height of the "New International Economic Order." Most developing country delegations felt they had no choice but to sign on the dotted line.

Over the next few years, however, these countries realized that they had signed away their right to employ a variety of critical trade measures for development purposes.

In contrast to the loose GATT framework, which had allowed some space for development initiatives, the comprehensive and tightened Uruguay Round was fundamentally anti-development in its thrust which is evident in the loss of trade policy as development tool, the agreement on trade-related investment measures and the agreement on trade-related intellectual property rights.

WATERING DOWN THE "SPECIAL AND
DIFFERENTIAL TREATMENT" PRINCIPLE

The central principle of UNCTAD—an organization dis-empowered by the establishment of the WTO—is that owing to the critical nexus between trade and development, developing countries must not be subjected to the same expectations, rules, and regulations that govern trade among the developed countries. Owing to historical and structural considerations, developing countries need special consideration and special assistance in leveling the playing field for them to be able to participate equitably in world trade. This would include both the use of protective tariffs for development purposes and preferential access of developing country exports to developed country markets.

While GATT was not centrally concerned with development, it did recognize the "special and differential status" of the developing countries. Perhaps the strongest statement of this was in the Tokyo Round Declaration in 1973, which recognized "the importance of the application of differential measures in developing countries in ways which will provide special and more favorable treatment for them in areas of negotiation where this is feasible."[6]

Different sections of the evolving GATT code allowed developing countries to renegotiate tariff bindings in order to promote the establishment of certain industries; to use tariffs for economic development and fiscal purposes; to use quantitative restrictions to promote infant industries; and conceded the principle of non-reciprocity by developing countries in trade negotiation.[7] The 1979 framework agreement known at the enabling clause also provided a permanent legal basis for general system of preferences (GSP) schemes that would provide preferential access to developing country exports.[8]

A significant shift occurred in the Uruguay Round. GSP schemes were not bound, meaning tariffs could be raised against developing country until they equaled the bound rates applied to imports for all sources. During the negotiations, the threat to remove GSP was used as "a form of bilateral pressure on developing countries."[9] Special and differential treatment (SDT) was turned from a focus on a special right to protect and special rights of market access to "one of responding to special adjustment difficulties in developing countries stemming from the implementation of WTO decisions."[10] Measures meant to address the structural inequality of the trading system gave way to measures, such as a lower rate of tariff reduction or a longer time frame for implementing decisions, which regarded the problem of developing countries as simply that of catching up in an essentially even playing field.

SDT has been watered down in the WTO, and this is not surprising for the neoliberal agenda that underpins the WTO philosophy which differs from the Keynesian assumptions of GATT: that there are no special rights, no special protections needed for development. The only route to development is one that involves radical trade (and investment) liberalization.

FATE OF THE SPECIAL MEASURES FOR DEVELOPING COUNTRIES

Perhaps the best indicators of the marginal consideration given to developing countries in the WTO is the fate of the measures that were supposed to respond to the special conditions of developing countries. There were three key agreements which promoters of the WTO claimed were specifically designed to meet the needs of the South:

> The special ministerial agreement approved in Marrakech in April 1994, which decreed that special compensatory measures would be taken to counteract the negative effects of trade liberalization on the net food-importing developing countries.

> The Agreement on Textiles and Clothing, which mandated that the system of quotas on developing country exports of textiles and garments to the North would be dismantled over ten years.

> The Agreement on Agriculture (AOA), which, while "imperfect," nevertheless was said to promise greater market access to developing country agricultural products and begin the process of bringing down the high levels of state support and subsidization of EU and

US agriculture, which was resulting in the dumping of massive quantities of grain on Third World markets.

WHAT HAPPENED TO THESE MEASURES?

The special ministerial decision taken at Marrakech to provide assistance to "net food importing countries" to offset the reduction of subsidies that would make food imports more expensive for the "net food importing countries" has never been implemented. Though world crude oil prices more than doubled in 1995–1996, the World Bank and the IMF scotched any idea of offsetting aid by arguing that "the price increase was not due to the agreement on agriculture, and besides there was never any agreement anyway on who would be responsible for providing the assistance."[11]

The Agreement on Textiles and Clothing committed the developed countries to bring under WTO discipline all textile and garment imports over four stages, ending on January 1, 2005. A key feature was supposed to be the lifting of quotas on imports restricted under the multifiber agreement (MFA) and similar schemes which had been used to contain penetration of developed country markets by cheap clothing and textile imports from the Third World. However, developed countries retained the right to choose which product lines to liberalize and when, so that they first brought mainly unrestricted products into the WTO discipline and postponed dealing with restricted products until much later. Thus, in the first phase, all restricted products continued to be under quota, as only items where imports were not considered threatening—like felt hats or yarn of carded fine animal hair—were included in the developed countries' notifications. Indeed, the notifications for the coverage of products for liberalization on January 1, 1998 showed that "even at the second stage of implementation only a very small proportion" of restricted products would see their quotas lifted.[12]

Given this trend, John Whalley notes that "the belief is now widely held in the developing world that in 2004, while the MFA may disappear, it may well be replaced by a series of other trade instruments, possibly substantial increases in anti-dumping duties."[13]

When it comes to the Agreement on Agriculture, which was sold to developing countries during the Uruguay Round as a major step toward providing market access to developing country imports and bringing down the high levels of domestic support for First World farming interests that results in dumping of commodities in Third World markets, little gains in market access after five years into developed country markets have been accompanied by even higher levels of overall subsidization—through ingenious combinations of export subsidies, export credits, market support, and various kinds of direct income payments.

The figures speak for themselves: the level of overall subsidization of agriculture in the Organization for Economic Cooperation and Development (OECD) countries rose from $182 billion in 1995 when the WTO was born, to $280 billion in 1997 to $362 billion in 1998! Instead of the beginning of a New Deal, the AOA, in the words of a former Philippine secretary of trade, "has perpetuated the unevenness of a playing field which the multilateral trading system has been trying to correct. Moreover, this has placed the burden of adjustment on developing countries relative to countries who can afford to maintain high levels of domestic support and export subsidies."[14]

The collapse of the agricultural negotiations in Seattle is the best example of how extremely difficult it is to reform the AOA. The European Union opposed until the bitter end language in an agreement that would commit it to "significant reduction" of its subsidies. But the US was not blameless. It resolutely opposed any effort to cut back on its forms of subsidies such as export credits, direct income for farmers, and "emergency" farm aid, as well as any mention of its practice of dumping products in developing country markets.

OLIGARCHIC DECISION MAKING
AS A CENTRAL, DEFINING PROCESS

Can the system of WTO decision making be reformed? While far more flexible than the WTO, the GATT was, of course, far from perfect, and one of the bad traits that the WTO took over from it was the system of decision making. GATT functioned through a process called "consensus." Now consensus responded to the same problem that faced the IMF and the World Bank's developed country members: how to assure control at a time that the numbers gave the edge to the new countries of the South. In the Fund and the Bank, the system of decision making that evolved had the weight of a country's vote determined by the size of its capital subscriptions, which gave the US and the other rich countries effective control of the two organizations. In the GATT, a one-country/one-vote system was initially tried, but the big trading powers saw this as inimical to their interests. The last time a vote was taken in GATT was in 1959.[15]

The WTO has continued this tradition of being an undemocratic institution where decisions are arrived at informally through consensus which renders non-transparent a process where smaller, weaker countries are pressured, browbeaten, or bullied to conform to the "consensus" forged among major trading powers.

With surprising frankness, at a press conference in Seattle, US trade representative Charlene Barshefsky, who played the pivotal role in all three ministerials, described the dynamics and consequences of this system of decision making: "The process, including even at Singapore as recently as three years ago, was a rather exclusionary one. All meetings were held between 20 and 30 key countries… And that meant 100 countries, 100, were never in the room…[T]his led to an extraordinarily bad feeling that they were left out of the process and that the results even at Singapore had been dictated to them by the 25 or 30 privileged countries who were in the room."[16]

Then, after registering her frustration at the WTO delegates' failing to arrive at consensus via supposedly broader "working groups" set up for the Seattle ministerial, Barshefsky warned delegates: "…[I] have made very clear and I reiterated to all ministers today that, if we are unable to achieve that goal, I fully reserve the right to also use a more exclusive process to achieve a final outcome. There is no question about either my right as the chair to do it or my intention as the chair to do it…."[17]

And she was serious about ramming through a declaration at the expense of non-representation, with India, one of the key developing country members of the WTO, being "routinely excluded from private talks organized by the United States in last ditch efforts to come up with a face-saving deal."[18]

In damage-containment mode after the collapse of the Seattle ministerial, Barshefsky, WTO director general Mike Moore, and other rich country representatives have spoken about the need for WTO "reform." But none have declared any intention of pushing for a one-county/one-vote majority decision making system or a voting system weighted by population size, which would be the only fair and legitimate methods in a democratic international organization. The fact is, such mechanisms will never be adopted, for this would put the developing countries in a preponderant role in terms of decision making.

SHOULD ONE TRY TO REFORM A JURASSIC INSTITUTION?

Reform is a viable strategy when the system is question is fundamentally fair but has simply been corrupted such as the case with some democracies. It is not a viable strategy when a system is so fundamentally unequal in purposes, principles, and processes as the WTO. The WTO systematically protects the trade and economic advantages of the rich countries, particularly the United States. It is based on a philosophy that denigrates the right to take activist measures to achieve development on the part of less developed countries, thus leading to a radical dilution of their right to "special and differential treatment." The WTO raises inequality into a principle of decision making.

The WTO is often promoted as a "rules-based" trading framework that protects the weaker and poorer countries from unilateral actions by the stronger states. The opposite is true: the WTO, like many other multilateral international agreements, is meant to institutionalize and legitimize inequality. Its main purpose is to reduce the tremendous policing costs to the stronger powers that would be involved in disciplining many small countries in a more fluid, less structured international system.

It is not surprising that both the WTO and the IMF are currently mired in a severe crisis of legitimacy. For both are highly centralized, highly unaccountable, highly non-transparent global institutions that seek to subjugate, control, or harness vast swathes of global economic, social, political, and environmental processes to the needs and interests of a global minority of states, elites, and transnational corporations. The dynamics of such institutions clash with the burgeoning democratic aspirations of peoples, countries, and communities in both the North and the South. The centralizing dynamics of these institutions clash with the efforts of communities and nations to regain control of their fate and achieve a modicum of security by de-concentrating and decentralizing economic and political power. In other words, these are Jurassic institutions in an age of participatory political and economic democracy.

BUILDING A MORE PLURALISTIC SYSTEM OF INTERNATIONAL TRADE GOVERNANCE

If there is one thing that is clear, it is that developing country governments and international civil society must not allow their energies to be hijacked into reforming these institutions. This will only amount to administering a facelift to fundamentally flawed institutions. Indeed, today's need is not another centralized global institution, reformed or unreformed, but the decentralization of institutional power and the creation of a pluralistic system of institutions and organizations interacting with one another amid broadly defined and flexible agreements and understandings.

It was under such a more pluralistic global system, where hegemonic power was still far from institutionalized in a set of all encompassing and powerful multilateral organizations that the Latin American countries and many Asian countries were able to achieve a modicum of industrial development in the period from 1950–1970. It was under a more pluralistic world system, under a GATT that was limited in its power, flexible, and more sympathetic to the special status of developing countries, that the East and Southeast Asian countries were able to become newly industrializing countries through activist state trade and industrial policies that departed significantly from the free market biases enshrined in the WTO.

The alternative to a powerful WTO is not a Hobbesian state of nature. The reality of international economic relations in a world marked by a multiplicity of international and regional institutions that check one another is a far cry from the propaganda image of a "nasty" and "brutish" world. Of course, the threat of unilateral action by the powerful is ever present in such a system, but it is one that even the powerful hesitate to take for fear of its consequences on their legitimacy as well as the reaction it would provoke in the form of opposing coalitions.

What developing countries and international civil society should aim at is not to reform the WTO but, through a combination of passive and active measures, to radically reduce its power and make it simply another international institution coexisting with and being checked by other international organizations, agreements, and regional groupings. These would include such diverse actors and institutions as UNCTAD, multilateral environmental agreements, and the International Labor Organization, involving trade blocs such as the Common Market of the South (Mercosur) in Latin America, the South Asian Association for Regional Development (SAARC) in South Asia, the Southern Africa Development Coordination Conference (SADCC) in Southern Africa, and the Association of Southeast Asian Nations (ASEAN) in Southeast Asia. It is in such a more fluid, less structured, more pluralistic world with multiple checks and balances that the nations and communities of the South will be able to carve out the space to develop based on their values, their rhythms, and the strategies of their choice.

NOTES

1. Press briefing, Seattle, Washington, December 2, 1999.
2. Quoted in "Deadline set for WTO reforms," *Guardian News Service*, January 10, 2000.
3. Figures from *World Trade Organization, Annual Report 1998: International Trade Statistics* (Geneva: WTO, 1998), pg. 12.
4. Quoted in "Cakes and caviar: The Dunkel draft and Third World agriculture," *The Ecologist*, Vol. 23, No. 6 (November–December 1993), pg. 220.
5. C. Fred Bergsten, director, Institute for International Economics. Testimony before US Senate, Washington, DC, October 13, 1994.

6. Quoted in John Whaley, "Special and differential treatment in the millennium round," *CSGR Working Paper,* No. 30/99 (May 1999), pg. 3.

7. Ibid., pg. 4.

8. Ibid., pg. 7.

9. Ibid., pg. 10.

10. Ibid., pg. 14.

11. "More power to the World Trade Organization?" Panos briefing, November 1999, pg. 14.

12. South Center. *The Multilateral Trade Agenda and the South* (Geneva: South Center, 1998), pg. 32.

13. Whalley, John. "Building poor countries' trading capacity," *CSGR Working Paper Series* (Warwick: CSGR, March 1999)

14. Secretary of trade Cesar Bautista, address to second WTO ministerial, Geneva, May 18, 1998.

15. C. Fred Bergsten testimony.

16. Press briefing, Seattle.

17. Ibid.

18. "Deadline set for WTO reforms."

3

JURASSIC FUND: SHOULD
DEVELOPING COUNTRIES PUSH
TO DECOMMISSION THE IMF?

(An expanded version of the author's column in the
Far Eastern Economic Review, December 6, 1999.)

When the International Monetary Fund (IMF) made a surprise announcement at the World Bank-IMF annual meeting at the end of September 1999 that it would now put "poverty reduction" at the center of its approach toward developing countries, there was widespread speculation among Washington watchers that Michel Camdessus' days as managing director were numbered.

Camdessus resigned in mid-November 1999, shortly after Larry Summers, the new US Treasury secretary and one of Camdessus' biggest backers, told the US Congress that the US would support a "new framework for providing international assistance to [developing] countries—one that moves beyond a closed IMF-centered process that has too often focused on narrow macroeconomic objectives at the expense of broader human development."[1]

The Frenchman's 13-year reign had been identified with a paradigm of development that he fervently believed in: structural adjustment. In the two decades since 1980, structural adjustment programs (SAPs) were imposed jointly by the World Bank and the IMF on close to 90 developing countries, from Guyana to Ghana. Despite important differences among the various economies, SAPs had the same basic elements: long-term "structural" reforms to deregulate the economy, liberalize trade and investment, and privatize state enterprises, coupled with short-term stabilization measures like cutbacks in government expenditures, high interest rates, and currency devaluation.

SAPs multiplied during the Third World debt crisis of the early

1980s. An important reason was strong pressure from the Bank and IMF on governments to restructure their economies along lines designed to yield the financial resources to pay off their massive debts to the international commercial banks. But the objective of SAPs went beyond debt repayment or the attainment of short-term macroeconomic stability. The Bank and the Fund sought nothing less than the dismantling of protectionism and other policies of state-assisted capitalism that IMF and World Bank theorists judged to be the main obstacles to sustained growth and development.

When the socialist economies of Eastern Europe and Russia collapsed in the early 1990s, structural adjustment was also extended to that part of the world, and in a manner that was even more radical than in the South—a process that Harvard's Jeffrey Sachs, then one of its vocal proponents, appropriately labeled "shock therapy." IMF technocrats went to these countries with even more dogmatic confidence in their one true model than the Marxist bureaucrats they supplanted had in theirs. By the early 1990s, shock therapy and structural adjustment had become cornerstones of what economist John Williamson called "the Washington consensus" on the desired macroeconomic framework that would create a truly global economy fueled by market forces.

RETREAT

Two decades after the first structural adjustment loan, the Bank has formally abandoned structural adjustment, replacing it with the "comprehensive development framework." The new paradigm, according to a statement of the Group of Seven (G-7) finance ministers and Central Bank governors,[2] has the following elements:

- Increased and more effective fiscal expenditures for poverty reduction with better targeting of budgetary resources, especially on social priorities in basic education and health.

- Enhanced transparency, including monitoring and quality control over fiscal expenditures.

- Stronger country ownership of the reform and poverty reduction process and programs, involving public participation.

- Stronger performance indicators that can be monitored for follow-through on poverty reduction.

- Ensure macroeconomic stability and sustainability, and reduce barriers to access by the poor to the benefits of growth.

What brought about the 180 degree turn? Failure, spectacular failure, that could no longer be denied at the pain of totally losing institutional credibility.

The World Bank—or rather James Wolfensohn, President Bill Clinton's nominee to head the Bank in 1993—was the first to recognize that something was amiss. Coming from outside orthodox development circles, Wolfensohn sensed what most World Bank officials did not want to acknowledge: that with over 100 countries under adjustment for over a decade, it was strange that the Bank and the Fund found it hard to point to even a handful of success stories. In most cases, as Rudiger Dornbusch of the Massachusetts Institute of Technology put it, structural adjustment caused economies to "fall into a hole,"[3] wherein low investment, reduced social spending, reduced consumption, and low output interacted to create a vicious cycle of decline and stagnation, rather than a virtuous circle of growth, rising employment, and investment, as originally envisaged by World Bank-IMF theory.

With much resistance from the Bank's entrenched bureaucracy, Wolfensohn slowly moved to distance the Bank from hard-line adjustment policies. He even got some of his staff to (grudgingly) work with civil society groups to assess SAPs in the so-called "structural adjustment review initiative" (SAPRI). For the most part, however, the change of attitude did not translate to changes at the operational level owing to the strong internalization of the structural adjustment approach among Bank operatives.

In contrast, while doubt began to engulf the Bank, the IMF plowed confidently on, and the lack of evidence of success was interpreted to mean simply that a government lacked political will to push adjustment. Through the establishment of the extended structural adjustment facility (ESAF), the Fund sought to fund countries over a longer period in order to more fully institutionalize the desired free market reforms and make them permanent.

THE PHILIPPINE CASE

The Philippines, together with Turkey and Costa Rica, was one of the guinea pigs of structural adjustment. Its experience under adjustment was representative of the Third World experience. Between 1980 and 1999, the Philippines became the recipient of nine structural adjustment loans from the World Bank, participating in three standby programs, two extended fund programs, and one precautionary standby arrangement with the IMF.[4] The country, in short, was in continuous adjustment for nearly 20 years, its macroeconomic policies being micromanaged by the Bretton Woods twins.

The first phase of adjustment focused on trade liberalization, and saw quantitative restrictions removed on more than 900 items, while the nominal average tariff protection was brought down from 43 percent in 1981 to 28 percent in 1985. But the program failed to factor in the onset of a global recession, so that instead of rising, exports fell, while imports coming in to take advantage of the liberalized regime severely eroded the home industries. As the late economist Charles Lindsay noted, "Whatever the merits of the SAP, its timing was deplorable."[5] Instead of allowing the government to set in motion countercyclical mechanisms to arrest the decline of private sector activity, the structural adjustment framework intensified the crisis with its policy of high interest rates and tight government budgets. Not surprisingly, the GNP shrank precipitously two years in a row, contributing to the political crisis that resulted in the ouster of Ferdinand Marcos in February 1986.

Under Corazon Aquino the second phase of adjustment saw economic recovery subordinated to the repayment of the foreign debt of the country's $26 billion foreign debt. This was achieved via fiscal austerity and much more intensified export of natural resources and export-oriented production. A financial hemorrhage ensued, with the net transfer of financial resources coming to a negative $1.3 billion a year on average between 1986 and 1981, according to the Freedom from Debt Coalition.[6] To service the debt, the Aquino administration was forced to borrow heavily from domestic financial sources, forcing it to channel much of its budgetary expenditures from development and social spending to meeting both domestic and foreign debt obligations. By 1987, some 50 percent of the budget was going to service the national debt.[7]

Not surprisingly, this "model debtor" via structural adjustment institutionalized stagnation, with the country registering zero average GNP growth between 1983 and 1993. Stagnation led to a worsening of social conditions, with families living under the poverty line coming to 46.5 percent of all families in 1991 and share of the national income going to the lowest 20 percent of families dropping from 5.2 percent in 1985 to 4.7 in 1991.[8] The Philippines also provided one of the best documented studies of the correlation between environmental destruction and structural adjustment, with a World Resources Institute study concluding that adjustment "created so much unemployment that migration patterns changed drastically. The large migration flows to Manila declined, and most migrants could only turn to open access forests, watersheds, and artisanal fisheries. Thus the major environmental effect of the economic crisis was overexploitation of these vulnerable resources."[9]

When the Ramos administration took over in 1992, the focus of adjustment shifted back to accelerated privatization, deregulation, and liberalization of trade, investment, and finance. Petron and several government enterprises and services passed to the private sector; a substantially free trade regime was targeted for 2004, when tariff rates would be reduced to a uniform five percent or less for all products; and nationality restrictions on foreign investment were relaxed considerably. Capital account liberalization, an IMF prescription, resulted in massive inflows of speculative capital into the financial and real estate sector, triggering an artificial boom in Manila. But the liberalized capital account also became the wide highway through which billions of dollars exited in 1997 and 1998, at the onset of the Asian financial crisis, bringing the GNP growth rate to below zero in 1998.[10]

Adjusted and readjusted for nearly 20 years, Manila simply could not climb out of a deepening hole.

CRISIS OF LEGITIMACY

It was the Asian financial crisis that finally forced the IMF to confront reality. In 1997–1998 the Fund moved with grand assurance into Thailand, Indonesia, and Korea, with its classic formula of short-term fiscal and monetary policy *cum* structural reform in the direction of liberalization, deregulation, and privatization. This was the price exacted from their governments for the IMF financial rescue packages that would allow them to repay the massive debt incurred by their private sectors. But the result was to turn a conjunctural crisis into a deep recession, as government's capacity to counteract the drop in private sector activity was destroyed by budgetary and monetary repression.[11] If some recovery is now discernible in a few economies, this is widely recognized as coming in spite of, rather than because of, the IMF.

For a world that had long been resentful of the Fund's arrogance, this was the last straw. In 1998–1999, criticism of the IMF rose to a crescendo. The Fund went beyond its stubborn adherence to structural adjustment and its serving as a bailout mechanism for international finance capital to encompass accusations of its being non-transparent and non-accountable. Its vulnerable position was exposed during a debate in the US Congress in 1999 over a G-7 initiative to provide debt relief to 40 poor countries. Legislators depicted the IMF as the agency that caused the debt crisis of the poor countries in the first place, and some called for its abolition within three years. Said Representative Maxine Walters: "Do we have to have the IMF involved at all? Because, as we have painfully discovered, the way the IMF works causes children to starve."[12]

In the face of such criticism from legislators, the IMF's most powerful member, US Treasury secretary Larry Summers, claimed that the IMF-centered process would be replaced by "a new, more open and inclusive process that would involve multiple international organizations and give national policy makers and civil society groups a more central role."[13]

BUT IS THIS FOR REAL?

So structural adjustment is dead, and the Bretton Woods institutions have seen the light. But wait, isn't there something too easy about all this?

The fact is, in the case of the IMF as well as that of the World Bank and the Asian Development Bank (ADB), jettisoning the paradigm of structural adjustment has left them adrift. In the view of many critics, all that remains are the rhetoric and broad goals of reducing poverty, but without an innovative macroeconomic approach. Wolfensohn and his ex-chief economist Joseph Stiglitz talk about "bringing together" the "macroeconomic" and "social" aspects of development, but Bank officials cannot point to a larger strategy beyond increasing lending to health, population, nutrition, education, and social protection to 25 percent of the Bank's total lending. The ADB is even more of a new-comer in the anti-poverty approach, and its strategy paper issued this year is long on laudable goals but, even ADB insiders agree, breaks no new ground in terms of macroeconomic innovation. Most at sea are IMF economists, some of whom openly admitted to representatives from non-governmental organizations (NGOs) at the September IMF-World Bank meeting in 1999 that so far the new approach was limited to re-labeling the extended structural adjustment fund the "poverty reduction facility," and that they were looking to the World Bank to provide leadership.[14]

It is not surprising that in these circumstances, the old framework would reassert itself, with, for example, the IMF telling the Thai government, already its most obedient pupil, to cut its fiscal deficit despite a very fragile recovery; the Fund's pushing Indonesia to open its retail trade to foreign investors, despite the consequences in terms of higher unemployment; and technocrats of the ADB making energy loans and Miyazawa Plan funding contingent on the Philippine government's accelerating the IMF-promoted privatization of the National Power Corporation, despite the fact that consumers are likely to end up paying more to the seven private monopolies that will succeed the state enterprise.

"It's once again the old approach of deregulation, privatization, and liberalization but with safety nets," is the not an inappropriate description by one Filipino labor leader much consulted by the multilateral institutions.[15]

Then there is the issue of accountability. One cannot just walk away from the scene of the crime without admitting wrongdoing. The Bank and the Fund have been responsible for tremendous economic and social damage wrought on Third World economies for over two decades. Shouldn't they be held to account for that? Should not Camdessus and the whole top leadership of the IMF, including his deputy Stanley Fischer and Asia-Pacific division chief Hubert Neiss, who blindly embraced adjustment to the end, take responsibility for their massive blunders? Despite their announced resignations, both Camdessus and Neiss are unrepentant when it comes to their policies.

Many of the Fund's longtime critics have a darker view of things. To them, Camdessus served as a sacrificial lamb to blunt real efforts at reform at a time that the Fund "desperately needs" credibility and legitimacy, as *The Financial Times* put it.[16] This fear is well-grounded, for in his most recent statements, Larry Summers, the pivotal figure when it comes to the future of the IMF, appears to have forgotten about the need for a paradigm shift. When speaking about the elements of a "new" IMF strategy, Summers says that the "approach looks to the IMF to continue to certify that a country's macroeconomic policies are satisfactory before debt is relieved or new concessional lending is advanced."[17] Is this what is meant by "moving away from an IMF-centered process that has too often focused on narrow macroeconomic objectives at the expense of broader human development"?[18]

Bearing in mind that trade liberalization was one of the most controversial dimensions of the old structural adjustment approach, even more revealing is Summers' view that the new IMF must have as one of its priorities "strong support for market opening and trade liberalization."[19] Trade liberalization, Summers continues, "is often a key component of IMF arrangements. In the course of negotiations, the IMF has sought continued compliance with existing trade obligations and further commitments to market opening measures as part of a strategy for spurring growth. For example: As part of its IMF program, Indonesia has abolished import monopolies for soybeans and wheat;

agreed to phase out all non-tariff barriers affecting imports; dissolved all cartels for plywood, cement, and paper; removed restrictions on foreign investment in the wholesale and resale trades; and allowed foreign banks to buy domestic ones. Zambia's 1999 program with the IMF commits the government to reducing the weighted average tariff on foreign goods to ten percent, and to cutting the maximum tariff from 25 percent to 20 percent by 2001. In July, the import ban on wheat flour was eliminated."[20]

Calling this a "new approach" is, let us face it, stretching the truth.

RADICAL REFORM OR DECOMMISSIONING?

What would a real process of transformation look like? It would be something that would include more than the open selection process for the new managing director—one that would open the recruitment process to non-Europeans—endorsed by Jeffrey Sachs.[21] For the problem lies in the very structure and culture of the institution: a lack of accountability except to the US Treasury Department; a belief in non-transparency as an important condition for effectiveness; and a deeply ingrained elitism that renders the bureaucracy incapable of learning from outsiders.

If this is the heart of the matter, then surgery must be more radical which might include the following measures:

First, so embedded is the old adjustment framework in current programs that only a clean break with the past can take place, not just with a renaming but with the immediate dismantling of all structural adjustment programs in the Third World and the ex-socialist world and the IMF adjustment programs imposed on Indonesia, Thailand, and Korea following the Asian financial crisis.

Second, immediate reduction of the IMF professional staff from over 1000 to 200, and major cuts in both capital expenditures and operational expenses of the agency. Most of the Fund's economists are today employed in micromanaging adjustment programs and would definitely cease to be necessary if, as the G-7 finance ministers and Central Bank governors suggest, developing countries be given more authority in formulating and implementing their poverty reduction programs, and if, as Jeffrey Sachs advises, the Fund's main work is limited to monitoring world capital markets and the world's monetary system.[22]

Third, and most important, is the creation of a global commission on the future of the IMF to decide if the Fund is to be reformed along the lines suggested by Sachs and others or, to borrow a phrase applied to aging nuclear plants, it is to be decommissioned. Half of the members of such a body should come from civil society organizations since it is these groups that were instrumental in bringing to light the destructive impact of adjustment programs and are now engaged in many of the most innovative experiments in grassroots social development. Energy from below and decentralized operations are the trademarks of so many successful organizations that the top-down centralized IMF looks positively Jurassic.

With its credibility and legitimacy in tatters, the Fund is in severe crisis. Unless international civil society intervenes, and intervenes forcefully now, the powers will wait for the storm to blow over while talking, as Larry Summers did, about reform. Radical reform or decommissioning? That is the question of the hour around which we must frame our strategies for intervention.

NOTES

1. Op-ed piece in *Washington Post,* reproduced in *Today* (Manila), November 15, 1999.

2. Communique, September 25, 1999.

3. Rudiger Dornbusch, quoted in Jacques Polak, "The changing nature of IMF conditionality," *Essays in International Finance,* Princeton University, No. 184 (September 1991), pg. 47.

4. Data from Freedom from Debt Coalition (Philippines).

5. Lindsey, Charles. "The political economy of economic policy reform in the Philippines: continuity and restoration," in Andrew MacIntyre and Kanishka Jayasuriya, eds., *The Dynamics of Economic Policy Reform in Southeast Asia and the Southwest Pacific* (Singapore: Oxford University Press, 1992).

6. Freedom from Debt Coalition. "Revisiting Philippine debt," paper presented at the National Debt Conference, Innotech, Commonwealth Avenue, October 9–10, 1997.

7. Freedom from Debt Coalition. *Primer on Philippine Debt* (Quezon City: FDC, 1997).

8. Briones, Leonor and Jenina Joy Chavez-Malaluan. "New social and political challenges within the framework of the structural adjustment process in Southeast Asia (with focus on the Philippines): effects on new population trends and quality of life," paper prepared for the Population and Quality of Life Independent Commission, Manila, May 1994. Unpublished.

9. Cruz, Wifredo and Robert Repetto. *The Environmental Effects of Stabilization and Structural Adjustment* (Washington, DC: World Resources Institute, 1992), pg. 48.

10. See Walden Bello, *Addicted to Capital: the Ten-Year High and Present Day Withdrawal Trauma of Southeast Asia's Economies* (Bangkok: Focus on the Global South, 1997).

11. See Nicola Bullard, Walden Bello, and Kamal Malhotra, *Taming the Tigers: The IMF and the Asian Crisis* (Bangkok: Focus on the Global South, 1998).

12. Quoted in Associated Press, reproduced in *Business World,* November 15, 1999.

13. Op-ed, *Washington Post,* reproduced in *Today,* November 15, 1999.

14. Personal communication, Ted Van Hees of Eurodad, New York, November 1, 1999.

15. Comment of Luis Corral, political affairs director of TUCP, November 6, 1999.

16. "The IMF's new leader," *The Financial Times,* November 18, 1999, pg. 16.

17. US Treasury secretary Larry Summers, "The right kind of IMF for a stable global financial system," remarks to the London School of Business, London, England, December 14, 1999.

18. Op-ed piece in *Washington Post,* reproduced in *Today,* November 15, 1999.

19. US Treasury secretary Larry Summers, testimony before the US Senate Committee on Foreign Relations, Washington, DC, November 5, 1999.

20. Ibid.

21. Sachs, Jeffrey. "Time to end the backroom poker game," *The Financial Times,* November 15, 1999.

22. Ibid.

4

MELTZER REPORT ON BRETTON WOODS
TWINS BUILDS CASE FOR ABOLITION

Focus on Trade, April 2000

During the heated debate on whether or not to raise the US quota in the International Monetary Fund (IMF) in 1998, the US Congress voted for the quota increase but attached several conditions, including the creation of an independent body to look at the mission and performance of the World Bank and the IMF.

The report of the International Financial Institution Advisory Commission, better known as the Meltzer Report, after its chairman Alan Meltzer, serves as a striking confirmation from the mainstream of what progressive critics of the Bretton Woods institutions have been saying for the last 25 years. Among the most important claims in the corpus of critical literature that the report supports are the following:

Instead of promoting economic growth, the International Monetary Fund institutionalizes economic stagnation.

The World Bank is irrelevant rather than central to the goal of eliminating global poverty.

Both institutions are to a great extent driven by the interests of key political and economic institutions in the Group of Seven (G-7) countries—particularly, in the case of the IMF, the US government, and US financial interests.

The dynamics of both institutions derive not so much from the external demands of poverty alleviation or promoting growth, but to the internal imperative of bureaucratic expansionism or empire-building.

There is little in the report that was not earlier documented in such works as Cheryl Payer's *The Debt Trap*, Bruce Rich's *Mortgaging the Future*, Susan George's *Faith and Credit*, and the Food First trilogy *Aid as Obstacle, Development Debacle: The World Bank in the Philippines*, and *Dark Victory: The US, Structural Adjustment, and Global Poverty*. But then the importance of the document lies not only in its critique but in the fact that a significant part of the establishment has embraced much of the progressive analysis, and even more significantly, made fairly radical proposals for the future of the Bretton Woods twins.

Criticisms of the IMF have found a very receptive global audience recently owing to the devastating performance of the Fund during the Asian financial crisis. To the credit of its authors, the Meltzer Report was not taken in by the World Bank's propaganda that, in contrast to the IMF, it has turned a new leaf. The report shows that the much vaunted poverty reduction strategy or comprehensive development framework articulated by ideological entrepreneur James Wolfensohn is largely a public relations effort to save the Bank and that, although it is billed as a brand new development paradigm, it is largely devoid of substance.

THE IMF: NO REDEEMING VALUE

While diplomatic in its language when discussing the IMF, the report finds little of redeeming value in the institution. It shows that the Fund's foray into macroeconomic reform via structural adjustment institutionalized economic stagnation, poverty, and inequality in Africa and Latin America in the 1980s and 1990s—precisely what Food First had documented in detail in its 1994 book *Dark Victory: The US, Structural Adjustment, and Global Poverty.*

It confirms that the Fund's duty of ensuring a stable global financial order was derailed by its prescription of indiscriminate capital account liberalization for developing countries, its habit of assembling financial rescue packages that simply encouraged moral hazard or irresponsible lending and speculative investment, and its prescribing tight fiscal and monetary policies that merely worsened the situation in the crisis countries instead of reversing it.

The report is on the right track when it recommends the closure of the structural and extended structural adjustment programs, now renamed the "poverty and growth facility." And it is correct in recommending downsizing the IMF in both size and its scope of responsibilities, though as we shall argue below, it would do better to recommend an outright abolition of the Fund.

The report is, however, wrong in its recommendation that the IMF should serve as a "quasi-lender of last resort" to countries suffering a liquidity crisis. The IMF, by the Commission's own account, has handled this function badly in the past. Moreover, the Commission's recommending of strict conditions under which the IMF may extend credit contradicts its own criticism of "the use of IMF resources and conditionality to control the economies of developing nations."

Particularly objectionable is the Commission's proposal that the Fund provide liquidity assistance only to those countries that "permit freedom of entry and operation for foreign financial institutions" on the ground that these entities would, among other things, "stabilize and develop the local financial system." This recommendation is problematic for two reasons. First, foreign financial institutions such as hedge funds, which have taken full advantage of "free entry and operation," have helped precipitate one financial crisis after another. Second, forcing countries to adopt western-style free market norms governing ownership of foreign financial subsidiaries and their local operations violates the first core principle it proposes for IMF reform— that is, "sovereignty—the desire to ensure that democratic processes and sovereign authority are respected in both borrowing and lending countries."

This contradiction between the logic of the analysis and the prescription reminds us that the Commission is, after all, a US government-appointed body, many of whose members come from the banking sector, conservative think tanks, and establishment universities who are very wary about placing significant restrictions on the free flow of finance capital globally, even when the evidence they are staring at underlines the destructiveness of unchecked capital mobility.

THE WORLD BANK: HYPE VERSUS SUBSTANCE

When it comes to the World Bank, the report is equally devastating. The rhetoric about focusing on poverty alleviation, it says, is contradicted by the reality that 70 percent of the Bank's non-aid lending is concentrated in 11 countries, while the Bank's 145 other member countries are left to divide the remaining 30 percent. Moreover, 80 percent of World Bank resources have gone, not to poor countries with poor credit ratings and investment ratings, but to countries that could have raised the money in international private capital markets owing to their having investment grade or high yield ratings.

In terms of achieving a positive development impact, the Bank's own evaluation of its projects shows an outstanding 55–60 percent failure rate. The failure rate is particularly high in the poorest countries, where it ranges from 65 percent to 70 percent. And these are the very countries that are supposed to be the main targets of the Bank's antipoverty approach.

The picture that is drawn of the World Bank is that of a massive institution that is driven to lend more by institutional imperatives than actual need in the recipient countries, that is burdened by high failure rates both in its project lending and its program (adjustment) lending, that has poor monitoring capabilities of the sustainability of its projects, that competes with rather than supplements the regional development banks (Asian Development Bank, Inter-American Development Bank, and African Development Bank). The stark reality is that of a dinosaur that is slowly sinking in a bog of its own making but which flags a "new approach" of "poverty reduction" or "comprehensive development" to mask a fundamental crisis of identity and direction.

REFORM OR ABOLITION?

The Meltzer Report's basic conclusion is that the IMF and the Bank are monolithic institutions that have outlived their usefulness. Now, institutions should be saved and reformed if their functioning, while defective, nevertheless broadly achieves their basic objectives. They should be abolished if they have become fundamentally dysfunctional in achieving their basic objectives. The IMF, in the Report's view, has become part of the problem rather than part of the solution in global development and financial governance. The World Bank likewise has become irrelevant rather than central to the alleviation of poverty. Despite adjustments here and there, the two institutions are imprisoned within paradigms and structures that cannot handle the multiple problems confronting the world economy during this phase of globalization.

To borrow the language of Thomas Kuhn's classic *Structure of Scientific Revolutions,* both institutions are like paradigms in crisis. The solution when a paradigm is in fundamental crisis is not to try to reform it with endless minute adjustments that merely prolong its inevitable demise, but to cut cleanly from it in favor of a simpler, more relevant, and more useful paradigm—in a manner similar to the way the founders of early modern science simply junked the old, hopelessly complex Ptolemaic paradigm for explaining the cosmos (the sun and other celestial bodies moving around the earth) in favor of the simpler Copernican paradigm (the earth moving around the sun).

Rather than trying to find a function for the Fund and assigning to it the role of being a lender of last resort, we would do better to scrap it totally and create a new institution that does not have the baggage of institutional failure and an obsolete institutional mindset, and thus better positioned to manage financial crises in this era. Rather than expect the highly paid World Bank technocrats who live in the affluent suburbs of Northern Virginia to do the impossible—designing anti-poverty programs for folks from another planet: poor people in the Sahel—it would be more effective to abolish an institution that has made a big business out of "ending poverty," and completely devolve the work to local, national, and regional institutions better equipped to attack the causes of poverty. And this task should not fall to the regional development banks so long as they are imprisoned by World Bank-type structures.

The Meltzer Report does not go far enough. It does not follow the logic of its analysis to its inevitable conclusion: the abolition of the Jurassic Bretton Woods institutions. It is up to the grassroots movements around the world to uncompromisingly deliver that message to the powers that be.

PART TWO

Speculative Capital and the Asian Financial Crisis

5

ASIAN FINANCIAL CRISIS: THE MOVIE

Food First Backgrounder, Winter 1999

After seeing Steven Spielberg's syrupy tribute to Yankee patriotism, *Saving Private Ryan*, I told myself that surely I could manage something better on the Asian financial crisis. Anyway, here's the screenplay for a movie tentatively titled *Asian Financial Crisis: The Movie—Heroes, Villains, and Accomplices*.

First of all, there are no heroes. The Japanese could have played the role of knight in shining armor in 1998, when they had the chance to reverse the descent into depression via the proposed Asian Monetary Fund (AMF)—a mechanism capitalized to the tune of $100 billion that was designed to defend the region's currencies from speculative attacks. But in typical fashion, they shelved their proposal when Washington opposed it. Though the AMF was resurrected as the Miyazawa Plan that would give the troubled Asian economies $30 billion in financial aid, it was too little and too late.

VILLAIN OF THE PIECE: CRONY CAPITALISTS OR FOREIGN SPECULATIVE INVESTORS?

On the other hand, there are a number of candidates for the role of principal villain. Taking the cue from the western press, one might begin with the practices and institutions that are usually presented to the public as the villains of the piece—that is, aside from prime minister Mohamad Mahathir of Malaysia, who became the US media's favorite whipping boy—at the same time, it must be noted, that they elevated Philippine actor-president Joseph Estrada to the status of Asia's new hero.

One might begin by quoting a person who has come to be the chief screenwriter of one version of the crisis, US Treasury secretary Robert Rubin. In assigning the blame for the financial crisis, Mr. Rubin assigned pride of place to lack of information on the part of investors. In a speech he gave at the Brookings Institution in April 1998, Rubin said:

> [T]here are obstacles to getting good information about economic and financial matters. One is the temptation in the private sector and in government to avoid disclosing problems. But sooner or later, as we have seen in Asia, the problems will make themselves known. In many cases, lack of data meant that no one had a true understanding of this build-up or these economies vulnerabilities.[1]

This lack of transparency on the part of financial institutions went hand-in-hand with distorted incentives, lack of supervision, and the absence of so-called prudent regulation. All this was, in turn, part of a witches brew of unsound and corrupt practices known as "crony capitalism," which Larry Summers, the famous economist and Rubin's undersecretary, said was "at the heart of the crisis."[2] Interestingly, it might be pointed out, Summers and others picked up a term—crony capitalism—that we Filipinos coined during the Marcos period.

Before going on, one might also briefly note here that this is a massive reversal of the view that held sway at the World Bank when Summers, who now plays an overweight, over-the-hill Sundance Kid to Rubin's Butch Cassidy on CNN, was that institution's chief economist in the late 1980s and early 1990s. For those too young to remember what the orthodoxy was then, one might cite the Bank's famous *East Asian Miracle,* published in 1993:

In each HPAE [high performing Asian economy], a technocratic elite insulated to a degree from excessive political pressure supervised macroeconomic management. The insulation mechanisms ranged from legislation, such as balanced budget laws in Indonesia, Singapore, and Thailand, to custom and practice in Japan and Korea. All protected essentially conservative macroeconomic policies by limiting the scope for politicians and interest groups to derail those policies.[3]

Economic policy making by Asian technocrats was largely insulated from political and business pressures, and this was a large part of the explanation for the so-called Asian miracle. Every mortal is, of course, entitled to an about face. But the problem with the latest intellectual fashion from the Summers' salon is that the practices of "crony capitalism" were very much part of economic life in the three decades that East Asian countries led the world in the rate of growth of the gross national product (GNP). If crony capitalism was the chief cause of the Asian collapse, why did it not bring it about much sooner? How could economies dominated by these practices of rent-seeking that supposedly suffocate the dynamism of the market—including Japan and South Korea—even take off in the first place?

Moreover, crony capitalism has become so elastic in its connotations—which range from corruption to any kind of government activism in economic policy making—as to become useless as an explanatory construct. It is one thing to say that corruption has pervaded relations between government and business in East Asia. Corruption takes place in Italy or in the United States, where it is legalized through such mechanisms as "political action committees" (PACs) that make politicians' electoral fortunes dependent on favorable treatment of corporate interests. It is quite another thing to say that corruption and its companions, lack of regulation and lack of transparency, constitute the principal reason for the downfall of the East Asian economies.

Criticizing the crony capitalist thesis might strike those who have followed events in Asia closely as beating a dead horse. It is, but this dead horse deserves to be beaten and buried because it has a way of resurrecting in Dracula-like fashion periodically. After the Russian crash in 1998 and the collapse and bail-out of the hedge fund Long-Term Capital by the US Federal Reserve, and Brazil's teetering on the edge, there is now little doubt that the central cause of the financial crisis was the quick, massive flow of global speculative capital and bank capital into East Asia in the early 1990s and its even more massive and even swifter exit in 1997.

There seems to be little doubt as well that the multilateral institutions, in particular, the International Monetary Fund (IMF), played a key facilitating role by pressing the Asian governments incessantly to liberalize their capital accounts, in order to encourage massive foreign capital inflows into their economies in the belief that foreign capital was the strategic factor in development. One can say that the IMF has been the cutting edge of globalization in the region, since it is financial liberalization that is the cutting edge of the integration of these national economies into the global economy.

Northern speculative funds came to Asia not because they were conned by crafty and dishonest Asian financial operators. Don't get us wrong: Asia was swarming with crooked financial operators. But that these western investors were conned or fooled? Come on. Speculative investors came into Asia because they perceived the opportunities to gain greater margins of profit on financial investments here to be greater than in the northern money centers in the early 1990s, owing to the much higher interest rates, the low stock prices, and—not to be underestimated—the incredible hype created around the so-called Asian economic miracle.

The fact is, money was very eager to get into Asian capital markets in the early 1990s, and whether or not the information was available, investors and fund managers were quite nondiscriminating in their moves into these markets. As Rubin himself admitted in a speech at Chulalongkorn University in 1998:

> One of the things that has most struck us about the Asian crisis, is that after the problems began to develop and we spoke to the institutions that had extended credit or invested in the region, so often we found these institutions had engaged in relatively little analysis and relatively little weighing of the risks that were appropriate to the decisions.[4]

The fund managers were going to see what they wanted to see. Not only did many not assess their investments and local partners or borrowers, but they actually made their moves mainly by keeping an eagle eye on the moves of other investors—especially those with great reputations for canny investing like George Soros or Long-Term Capital's John Merriwether. But if there was little room or desire for serious analysis of markets in the entry phase, there was even less in the exit phase, as the rush of investment leaders communicated panic to one and all.

In the first months of the crisis, Stanley Fischer, the American deputy managing director of the IMF, was attributing the crisis not to politicians or lack of transparency or crony capitalism, but to the investors' herd behavior:: "[M]arkets are not always right," he said. "Sometimes inflows are excessive, and sometimes they may be sustained too long. Markets tend to react late; but they tend to react fast, sometimes excessively."[5]

Bangkok was a debtor's rather than a creditor's market in the early 1990s. With so many foreign banks and funds falling over themselves to lend to Thai enterprises, banks, and finance companies, they were willing to forego the rigorous checks on borrowers that western banks and financial institutions are supposedly famous for. The bad—indeed, shady—financial history of the Thai finance companies was not a secret.[6] In the 1970s and 1980s, many finance companies resorted to questionable business practices to raise capital, including widespread speculation and manipulation of stock prices, leading to the closure of some of them. Any neophyte in Bangkok's financial club knew this history. Yet the finance companies were flush with foreign cash, often times urged on to them by foreign lenders unwilling to forego what could turn out to be a gold mine.

Throughout Asia, American chambers of commerce, foreign correspondents' clubs, and expatriate circles were replete with stories of rigged bids, double—sometimes triple—accounting, false statistics, cronyism in high places, but everyone accepted that these were the risks of doing business in Asia. You had to live with them if you were going to have your share of the bonanza. In the end, what really served as the ultimate collateral or guarantee for the investments foreign operators made in Asian enterprises and banks was the six to ten percent growth rates that they expected to go on far into the future. Now you might end up with some duds, but if you spread your investments around in this region of limitless growth, you were likely to come out a winner.

SUPPORTING CAST

This brings up the role of strategic expectations, and of certain players and institutions that encouraged and maintained those expectations. There was a whole set of actors that played a supporting but critical role, and the speculative investors were operating in a context where they were locked into mutually reinforcing psychology of permanent boom with these other players.

A key player here is much of the business press. Business publications proliferated in the region beginning in the mid-1980s. But proliferation alone is not adequate to convey the dynamics of the business press, since there was also a process of monopolization at work. The Asian prosperity started attracting the big players from the West, and among the more momentous deals was the purchase of the famous *Far Eastern Economic Review* by Dow Jones, of *Asiaweek* by Times-Warner, and of Star Television in Hong Kong by Rupert Murdoch. CNN, another Time Warner subsidiary, and CNBC also moved in, with much their programming devoted to business news.

These news agents became critical interpreters of the news in Asia to investors located all over the world and served as a vital supplement to the electronic linkages that made real-time transactions possible among the key stock exchanges of Singapore, Hong Kong, Tokyo, Osaka, New York, London, and Frankfurt a reality.[7]

For the most part, these publications and media, whether they were independent or part of the big chains, highlighted the boom, glorified the high growth rates, and reported uncritically on so-called success stories, mainly because their own success as publications was tied to the perpetuation of the psychology of boom. A number of writers writing critical stories on questionable business practices, alarming developments, or failed enterprises complained that they could not place their stories, or that their editors told them to accentuate the positive.

Parachute journalism, a phrase applied to writers who flew in, became instant experts on the Vietnam War or the Philippines under Marcos, then left after filing their big stories, became a practice as well in economic journalism in the 1990s, with *Fortune, Business Week, Newsweek*, and *Time* setting the pace. It was, for instance, Dorinda Elliot of the *Newsweek* airborne brigade, who, more than anybody else, sanctified the Philippines' status as Asia's newest tiger during the Subic APEC Summit of November 1996—a status that lasted less than eight months, until the collapse of the peso in July 1997.

Many of these business publications, in turn, developed an unwholesome reliance on a character type that proliferated in the region in the early 1990s, the investment adviser or strategist—an "expert" connected with the research arms of banks, investment houses, brokerage houses, mutual funds, and hedge funds. In many instances, notes Philip Bowring, former editor of *Far Eastern Economic Review*, economic journalism degenerated into just stringing along quotes from different investment authorities.[8]

Interestingly enough, many of these people were expatriates, or "expats," to use a Bangkok term, some of them refugees from the collapse of stock markets in New York and London in the late 1980s. Some of them were Generation X or pre-Generation X types who had been too young to participate in the junk bond frenzy in Wall Street in the Reagan years but discovered similar highs in the East. Many of these people were as young as Nick Leeson, the 26-year-old broker who brought down the venerable Baring Brothers. But to the reporters in the business press, their advice on going underweight or overweight in certain countries or taking short or long positions in dollars or moving into equities and out of bonds and vice versa were dispensed to readers as gospel truth. This is not to say that all of these actors dispensed uniformly optimistic advice to investors playing the region. It did mean, however, that they could not afford to paint too pessimistic a picture of any country in the region since after all their bread and butter came from bringing global capital into Asia.

A good illustration of the modus operandi of these operators is provided by a prominent Singapore-based "expat" expert, who was widely cited in *The Economist, Far Eastern Economic Review, The Financial*

Times, Reuters, and *The Asian Wall Street Journal* as the last word on the Southeast Asian investment scene. This is how this expert assessed Thailand in December 1996, when it was becoming clear to the rest of us mortals in Bangkok that the economy was in real deep trouble:

> We believe that current pessimism about the Thai economy is based on a number of key misconceptions. We do not believe any of the following:
>
> Thailand is entering a recession.
> Investment is collapsing.
> Export growth is collapsing.
> The Bank of Thailand has lost control.
> Current account deficit is unsustainable.
> Thailand faces a debt crisis.
> There is a chance that the baht will devalue.
> Economic prospects for 1997: Expect a rebound.[9]

Neil Saker of Singapore's SocGen-Crosby Securities is one of the best examples of the way markets operated in East Asia. One would have expected that after such a massive misreading of the situation, he would have been run out of Asia by irate investors. But lo and behold, Saker was able to transform himself from the prophet of permanent boom into the prophet of doom after the financial collapse of 1997, this time issuing statements about how investors would be wise to go underweight in their investments in the region for a long time to come. Lately, he has again reinvented himself, this time as the prophet of the "Asian recovery," advising investors to go "overweight" in Thailand and Singapore, which so happened to move into recession on the day he issued his recommendation.[10]

And worse, he is quoted just as frequently today in *The Financial Times, Far Eastern Economic Review, Asiaweek,* and *The Asian Wall Street Journal.* The market has such a short memory that it rewards charlatans instead of punishing them.

ACADEMICS: BYSTANDERS OR ACCOMPLICES?

To lay the blame only on the business press and the investment advisers for the creation of an atmosphere of inflated expectations would not be fair, for the academic world played a key role. It was economists and political scientists in the West, who when seeking to explain the high growth rates of the Asian countries from the 1960s on, formulated the interrelated propositions that an economic miracle had come about in Asia, that high growth was likely to mark the region in the forseeable future, and that Asia would be the engine of the world economy far into the twenty-first century. What is even more amazing is that there was a remarkable consensus between the left and the right in the academic world that Asian growth was exceptional—though for diametrically opposite reasons. The right insisted that it was because of free markets, the left because of the role of the interventionist state.[11]

Writing on why and how the tigers evolved and why Asia would be the center of the world economy in the coming century became big business, and here the most thriving business were those books that sought to equip American businessmen and politicians with insights on how to deal with those formidable Asians, like James Fallows' *Looking at the Sun*. Not to be left out of the boom, the security experts sought to cash in on the Asian miracle mania by writing on how Asian prosperity could produce either peace or war, with crass pop analysts writing on "the coming war with Japan" or "the coming war with China," or, like Harvard guru Samuel Huntington, expatiating on the long twilight struggle against the "Islamic-Confucian connection." But whether they liked Asia or saw it as a threat, most academics and policy analysts believed in the long Asian boom.

The few who dissented from this consensus were attacked by both sides. Our critique of the increasing stresses of the newly industrialized countries (NIC) growth model on account of collateral damage in the form of environmental devastation, the subjugation of agriculture to industry, the growing income disparities, and the growing technological dependency that was behind the creation of structurally determined trade deficits was dismissed by the right as well as the academic liberals center of as a case of "leftist" pessimism.

But we were also dismissed by the academic left, who saw us as adhering to old-fashioned dependency theory or to obsolete variants of Marxism. Indeed, the most savage criticisms sometimes came from the left. To cite one example, a reviewer of *Dragons in Distress* in a progressive journal said that our suggestion in 1990 that Korea's problem in a few years' time would not be how to enter the First World but how to avoid being hurled back into the Third World was simply laughable.

In any event, the World Bank stepped in to serve as an arbiter between the left and right interpretations in the early 1990s and found merit on both sides of the argument—though more merits, it said, resided on the right than on the left. But what is particularly significant for this discussion is that the Bank declared that, despite slight deviations here and there, the Asian tigers had the economic fundamentals right and were thus geared to enter a period of even greater prosperity. Since the World Bank is the equivalent in development circles of the papacy in the Roman Catholic Church, the World Bank book, *The East Asian Miracle*, which came out in 1993, became a kind of bible, not only in the academic world but in financial and corporate circles. The rush into Asia of speculative capital in the next few years must certainly be at least partly tied to its thesis of Asian exceptionalism, to Asia as the land of the never-ending bonanza.

THE STORY SO FAR

Crony capitalist practices pervaded Asian capitalism, but they were definitely not the cause of the financial collapse. Northern finance capital was not conned into coming into investing in the region by dishonest Asian banks and enterprises that concealed the actual state of their finances. That is, they cooked their books but they fooled nobody. Portfolio investors and banks moved vast quantities in and out of the region, oftentimes without any real effort to arrive at an assessment of local conditions and borrowers and largely as a result of herd behavior.

The fundamentals of borrowers were often ignored in favor of what many investors and lenders saw as the real collateral or guarantee that they would eventually get a high rate of return from their investments, which was the eight to ten percent growth rate of the country and this was expected to extend far into the future. With such a perspective, you should expect to end up with some bad eggs among your debtors, but if you spread your investment around in this region of everlasting prosperity, you were likely to come out ahead in the end.

Playing a critical role as accomplices in the Asian financial crisis were three institutional actors: the business press, the investment analysts, and, last but not least, the majority of academic specialists on the East Asian economies and political systems.

A global network of investors, journalists, investment analysts, and academics were locked into a psychology of boom, where growth rates, expectations, analysis, advice, and reporting interacted in a mutually reinforcing inflationary fashion characteristic of manic situations. Just as in the case of the Cold War lobby in the US, there was a whole set of actors that—perhaps half consciously, one must concede—developed an institutional interest in the maintenance of the illusion of a never-ending Asian bonanza so that, whether in the press, in the boardroom, or in the academy, alternative viewpoints were given short shrift.

But not to worry, many of the prophets of boom quickly adjusted and became prophets of doom or sanctimonious exponents of the crony capitalist explanation for Asia's problems. Many are coming through with their reputations intact and some are realizing that books on why Asia collapsed can be just as profitable as books on why Asia was going to be the driver of the twenty-first century during the boom.

But wait a minute: this only brings the story to July 1997, the day the floating of the Thai baht triggered the crisis. The screenplay to the sequel, from July 1997 up until today, still needs to be written, but for this part the story line is much clearer, with the IMF and the US Treasury, Japan, and Prime Minister Mahathir serving as chief protagonists, with brief cameos by China, Hong Kong, and the World Bank.

HOW WILL THIS FILM END?

That part of the story remains to be written by the peoples of East and Southeast Asia. In the movie script for the first part, quite a number of characters—indeed, hundreds of millions of ordinary Asians—have not been brought in. This is because they were largely passive participants in this drama. Rather than acting, they were acted on. That may no longer be the case, judging from events in the streets of Jakarta, Kuala Lumpur, and Bangkok. In the coming period, the region is likely to see the emergence of movements motivated by resistance not only to indiscriminate financial and economic globalization but to its cultural and political aspects as well.

Within the region, we are likely to see a move away from dependence on foreign financial flows and foreign markets toward economic strategies based principally on domestic financial resources and the local market. That means greater pressure on governments for redistribution of assets and income in order to create the dynamic domestic market that can serve as the engine of growth in place of the rollercoaster global economy.

Elements of the domestic alternative are already being discussed actively throughout the region. What is still unclear is how these elements will hang together. The new political economy may be embedded in religious or secular discourse and language. Its coherence is likely to rest less on considerations of narrow efficiency than on a stated ethical priority given to community solidarity and security.

Moreover, the new economic order is unlikely to be imposed from above in Keynesian technocratic style, but is likely to be forged in social and political struggles. For one thing is certain: mass politics with a class edge—frozen by the superficial prosperity before the crash of 1997—is about to return to center stage in Asia.

In short, *Asian Financial Crisis* is likely to end with a bang, not a whimper.

NOTES

1. Rubin, Robert. "Strengthening the architecture of the international financial system," speech delivered at Brookings Institution, Washington, DC, April 14, 1998.

2. Summers, Larry. "The global economic situation and what it means for the United States," remarks to the National Governors Association, Milwaukee, Wisconsin, August 4, 1998.

3. World Bank. *The East Asian Miracle* (New York: Oxford University Press, 1993), pp. 348–349.

4. Rubin, Robert. Remarks at the Sasin Institute of Business Administration, Chulalongkorn University, Bangkok, June 30, 1998.

5. Fischer, Stanley. "Capital account liberalization and the role of the IMF," paper presented at the Asia and the IMF Seminar, Hong Kong, September 19, 1997.

6. See Pakorn Vichyanond, *Thailand's Financial System: Structure and Liberalization* (Bangkok: Thailand Development Research Institute, 1994).

7. A good study of how these global, real-time linkages made possible moneymaking among these far-flung stock markets via arbitrage is John Gapper and Nicholas Denton's *All That Glitters: The Fall of Barings* (London, UK: Penguin, 1996).

8. Bowring, Philip. Comments at seminar on "Improving the flow of information in a time of crisis: the challenge to the Southeast Asian media," Subic, Philippines, October 29–31, 1998.

9. Saker, Neil. "Guest viewpoint: Thailand update: market pessimism is overblown," *BOI Investment Review 2*, December 31, 1996.

10. Quoted in "Confidence returning to Asia says report," *Reuters,* November 11, 1998.

11. On the right, see Anne Krueger, "East Asia: lessons for growth theory," paper presented at the fourth annual East Asian Seminar on Economics, National Bureau of Economic Research, San Francisco, California, June 17–19, 1993; Ian D. Little, *Economic Development* (New York: Basic Books, 1982); Helen Hughes, "East Asian export success," Research School of Pacific Studies, Australian National University, Canberra, 1992. On the left, Robert Wade, *Governing the Market: Economic Theory and the Role of Government in East Asian Industrialization* (Princeton: Princeton University Press, 1990); and Alice Amsden, *Asia's Next Giant: South Korea and Late Industrialization* (New York: Oxford University Press, 1989).

6

FAST TRACK CAPITALISM, GEOECONOMIC COMPETITION, AND THE SUSTAINABLE DEVELOPMENT CHALLENGE IN EAST ASIA

From *Globalization in the South*
(New York: St. Martin's Press, 1997)

The explosive economic growth in the Asia-Pacific region attracted the attention of economic policy makers, corporate leaders, and academic thinkers throughout the world. For the US economic and political establishment, East Asia moved from being a partner in the Cold War to being a competitor for global economic hegemony. In Europe, there was much worry in government and corporate circles about the contrast between what is fashionably termed "Eurosclerosis" and East Asian dynamism. And in much of the South, "Asian capitalism" replaced socialism as the new paradigm of development.

Within the region itself, "fast track" capitalism was accompanied by a region-wide consensus celebrating East Asian economic growth. This consensus was a powerful, persuasive, and ideologically hegemonic alliance of government technocrats, private interests, and established intellectuals. This consensus stressed that much of East and Southeast Asia had left or was leaving the Third World; that high-speed growth marked the region far into the twenty-first century; and that East Asia would increasingly be the "driver" of the world economy as the US and European economies continued to be marked by weak or low growth. In short, it was the Asia-Pacific's turn to be at the center of the world stage.

But while there was a consensus on the celebration of high-speed growth and its desirability, there was intense debate on the causes of this growth and, related to this, on the policies to be followed to sustain it. Moreover, while the consensus was hegemonic, it was not total, for other voices were questioning both the impact and the direction of high speed growth.

THE FREE MARKET EXPLANATION

Within establishment circles, two competing schools emerged to explain the so-called "East Asian miracle." One saw Asian growth as the flowing of free market policies. The other attributed it to a combination of neo-mercantilism, protectionism, and government activism that can appropriately be termed "state-assisted capitalism."

The free market model of East Asian development was espoused by orthodox economists such as those connected with the World Bank, the International Monetary Fund (IMF), and the "eminent persons' group" (EPG) identified with the Asia-Pacific Economic Cooperation (APEC) initiative. In their view, the market was the central mechanism of rapid growth in Japan and the newly industrializing countries (NICs) in the past, and freeing market forces even more fully from government controls was the key to even more dynamic growth in the future.

The free market/free trade approach was institutionalized in World Bank and IMF-imposed structural adjustment programs (SAPs) which promoted radical deregulation, sweeping privatization, trade and investment liberalization, export-oriented trade and investment strategies, containment of wages, and cutting back of government expenditure. Purportedly inspired by the East Asian experience, SAPs were generalized to sub-Saharan Africa, North Africa, Latin America, and South Asia.

The problem with this model, say its critics, is that hardly any of the fast-growing countries of the region achieved "NIC-hood" by following the free market formula, except possibly Hong Kong and Singapore, which are really dependent urban economies masquerading as national economies. The Southeast Asian "stars" of the last ten years—Malaysia, Thailand, and Indonesia—are often portrayed in the business press as examples of growth through the implementation of liberal economic policies. But this interpretation is problematic. Certainly, these three countries did engage in some liberalization in the mid-1980s, but these programs did not substantially reduce the state's leading economic role:

Malaysia, which had a growth rate of ten percent per annum before the Asian financial crisis, is one of the few Third World countries that escaped stabilization or structural adjustment by the World Bank and the IMF in the 1980s, though its leadership on its own did undertake some liberalization. For the most part, the Malaysian state intervened heavily in economic life to give Malaysia more control of the national economy, maintained a protectionist trade regime, and engaged in what is called "picking winners," or targeting certain industries to develop through various incentives, including direct government participation in production. It was not unfettered market forces that produced the Malaysian industry's crown jewel, the Proton Saga, also known as the national car. It was a partnership between a state enterprise and the Japanese corporation Mitsubishi that produced the car as part of a state-managed rationalization of the car industry.[1] With close to 80 percent of its components sourced locally, the Proton Saga was trumpeted by official circles as an example of how foreign investment can be manipulated not to marginalize but to strengthen an activist government role in the economy.

Indonesia's growth rate of five to six percent was often attributed by World Bank officials to free market policies. But the reality is that economic liberalization had been quite limited, with the economy continuing to be marked by a high degree of protectionism, control by monopolies linked to key individuals or groups in government, and significant state influence on foreign investors. While the Malaysian state targeted the car industry, the Indonesian government heavily subsidized the creation of an increasingly sophisticated aircraft industry, which was roundly criticized by World Bank and other neo-classical economists.[2]

Of all the large economics of Southeast Asia, Thailand was the closest to a market-dominated economy. Yet one finds the seeming anomaly that the Thai economy actually became more protectionist as it moved to a second stage of import substitution in the mid- and late 1980s, precisely the period when it began to register the eight to 12 percent growth rates that dazzled the world.[3]

STATE-ASSISTED CAPITALISM

Dissatisfaction with both the explanatory power and prescriptive thrust of the free market school has spawned a perspective on East Asian growth that goes in the opposite direction, to claim that state intervention in the bigger NICs or "Near NICs" was the central factor in the take-off of these economies. Specifically, development was produced by a strategy consisting of:

1. Strategic economic planning managed by government, exemplified in some countries by five and ten year plans.
2. Government targeting of specific industries for development, and generous subsidy of private enterprises to support the targeted industries.
3. Building strategic economic depth by moving in a planned fashion from the development of consumer goods industries to intermediate goods and capital goods enterprises.
4. Reserving the domestic market for local entrepreneurs by maintaining tight restrictions on imports and foreign investments.
5. Adopting a mercantilist trade strategy consisting of limiting the entry of foreign imports into the domestic market while aggressively winning and dominating export markets, resulting in a growing trade surplus.
6. Bold, Keynesian-style manipulation of macroeconomic mechanisms such as deficit spending, loose credit policies, massive borrowing, and strict undervaluation of the currency relative to hard currencies in order to keep exports competitive in world markets.

The mix of these policies, of course, differed from economy to economy, and in some economies some elements of these formulas were not even implemented. Taiwan did not engage in massive foreign borrowing, but resorted to the massive dollar reserves it had built up from exports. However, the main thrust of economic policy in all the key NICs was government leadership of the economic process via activist, interventionist policies that disciplined the private sector and controlled the market. To borrow economist Alice Amsden's phrase in her classic study of Korean industrialization, "not only has Korea not gotten relative prices right, it has deliberately gotten them wrong."[4]

True, market mechanisms operated, but they were deliberately distorted and much inefficiency was tolerated in the short term to build up strategic economic depth. For instance, Korean technocrats deliberately violated the classical free market principle of consumer sovereignty—"Give the consumer the best product at the lowest price"—for the larger strategic goal of strengthening national economic sovereignty. If the price of Korean-made computers in the domestic market was three to four times that in export markets, this was in order to allow local conglomerates and monopolies to recoup the losses they incurred in battling against the formidable Japanese in highly competitive export markets.

To take another example, in contrast to the neo-classical dictum that macroeconomic stability is a key condition of growth, proponents of state-assisted capitalism see imbalance as a necessary feature of development. They point to the fact that the heavy and chemical industry drive in Korea in the 1970s may have provoked many short-term dislocations and triggered inflation, but also laid the basis for Korea's successful push to export capital-intensive high-tech products like microchips and cars in the 1980s.[5]

THEORETICAL MODELS AND ECONOMIC REALPOLITIK

Exasperated by what it saw as the World Bank-IMF's doctrinal commitment to the free market/free trade paradigm, Japan's famous Ministry of Industry (MITT) has been known to become cautiously critical of World Bank-lMF structural adjustment programs. Japan has argued that it might be the dismantling of an activist economic role for the state through indiscriminate liberalization, deregulation, and privatization that is prolonging economic stagnation in countries being subjected to adjustment.

More important, the Japanese prodded the World Bank to review the Asian region's development experience and came forward with the bulk of funding for the study. Released in late 1993, the World Bank study, entitled *The East Asian Miracle,* grudgingly agreed that Japan, Korea, and some other NICs had not unsuccessfully employed state activist policies such as "picking winners," compensating market failure through subsidized loans to the private sector, and strategic protectionism. But much to the consternation of the Japanese, the World Bank insisted that these policies, while possibly successful in the earlier NICs. were not applicable to other developing countries in East Asia and elsewhere, and that they were constructive for certain countries only during a specific historical period, which had passed.[6]

The study's guiding lessons for countries still seeking to break out of underdevelopment was: "It is still better not to intervene than to intervene." Interestingly, this advice against replicating the NICs' experience with industrial policy drew the following response from a prominent critic of the free market school:

> There is reason to worry whether the World Bank's refusal to countenance selective industrial policies for industries high entry barriers reflects an underlying unwillingness to help developing countries enter industries that are already well established in the West, especially when Western plants have excess capacity.... Given the governing structure of the Bank, it is not difficult to imagine why.[7]

Some may dismiss this as crude conspiracy theory, but the Bank study's readiness to attribute success to market policies, while raising the standard of proof when it comes to assessing interventionist industrial policies, does reflect the fact that more than just academic and technocratic issues are at stake in the NIC debate.

The debate over models became caught up with the ongoing conflict between the US and Asian economies. The 1980s and early 1990s saw the aggressive pursuit of unilateralist trade policy in the name of free trade. Japan was, of course, a key target for the US. But practically all the other East Asian countries have been assaulted by American unilateralist trade policy. Korea, in particular, is often cited as a *prima facie* case of the opportunistic use of free trade to aggressively push US economic interests. In bilateral trade negotiations with Korea, free trade has been the slogan deployed by US trade negotiators in what Koreans have seen as an effort that goes beyond rectifying the trade balance to transforming the very foundations of their economy. Free trade and free markets have been invoked to legitimize an assault on a broad front that includes completely opening up an agricultural market that is already one of the US's biggest markets, doing away with restrictions on foreign investment aimed at the domestic market, limiting Korean access to high technology, and even seeking to change Korean consumer behavior to favor imports over domestic products and consumption over saving. Appeals to free trade were, of course, coupled with the threat to invoke Super 301 and Special 301 provisions of the US Trade Act, which mandated the president to take retaliatory action against "unfair traders" and "intellectual pirates."

Though they were not subjected to a full court press in the same way Korea was, the other Asian countries were also subjected to US trade offensive. Taiwan, Singapore, and Hong Kong were "graduated" from the General System of Preferences (GSP), which essentially accorded developing countries preferential tariff rates. The US also forced Taiwan to revalue its currency to make its products more expensive to US consumers, subjected a number of its electronics exporters to additional duties on anti-dumping grounds, imposed tight limits on its farm and textile exports, and placed it on the Special 301 watch list.

Indonesia was also placed on the Special 301 watch list for prohibiting foreign film distributors from directly importing or distributing their films in the country.

As for Thailand, it lost up to $644 million in GSP benefits following the US Department of Commerce's determination that it "did not fully provide adequate and effective intellectual property protection."[8] The country was also designated a "priority foreign country" under Special 301. Some US moves bordered on the outrageous and absurd, as when the US trade representative's office made Thailand the target of investigation for allegedly "exploiting its [monsoon] climate to hold on to the number one slot in world rice export markets." The investigation was triggered by the American Paddy and Rice Industry

League's claim that "[t]he last straw was the 1988 logging ban in Thailand," a move which "would further reduce the opportunity for the US to gain its rightful place as the world's top rice exporter."9 The logging ban, it must be noted, was enacted to reverse the rapid rate of deforestation that is producing an ecological calamity in that country.

APEC AS A BATTLEGROUND

The Asian political and economic elites suspicion of the free market/free trade model and their increasing identification with state-assisted capitalism was heightened by US initiatives connected with the Asia Pacific Economic Cooperation (APEC), a loose consultative grouping founded in 1989. At the first APEC summit in Seattle in November 1993, Washington, backed by Australia, pushed hard to have the association transformed from a consultative forum to a formal trading bloc with a timetable for the disappearance of trade and investment barriers. This effort, which was also promoted heavily at the second summit a year later in Bogor, Indonesia, has been seen almost universally by Asian governments as an "end run," to borrow a term from American football—as an American effort to outmaneuver them by institutionalizing, via a multilateral organization, the free trade agenda that it had been trying to force the Asians to swallow in bilateral trade negotiations.

A key element in the American game plan was the creation of an APEC "eminent persons' group," to provide the intellectual muscle for the creation of an APEC free trade area. Made up largely of pro-free trade economists, technocrats, and policy makers from the APEC member countries, this quasi-official body was largely set up with the blessings of the US trade bureaucracy, by Dr. C. Fred Bergsten, head of the Washington-based Institute of International Economics, to push the US free trade agenda. A stalwart of Washington's economics establishment, Bergsten is widely known as an unabashed promoter of US economic interests via free trade, and has served as a lobbyist not only for APEC, but also for the General Agreement on Tariffs and Trade (GATT) and the North American Free Trade Area (NAFTA). According to one report on his comments to a forum in Washington,

DC, in Bergsten's view, "Given the fact that all of the countries in the region, outside North America in particular, have lots of trade barriers ... very little would actually be required from the United States." Thus, "trade liberalization or moving to totally free trade in the region means enormous competitive gain to the United States."[10]

With aggressive self-promotion, Bergsten and the EPG managed to project themselves as a quasi-official body pushing a multilateral consensus rather than a body whose ideological agenda coincided with the US trade agenda. The blueprint they came out with, the so-called "2020 plan," was, in fact, adopted at the Bogor Summit in November 1994. The 2020 plan would commit APEC member countries to the formation of a free trade area, eliminating all trade and investment barriers among them by the year 2020. But the surface unanimity of the document masked deep rifts among the participants. The United States, Australia, New Zealand, Canada, Mexico, and Chile are earnest believers in the 2020 Plan. But these countries are seen by Asian technocrats as the outsiders seeking to gatecrash the party known as the "East Asian miracle." For most of the so-called "core" Asian members of APEC, agreeing to a statement that was long on vision but vague on implementation was less a declaration of belief than a relatively costless maneuver to accommodate American economic power. Indeed, shortly after the Bogor declaration, Thai and Malaysian officials declared that the 2020 plan was "non-binding."

In response to the APEC free trade area initiative, the Southeast Asian governments moved to speed up the timetable for their own subregional trading bloc, the ASEAN (Association of Southeast Asian Nations) Free Trade Area (AFTA). But more dramatic was the Malaysian prime minister's proposal to create the East Asia Economic Group (EAEG), a regional trade bloc that would include the ASEAN countries, China, Korea, and Japan but exclude Australia, Canada, the United States, and the Latin American countries. The EAEG resonated with the East Asian and Southeast Asian elites, and the reason it did so was that it addressed a central problem: the Asia-Pacific economies were becoming an integrated production base, but many of the economies of the region continued to be dependent on the US as their principal market. With Washington becoming more unilateralist in trade policy towards them, government and business elites realized their deep vulnerability to US trade retaliation. The EAEG promised to make the region itself the main market for its production, accelerating what was already a trend: the trade among the Western Pacific economies was growing faster than their trade with other regions. In 1994, Southeast Asia had overtaken the US to become Korea's biggest export market, while despite an official ban on direct transportation links, Taiwan's exports to China were expected to match in value those to the US. Earlier, Japan's trade with Asia had overtaken its trade with the US.

The US response was predictable. "We can never approve this regionalism which is designed to split the Asia-Pacific region and divide Japan and the United States," then secretary of state James Baker asserted when Malaysian prime minister Mahathir first floated the proposal in 1991. The Japanese response was a mixture of positive statements about the goals of the EAEG coupled with a studied hesitation to explicitly endorse the formation—to the chagrin of Mahathir. Japan's reticence is understandable. Endorsing EAEG would earn it the wrath of the US, something it could not at the moment afford. Indeed, for the Japanese the ideal situation was neither EAEG nor the APEC free trade area but the status quo, which one might characterize as a *de facto* trade and investment bloc dominated by Japan.

THE REGIONALIZATION OF THE JAPANESE ECONOMY

This *de facto* integration of the region around the Japanese economy can be traced to the Plaza Accord of the mid-1980s, when Japan was forced by the US and Europe to get the yen to appreciate *vis-a-vis* the dollar and other hard currencies in a draconian effort to reduce their trade surpluses with the former. With the rise in production costs that this move automatically produced, Japan manufacturers, in an effort to remain competitive in the US and other export markets, transferred a substantial part of their manufacturing operations to cheap labor sites in East and Southeast Asia. Between 1985 and 1990, some $40 billion worth of Japanese investment swirled through the region, in the process creating an impressive integrated regional platform composed of the Japanese conglomerates' complementary manufacturing operations located in different countries.

With the continuing rise in the value of the yen relative to the dollar, the transfer of Japan's industrial operations to that region accelerated, and many analysts talked about the "hollowing out" of Japan.[11] A survey of over 140 firms carried out by the Japan Machinery Exporters' Association in mid-1994 revealed that their companies expected their Japan-based production to decrease by eight percent during the fiscal year periods 1992–1994, while their Asian-based production rose by 41 percent.[12] By the end of that period, production in Asia was expected to reach the equivalent of a quarter of the surveyed firms' domestic production.[13] For some companies, overseas production had already outstripped production in their domestic factories. For example, the Japanese electronics producer Aiwa manufactured 90 percent of its output at Asian sites.[14]

One dimension of the Japan-sponsored regional integration taking place was horizontal; that is, splitting up the production of different goods or the components of one product among different countries. In Matsushita's strategy, each country was assigned specific items to produce for export: color TVs and electric irons in Malaysia, semiconductors in Singapore, and dry cell batteries, floppy disk drives, and electronic capacitors in the Philippines.[15] A more functional level of integration was undertaken by car companies like Nissan, Toyota, and Mitsubishi. In Toyota's scheme, Indonesia specialized in gasoline engines and stamped parts, Malaysia turned out steering links and electrical equipment, the Philippines produced transmissions, and Thailand manufactured diesel engines, stamped parts, and electrical equipment.

In addition to integration along lines of product specialization, a process of backward integration tightened the links of the region to the core economy. In the first phase of this process, which began in the mid-1980s, Japanese automobile and consumer electronics firms relocated their plants to the region. This was followed by the out-migration of smaller Japanese companies that supplied parts and components for the automobile and electronics manufacturers. A third phase of backward integration began with the relocation of heavy and chemical industries that provide basic inputs to both the big assemblers and their suppliers.[16]

Describing the process, one prominent Japanese diplomat, Hisahiko Okazaki, noted: "Japan is creating an exclusive Japanese market in which Asia-Pacific nations are incorporated in the so-called *keiretsu* (financial/industrial bloc) system."[17] The essential relationship between Japan and Southeast Asia, he contended, was one of trading "captive imports, such as products from plants in which the Japanese have invested," in return for "captive exports, such as necessary equipment and materials."[18]

But unlike the American design of integration via free trade, the Japanese design of integration via investment did not demand that the Asian governments change their investment laws. It did not require that they reduce their tariffs. It did not stipulate that they end their subsidies for local firms. It was all very informal, "very Asian," say envious US trade officials. As one Washington-based government analyst put it, "the Japanese don't need free trade" to create a trading and investment bloc.[19]

As a result, although Asian governments and business groups occasionally bemoaned the lack of technology transfer from the Japanese, most felt that they had a more strategic partnership with Japan than with the US, though the US continued to be the main export market for many of them. While some might have been upset at Japan's refusal to endorse the EAEG, they were likely to work with the Japanese behind the scenes to slow down, if not sabotage, the 2020 plan.

Increasingly, what Asian technocrats felt was at stake were not just trade relationships but their way of organizing economic life. The 2020 plan was ultimately threatening not only because the US may regain a strong foothold in Asian markets, but because the ideology and strategy of free trade that underpinned it aimed to dismantle the system of state-assisted capitalism that, in their view, had been responsible for their success.

Underneath the diplomatic maneuverings in Seattle, Jakarta, and the Osaka Summit in November 1995 was a struggle between contrasting ways of capitalist organization and the ideologies legitimizing these "capitalisms." Perhaps one of the best analyses of the implications of this conflict is provided by an Australian commentator, Kenneth Davidson:

> The unstated Anglo-Saxon assumption behind APEC is that if the Anglo-Saxon countries can persuade Asian countries to play the economic development game according to Anglo-Saxon rules, the game will be translated into a neoclassical, *laissez faire,* positive-sum game in which the players will be transmuted from countries or tribes into firms and individuals.[20]

However, managed capitalism of the Asian variety, Davidson continued, was proving more successful than the Anglo-Saxon variety and "more resistant to cultural and political convergence imposed by globalizing forces and the growth in Asian living standards that many in the West had hoped." In this context the Australian-American goal at APEC was "to try to get the Asian winners of the economic game to deny the cultural basis of their success in order to create the conditions whereby the losers can become winners."[21]

On the other hand, the Japanese and East Asian game plan was to emasculate any attempt to make APEC a free trade area, deflecting its energies instead to becoming an organization for economic cooperation and development (OECD) of the Pacific, a largely consultative group that would co-ordinate on eliminating not tariff and investment restrictions but "technical barriers" to trade.

THE SUSTAINABLE DEVELOPMENT CRITIQUE

While regional elites have battled to define the direction of Asia-Pacific development along free market lines or along the lines of state-assisted capitalism, many non-governmental organizations (NGOs), people's movements, and progressive academics, evolved a powerful critique of both approaches. The essence of this critique was that despite some very real differences, the free market model and the Asian capitalist or NIC model had more to unite them than to divide them:

1. Both the free market and NIC models fetishize economic growth as the be-all and end-all of development.

2. Both intrinsically generate and perpetuate social inequality even as, in the case of the Asian capitalist model, rapid growth took place. High growth rates are necessary to allow a rise in absolute incomes without having to undertake redistribution of wealth. This conjunction of a rise in absolute income and worsening income distribution has characterized Korea, Taiwan, Singapore, and Thailand in the last 20 years.

3. Both models—again intrinsically—are ecologically destructive and unsustainable. In the case of the market approach, there is a rundown of natural capital since ecological costs are typically not factored into the real costs of production. In the case of NIC capitalism, there was a deliberate sacrifice of the environment to attract local and foreign capital in order to deliver high-speed growth. Indeed, the prospect of zero investment in pollution control is one of the two cornerstones of the NIC model, the other being cheap labor. In the NICs, market and state act in a complementary fashion to create an accelerated plunder of the environment. In Taiwan, the policy of decentralized industrialization decreed by the KMT government pushed small and medium industries to settle helter-skelter throughout the country, in residential areas and close to waterways, in the process decentralizing pollution and converting the island into an ecological wasteland. In Thailand, the market, private interests, and state policy created the convergence of two ecological catastrophes: massive deforestation and massive water pollution.

4. Both strategies have detrimental effects on agricultural communities, with market signals and state policy channeling capital and personnel from agriculture to industry and promoting terms of trade adverse to agriculture.

5. Both approaches have very destructive effects on communities. In the case of the market approach, because of the dissolving effect of unchecked market forces on communal and community bonds. In the case of the NIC model of state-assisted capitalism, through the deliberate breaking up and resettling of organic communities that stand in the way of state-managed development projects. In Thailand, the

Philippines, Indonesia, and Malaysia, the story is depressingly similar: big dam schemes imposed from the center, uprooting and resettlement of communities, particularly indigenous communities, and the gradual erosion and silent destruction of resettled communities.

TOWARDS AN ALTERNATIVE DEVELOPMENT STRATEGY

Dissatisfaction with both the free market and NIC models is becoming increasingly vocal, especially among NGOs and peoples' organizations. East Asian NGOs have often been criticized as being long on critique and short on prescription. This has, however, changed in the last few years. Though their ways of expressing them may vary, NGOs throughout the region are beginning to articulate a similar set of core ideas that, for want of a better term, come under the rubric of "sustainable development."

1. In opposition to the blind play of market forces in the free market approach and to state fiat in the NIC model, the sustainable development perspective would make transparent, rational, and democratic decision making the fundamental mechanism of production, distribution, and exchange.

2. In contrast to the impersonal control by the "invisible hand" of the market and the hierarchical and centralizing thrust of decision making in the NIC model, the sustainable development model would centralize economic decision making and management to communities, regions, or ecological zones, and make national planning a bottom-up process.

3. In opposition to the premium put on economic growth by the free market and NIC models, the sustainable development model de-emphasizes growth in favor of equity, the quality of life, and ecological harmony.

4. Both the free market and NIC models are heavily biased towards

urban-based industry. Sustainable development would make agriculture and the reinvigoration of rural society the centerpiece of the development process.

5. In the free market and NIC models, the pursuit of profitability dictates the adoption of capital intensive high technology in industry and chemical intensive technology in agriculture. The sustainable development approach would try to reverse what it considers uncontrolled technological change at the expense of the people, favoring the development of labor-intensive appropriate technology for industry and organic, chemical-free agro-technology.

6. In the free market model, the private sector calls the shots, and in the NIC model, the state-big business partnership has a "duopoly" over political and economic decision making. The sustainable development approach would organize the popular sector, represented by NGOs, as the third pillar of the political and economic system—as a balance to state and business in the short term, but with the perspective of making it the dominant force in the triad in the long term.

7. Finally, in contrast to a property system based on the division between private and public ownership in both the free market and NIC models, the sustainable development approach supports the recognition, institutionalization, and expansion of the realm of the "commons," or community or ancestral property that cannot be disposed of by market transaction or state fiat.

Initiatives based on these principles are already taking place at both community and national levels, with some success. One thing is clear, however: a regional program of sustainable development is a must. Both the transnational capital (whose interests are served by the free market approach) and Asian capital must operate with perspectives and plans that are regional in scope.

The following ideas, though not making up a complete program, are being advanced in several quarters towards the elaboration of a progressive regional alternative to both the APEC free trade idea and EAEG.

On membership in an economic bloc, both Japan and the US should be excluded, for one of the key purposes of such a bloc is precisely to change the power relationship between the weaker countries and the economic superpowers. Including Japan in such a bloc, as Prime Minister Mahathir proposed, would defeat this. Preferential trading, investment, and technology sharing arrangements that build on the current strengths of the members of the bloc would be the key measures to move the region away from the high degree of dependence on both Japan and the United States for imports, exports, capital, and technology.

Rather than beginning with bringing down barriers to inter-corporate or intra-corporate trade, an alternative strategy for regional integration could begin by addressing the pressing cross-border problems that undercut the welfare of people and the environment. One such problem is posed by multinational corporations that pit one country against another by threatening to move their operations to a country with lower labor costs and a less strict enforcement of environmental laws. The creation of a common regional environmental code with tight standards, and a common labor code with guarantees of labor organization and decent wage standards, would be an important step in bringing about this people-based regional cooperation.

As another step in this people-based cooperation, a common front could be created to demand technology transfer from both Japanese and Western firms, a demand that can be easily ignored if it comes from individual governments and individual companies. But beyond strengthening their hand in technology transfer, a people-based Asia-Pacific economic bloc would pool together the region's capital and personnel resources for research and development programs not only in high tech but also in appropriate technology for industry and agriculture. This would be especially important in the area of agricultural technology, since farmers throughout the area are now in desperate need of appropriate alternatives to chemical intensive Green Revolution technology. The latter has had very significant long-term impacts on both the soil and the environment, which may have an impact on food security in the region.

In the area of trade itself, a people-based economic bloc would move towards connecting trading communities or regions directly, creating community trading organizations that would supplant the corporate middlemen that now siphon off most of the profits at both ends of the trading link, at the supplier end and at the consumer end. Trade would have to be taken away from its present dynamics of locking communities and countries into a division of labor that diminishes their capabilities in the name of "comparative advantage" and "interdependence." It must be transformed into a process that enhances the capacities of communities, that ensures that initial cleavages that develop owing to necessary division of labor do not congeal into permanent cleavages, and which has mechanisms, including income and technology sharing arrangements, that prevent exploitative relationships from developing among trading communities.

Needless to say, the formation of such a regional bloc must actively involve not only government and business but also NGOs and peoples' organizations. Indeed, the sustainable development agenda can only succeed if it is brought in democratically rather than imposed from above by regional elites. It is regional integration from below.

This vision of an alternative regional future is very different from the American corporate vision of regional integration via free trade, the Japanese corporate vision of integration via investment, and the economists' and technocrats' vision of never-ending high-speed growth. Articulating this alternative future is, more than ever, a necessity. While the rampant consumerism that comes with high speed growth continues to dazzle many in Asia, there is a growing feeling that a process which is accompanied by the decline of agriculture, increasing inequality, and uncontrolled ecological degradation is a recipe for an unlivable future.

NOTES

1. See the excellent analysis of Robert Doner's "Domestic coalitions and Japanese auto firms in Southeast Asia," (University of Michigan, Ann Arbor: Ph.D. dissertation, 1987), pp. 511–596.

2. For an interesting account of the development of the aircraft industry, see "Hero flying high on Indonesia's first passenger plane," *The Australian,* November 10, 1994,

pg. 15. See also J. McBeth, "In the clouds," *Far Eastern Economic Review,* August 24, 1995, pp. 38–45.

3. Sakasakul, C. *Lessons from the World Bank's Experience of Structural Adjustment Loans: A Case Study of Thailand* (Bangkok: Thailand Development Research Institute, 1992), pg. 19.

4. Amsden, A. *Asia's Next Giant: South Korea and Late Industrialization* (New York: Oxford University Press, 1989), pg. 139.

5. Bello, Walden and Stephanie Rosenfield. *Dragons in Distress: Asia's Miracle Economies in Crisis* (Oakland, CA: Food First Books, 1991), pp. 44–57.

6. World Bank. *The East Asian Miracle* (New York: Oxford University Press, 1993).

7. Wade, R. "Selective industrial policies in East Asia: Is the East Asian miracle right?" in A. Fishlow (ed.), *Miracle or Design: Lessons from the East Asian Experience* (Washington, DC: Overseas Development Council, 1994), pp. 74–75.

8. US Department of Commerce. *Thailand* (Washington, DC: US Department of Commerce, 1992), pg. 241.

9. "Environment, industry groups resist US trade accusations," *Bangkok Post,* April 1, 1992. Reproduced in *FBIS Environment Report,* May 1992, pg. 25.

10. "APEC to fulfill US goals," November 2, 1994, Kyodo News Agency. Reproduced in *FBIS Environment Report,* November 3, 1994, pg. 1.

11. "Nippon's choice," *Far Eastern Economic Review,* June 8, 1995, pp. 28–45.

12. Cronin, R. *Japan and US Economic Involvement in Asia and the Pacific: Comparative Data and Analysis* (Washington, DC: Congressional Research Service, 1994), pg. 23.

13. Ibid.

14. "Region expects greater Japanese investment," *Republika* [Jakarta], March 10, 1995. Reproduced in *FBIS Environment Report,* March 14, 1995, pg. 57.

15. Steven, R. *Japan's New Imperialism* (Armonk, NY: M.E. Sharpe, 1990), pg. 116.

16. "New strategies toward super-Asian bloc," *This Is* [Tokyo], August 1992. Reproduced in *FBIS Environment Report,* October 1992, pg. 18.

17. Ibid.

18. Ibid.

19. Nanto, D. (1989) *Pacific Rim Economic Cooperation* (Washington, DC: Congressional Research Service, 1989), pg. 10.

20. Davidson, K. "Hard lessons ahead as we learn to deal with Asia," *The Age,* November 15, 1994, pg. 19.

21. Ibid.

7

EAST ASIA: ON THE EVE
OF THE GREAT TRANSFORMATION?

Review of International Political Economy, Autumn 1998

Seven months after the outbreak of the Asian financial crisis, the International Monetary Fund (IMF) moved into the eye of the economic typhoon ravaging Asia. The Fund's high profile coincided with the spread of the deflationary and inflationary effects of the financial collapse on the real economy of the region, making the period potentially explosive.

THE IMF IN THE BREACH

In Indonesia, the Fund has admitted in an internal memo that it helped provoke the unraveling of the economy in October 1997, when its demand that the government shut down insolvent banks led not to the restoration of investor confidence but to panic selling of the rupiah for dollars, bringing down the value of the Indonesian currency by over 80 percent from mid-1997.[1]

In Thailand, the IMF prescription to regain investor confidence by drastically cutting back on government expenditures to achieve a budget surplus was seriously questioned by critics who found support in authorities like Harvard economist Jeffrey Sachs, who have written that:

the IMF arrived in Thailand in July filled with ostentatious declarations that all was wrong and that fundamental and immediate surgery was needed.... The IMF deepened the sense of panic not only because of its dire pronouncements but also because its proposed medicine—high interest rates, budget cuts, and immediate bank closures—convinced the markets that Asia indeed was about to enter a severe contraction. Instead of dousing the fire, the IMF in effect screamed fire in the theater.[2]

Thailand and the Asian region, warned Sachs, "does not need wanton budget cutting, credit tightening, and emergency bank closures. It needs stable or even expansionary monetary and fiscal policies to counterbalance the decline in foreign loans."[3]

The combination of the financial crisis and the IMF program provoked an economic contraction that led both IMF and Thai officials to revise their estimate of the 1998 gross domestic product (GDP) growth rate from a positive 3.5 percent (when the program with the Fund was signed in August) to a negative 3.5 percent in late February. According to the critics, this situation scared away the foreign capital that the Fund wanted to bring back to Thailand.

The Fund may be controversial in Indonesia and Thailand, but one cannot say that its prescriptions did not resonate with a significant sector of the population that saw the crisis as having been triggered by the corrupt Suharto economic monopoly in the case of Indonesia, and by greedy and irresponsible politicians in the case of Thailand. In Korea, the Fund was very unpopular, not only because it was seen as administering the wrong medicine, but because it was viewed as a surrogate for the US, imposing a program of deregulation and liberalization in trade, investment, and finance that Washington had been pushing on the country—with little success—before the outbreak of the financial crisis. US officials have, in fact, done little to hide that they see the Fund—where Washington has the biggest share of voting power—as doing their bidding. As US trade representative Charlene Barshefsky told the US Congress:

Policy-driven, rather than market-driven economic activity...meant that US industry encountered many specific structural barriers to trade, investment, and competition in Korea. For example, Korea maintained restrictions on foreign ownership and operation, and had a list of market access impediments.... The Korea stabilization package, negotiated with the IMF in December 1997, should help open and expand competition in Korea by creating a more market-driven economy.... [I]f it continues on the path to reform there will be important benefits not only for Korea but also the United States.4

The controversy over the role of the IMF is the latest phase in a regional economic drama that took the world by surprise when it broke in July 1996. The development experts from right to left who, while they might have differed in their analysis of the reasons behind the "Asian miracle," were nevertheless united in the consensus that the Asia-Pacific would be the engine of the world economy far into the twenty-first century. It might be said that the collapse of the Asian economies is probably the second biggest surprise of the last fifty years, the first being the collapse of Soviet socialism at the turn of the decade.

What brought about the crisis? Why were these economics so fragile after all? With events still moving rapidly, there is obviously a risk in advancing full-blown theories about the collapse. Nevertheless, it does seem that the dynamics of the collapse in Southeast Asia and Northeast Asia, while manifesting themselves dramatically in the financial sector, have been distinct; reflecting the different patterns of economic development in the two regions.

THE SOUTHEAST ASIAN COLLAPSE

In the case of the Southeast Asian countries, the crisis was definitely triggered by the rush of international capital out of the region in 1997—a movement that was more frenzied than its mad rush to get into the area in earlier years. The pendulum swing is illustrated by figures from the Institute of International Finance, which show net private inflows into Indonesia, Malaysia, South Korea, Thailand, and the Philippines jump from $40.5 billion in 1994 to $92.8 billion in 1996, then change into a $12 billion outflow in 1997.5 Even Stanley Fischer, deputy managing director of the IMF, has conceded that in the case of the Asian financial crisis, "[M]arkets am not always right. Sometimes inflows are excessive, and sometimes they may be sustained too long. Markets tend to react fast, sometimes excessively."6

It would, however, be simplistic to paint the region as being simply a victim of external forces. The elites of Southeast Asia in particular had institutionalized a pattern of development that was greatly dependent on huge infusions of foreign capital. As *The Nation* newspaper in Bangkok put it, "When Southeast Asia jumped on the global bandwagon, it should have been prepared for the downs as well as the ups."[7] Unlike the case of growth in the classical newly industrializing countries (NICS) of Taiwan and Korea, in the fast track capitalism of seven to ten percent GDP growth rates pursued by Southeast Asian technocrats, growth was sustained, not principally by domestic savings and investment, but by foreign investment.

Southeast Asia's growth was heavily dependent on Japanese direct investment in the late 1980s. The main cause of this inflow of capital was the Plaza Accord of 1985, whereby the United States forced the Japanese to drastically raise the value of the yen relative to the dollar in order to relieve the US trade deficit with Japan. The agreement did not do wonders for the US trade deficit, but by making production in Japan more expensive in dollar terms, it did do wonders for Southeast Asia by pushing the Japanese to relocate the more labor-intensive phases of their manufacturing to the region, touching off a decade of rapid growth. Between 1985 and 1990, some $15 billion worth of Japanese direct investment flowed into the region in one of the largest and swiftest movements of capital to the developing world in recent history.[8] Japanese direct investment brought with it billions of dollars more in Japanese bilateral aid and bank loans, as well provoking an ancillary flow of billions of dollars in foreign direct investment from the first generation newly industrializing economies of Taiwan, Hong Kong, and South Korea.

However, Japanese direct investment began to level off or, as in the case of Thailand, taper off in the early 1990s, prompting Southeast Asia's economic managers to search for alternative sources of capital for economies that had become addicted to massive inflows of foreign investment. These they found in the portfolio investors and big international banks that were scouring the globe in the early 1990s in search of alternatives to the "declining returns in the stock markets of industrial countries and the low real interest rates."[9]

To bring about this inflow of finance capital, Thailand's technocrats pioneered a formula that consisted of three key elements: liberalization of the capital account and of the financial sector as a whole; maintenance of high domestic interest rates relative to interest rates in northern money centers in order to suck in portfolio investment and bank capital; and the virtual fixing of. the local currency at a stable rate relative to the dollar in order to ensure foreign investors against currency risk. In the succinct description of one investment analyst:

> Since 1987 the Thai authorities have kept their currency locked to the US dollar in a band of [B]aht 25–26 while maintaining domestic rates 500–600 points higher than US rates and keeping their borders open to capital flows. Thai borrowers naturally gravitated towards US dollar borrowings and the commercial banks accommodated them, with the result that the Thai banks now have a net foreign liability position equivalent to 20 percent of GDP. The borrowers converted to baht with the Bank of Thailand, the ultimate purchaser of their foreign currency. Fuelled by cheap easy money, the Thai economy grew rapidly, inflation rose, and the current account deficit ballooned.[10]

Wildly successful in attracting foreign capital, the Thai formula was soon copied by finance ministries and central banks in Manila, Kuala Lumpur, and Jakarta. Instrumental in the diffusion of the Thai formula were the blessings of the IMF and the World Bank, which saw any move to eliminate barriers between the domestic and global financial markets as a step in the right direction. Indeed, the Bank of Thailand, the country's central bank, was held up by the Fund, the World Bank, and academic experts as a model for its neighbors, and its policies were regarded as the bedrock of Thailand's rise to tigerhood. Even as late as the second half of 1996, when it was becoming clear that the economy was headed for trouble, the IMF was still praising the Thai authorities for their "consistent record of sound macroeconomic management policies."[11]

In retrospect, Thailand exemplified the perils of the model of development based on huge infusions of foreign capital seeking quick and high returns. Net portfolio investment came to around $24 billion, while at least another $50 billion entered in the form of loans to Thai banks and enterprises. This massive inflow found its way not into the domestic manufacturing sector or agriculture, for these were considered low yield sectors that would provide a decent rate of return only after a long gestation period of huge blocks of capital. The high yield sectors with a quick turnaround time that foreign money inevitably gravitated to were the stock market, consumer financing and, in particular, real estate development.

Not surprisingly, a glut in real estate developed quite rapidly, so that by 1996 some $20 billion worth of new residential and commercial property remained unsold. Monuments to the property folly were evident everywhere, such as Bangkok Land Company's massive but virtually deserted residential complex near the Bangkok international airport and the sleek but empty thirty-story towers in the Bangna-trat area of the city.

The rest of the story unfolded quickly: commercial banks and finance companies found themselves horribly overexposed in real estate, with some estimates putting the exposure at 40 percent of total loans. Foreign portfolio investors and banks that had loaned to Thai entities soon discovered that their customers were carrying a huge load of non-performing loans. The zero growth in exports in 1996 was a sign that the vaunted export machine was growing non-competitive; and with a worsening balance of trade in goods and services, the country's future capacity to repay the debts incurred by the private sector became very cloudy. That the current account was in deficit to the tune of 8.2 percent of GDP in 1996 struck fear in the hearts of many investors, who were reminded by investment analysts that this was roughly the same figure as that of Mexico when that economy suffered its financial meltdown in December 1994.

By early 1997, many investors concluded that it was time to get out and to get out fast. With around $24 billion in baht parked in Thai stocks or paper or nestled in non-resident bank accounts,[12] the stampede was potentially catastrophic, for it meant unloading trillions of baht for dollars. With too many baht chasing too few dollars, the result was a massive downward push on the value of the baht and tremendous pressure on the authorities to devalue it officially relative to the dollar.

The scent of panic attracted the speculators, among them George Soros and his famous Quantum Fund. Gambling on the devaluation of the baht, Soros sought to make profits through well-timed purchases and unloading of baht and dollars. The Bank of Thailand sought to defend the baht at the sacrosanct $1:B25 rate by dumping its dollar reserves on the market. But the foreign investors' stampede that the speculators rode on was simply too strong. The result was that the central bank lost at least $9 billion in the spot market, and another $23.4 billion in forward swap commitments of its $39 billion reserves.[13] With such massive losses, the authorities threw in the towel and let the baht float to seek its "true" market value on July 2, 1997.

Speculators spotted the same skittish behavior among foreign investors in Manila, Kuala Lumpur, and Jakarta, where the same conjunction of commercial bank overexposure in the property sector, weak export growth, and a widening current account deficit was stoking fears of a devaluation of the local currency that could devastate their investments. As in Thailand, speculators rode on the exit of foreign investors from these economies, which accelerated tremendously after the devaluation of the baht on July 2. The Philippine peso was floated on July 11, followed by the Malaysian ringgit and the Indonesian rupiah over the next month. By the end of December 1997, these currencies had lost from 30 to 80 percent of their value. Foreign capital continued to exit, resulting in the catastrophic combination of skyrocketing import bills, a massive rise in the cost of servicing the foreign debt of the private sector, a steep hike in interest rates that spiked economic activity, and a chain reaction of bankruptcies.

The Southeast Asian miracle had come to a screeching stop.

TRAVAILS OF THE CLASSIC TIGER ECONOMY

Even as the economies of Southeast Asia were collapsing in dramatic fashion over the summer of 1997, things were building up to a climax in Korea, where seven of the country's mighty *chaebol* or conglomerates had come crashing down. The dynamics of the fall in Korea were, however, distinct from that in Southeast Asia.

Unlike the Southeast Asian economies, Korea, the classical NIC, had blazed a path to industrial strength that was based principally on domestic savings, carried out partly through equity-enhancing reforms such as land reform in the early 1950s. Foreign capital had played an important part, no doubt, but local financial resources extracted through a rigorous system of taxation plus profits derived from the sale of goods to a protected domestic market and to foreign markets opened up by an aggressive mercantilist strategy constituted the main source of capital accumulation.

The institutional framework for high-speed industrialization was a close working relationship between the private sector and the state, with the latter in a commanding role. By "picking winners," providing them with subsidized credit through a government-directed banking system, and protecting them from competition with transnationals in the domestic market, the state nurtured industrial conglomerates that it later pushed out into the international market.

In the early 1980s, the state-*chaebol* combine appeared to be unstoppable in international markets, as the deep pockets of commercial banks that were extremely responsive to government wishes provided the wherewithal for Hyundai, Samsung, LG Electronics, and other conglomerates to carve out market shares in Europe, Asia, and North America. The good years were from 1985 to 1990, when profitability was roughly indicated by the surpluses that the country racked up in its international trade account.

THE SQUEEZE

In the early 1990s, however, the tide turned against the Koreans. Three factors, in particular, appeared to be central: a failure to invest significantly in research and development, the massive trade blitz visited on Korea by the United States, and the Korean conglomerate's or *chabol's* ambitious global *modus operandi* of gaining, maintaining, or expanding market share at all costs.

Failure to invest significantly in research and development during the 1980s translated into continuing heavy dependence on Japan for basic machinery, manufacturing inputs, and technology, resulting in a worsening trade deficit with that country.

Government spending on research and development in the late 1980s came to only 0.4 percent of gross national product (GNP), and reforms needed to transform the country's educational structure so as to mass produce a more technically proficient workforce were never implemented.[14] By the end of the decade, there were only thirty-two engineers per 10,000 workers in Korea, compared to 240 in Japan and 160 in the United States.[15]

As for management, it took the easy way out. Many firms chose to continue to compete on the basis of low cost unskilled or semi-skilled labor by moving many of their operations to Southeast Asia. Instead of pouring money into research and development to turn out high-value-added commodities and develop more sophisticated production technologies, Korea's conglomerates went for the quick and easy route to profits, buying up real estate or pouring money into stock market speculation. In the 1980s, over $16.5 billion in *chaebol* funds went into buying land for speculation and setting up luxury hotels. As of the early 1990s, a single US corporation, IBM, was investing much more on research and development than all Korean corporations combined.[16]

Not surprisingly, most of the machines in industrial plants continued to be imported from Japan, and Korean-assembled products from color televisions to laptop computers continued to be made up mainly of Japanese components. For all intents and purposes, Korea was not able to graduate from its status as a labor-intensive assembly point for Japanese inputs using Japanese technology. Predictably, the result was a massive trade deficit with Japan, which came to over $15 billion in 1996.

As Korea's balance of trade with Japan worsened, so did its trade balance with the United States. Fearing the emergence of another Japan with which it would constantly be in deficit, Washington subjected Seoul to a broad-front trade offensive that was much tougher than the one directed at Japan, probably owing to Korea's lack of retaliatory capacity. Among other things, the United States:

• Hit Korean television manufacturers with anti-dumping suits.

- Forced Korea to adopt "voluntary export restraints" on a number of products, including textiles, garments, and steel.

- Forced the appreciation of the won, the Korean currency, relative to the dollar by 40 percent between 1986 and 1989 to make Korean goods more expensive to American consumers, thus dampening demand for them.

- Knocked Korea off the list of countries eligible for inclusion in the general system of preferences (GSP), which grants preferential tariffs to products from Third World countries in order to assist their development.

- Threatened Korea with sanctions for a whole host of alleged offences, ranging from violation of intellectual property rights to discriminatory tax treatment against large engine US car imports, under the Special 301 and Super 301 clauses of the 1988 US Trade Act (which mandates the US executive to take retaliatory action against countries that are adjudged unfair traders or seen as abetting the violations of the intellectual property rights of US corporations).

- Forced Korea to open up its markets to US tobacco products and to increase imports of beef.

- Forced Seoul to open an estimated 98 percent of industrial areas and 32 percent of service areas to foreign equity investments and stepped up the pressure for liberalization in telecommunications, maritime services, banking, government procurement, and many other areas.[17]

Hemmed in on all fronts, Korea saw its 1987 trade surplus of $9.6 billion with the US turn into a deficit of $159 million in 1992. By 1996, the deficit with the US had grown to over $4 billion, and Korea's overall trade deficit hit $21 billion.

Even as Korea's external accounts lurched sharply into the negative, the country's famed *chaebol* continued their bold strategies of carving out export markets and holding on to them even if they were a drain on corporate finances that were increasingly propped up by loans from both local and foreign sources. In the case of Samsung's VCR division, "[t]he more products it sold in the US, the more money it lost" because "rocketing labor costs and the strength of the Korean currency [resulted in] production costs in Korea...rising much faster than US-based prices for VCRs."[18]

But Samsung, like its rivals Daewoo and LG Electronics, refused to let go. In this sense, Korea's *chaebol* behaved very much like the Japanese military in the Pacific during the first six months of the WW II—quick expansion leading to perilous over-extension, to which the response was not to pull back into a viable defensive perimeter but to hang tightly on to far-flung holdings whose supply turned into a logistical nightmare. For example, even as Kia Motors was lurching into bankruptcy brought about by massive debt in 1996, it was planning a major new finance-intensive joint venture with Indonesian partners to monopolize the Indonesian car market.

DESPERATION MOVE

In a desperate attempt, to regain profitability to sustain their precarious global reach, the *chaebol* tried to ram through parliament in December 1996 a series of laws based on the American model. These laws would have given it significantly expanded rights to fire labor and reduce the workforce, along the lines of sloughing off "excess labor" and making the surviving workforce more productive. When this failed owing to fierce street opposition from workers, many *chaebol* had no choice but to fall back on their long-standing symbiotic relationship with the government, the banks, and external creditors, this time to draw ever greater amounts of funds to keep money-losing operations alive. By 1998, *chaebol* were operating with debt loads that were ten to forty times their own capital, even as the return to equity—a key index of profitability—had shrunk to a minuscule 0.8 percent.[19]

However, the lifeline could not be maintained without the banks themselves being run into the ground. By October 1997, it was estimated that non-performing loans by Korean enterprises had escalated to over $50 billion. As this surfaced, foreign banks, which already had about $200 billion worth of investments and loans in Korea, became reluctant to roll over debt coming due, much less release new funds. By late November, on the eve of the APEC Summit in Vancouver, Seoul, saddled with having to repay some $72 billion out of a total foreign debt of $110 billion within one year, joined Thailand and Indonesia in the IMF queue.

The Korean government was able to get a commitment of $57 billion to bail out the economy, but only on the condition that it would not only undertake a harsh stabilization program, but also do away with the key institutions and practices that had propelled the country into tigerhood. The miracle was over.

THE FUTURE

What happens next in a region that is now strewn with the wrecks of economic miracles?

It is certain that recession will spread owing to the exchange rate dislocations, capital flight and belt-tightening IMF stabilization programs. This will deepen as foreign direct investors increasingly follow the example of portfolio investors in reducing their profile in Southeast Asia. Already, nearly all the key Japanese vehicle manufacturers—Toyota, Mitsubishi, Isuzu, and Hino—have either reduced or shut down operations in Thailand.

While there is some talk about foreign capital returning soon to take advantage of fire sale prices to buy bankrupt firms, and some speculation that Southeast Asian countries will recover owing to competitive currencies that will allow them to regain export markets, the future is likely to be one of prolonged deflation rather than quick recovery.

In the years before the crash the main engine of East Asian growth was increasingly intra-regional trade, with intra-Asian trade as a proportion of total Asian trade, rising from 47 percent in 1990 to 53 percent in 1995. This strength has now turned into an Achilles' heel. Unlike the early 1990s, when Japan's recession was offset by the boom in Southeast Asia and continuing growth in Korea, today all three sources of regional demand have been doused (with Japan stubbornly refusing to increase demand through stepped-up government spending) while a fourth source, China, remains a weak stimulus, with significant protectionist barriers limiting import growth to a mere 2.5 percent in the first nine months of 1997.

This leaves Europe and the US as significant mass markets. Europe, however, is experiencing a slowdown in demand, with recession and high unemployment continuing to envelop key countries like Germany. As for the expansive US market, Southeast Asian exporters are likely to encounter an uphill battle for market share against ruthlessly competitive China and the newly competitive countries of Latin America.

AMERICA'S WINDOW OF OPPORTUNITY

How the US would respond to the crisis in East Asia was a matter of great concern to the Asian elites when the crisis broke in mid-1997. Would Washington stand back and see the crisis unfold, smug that its dynamic economy would remain relatively unaffected by the "Asian flu"? Or would America, as in Europe immediately after WW II, come up with an Asian version of the Marshall Plan? As it turned out, Washington's stance was neither isolation nor generous engagement, but an opportunistic one of taking advantage of the crisis to achieve what it has been trying to push over the last decade with little success: the free market transformation of economic systems that are best described as state-assisted capitalist formations.

US officials have long regarded the complex of protectionism, mercantilism, industrial policy, and activist state intervention in the economy that envelops most of the East and Southeast Asian countries as a system that handicaps US economic interests exporting to or investing in Asia while unfairly assisting Asian firms in penetrating the US market. As the Cold War wound down from the mid-1980s, Washington began to redefine its economic policy towards East Asia as the creation of a level playing field for its corporation via liberalization, deregulation, and privatization of the Asian economies.

It was a goal that the US pursued through various means in the late 1980s and early 1990s, including IMF and World Bank's "structural adjustment programs" in the mid-1980s; a harsh unilateralist trade campaign employing the threat of trade retaliation to open up markets and stop unauthorized use of US high technologies, a drive to create an APEC free trade area with a comprehensive liberalization program leading to borderless trade among eighteen countries; and a strong push on the Asian countries to implement the GATT Uruguay Round agreements that eliminated trade quotas, reduced tariffs, banned the use of trade policy for industrialization purposes, and opened up agricultural markets.

Prior to the crisis, the liberalization drive had brought meager results, except perhaps in the case of Korea whose trade surplus had been turned into a deficit. But even this development did not change US trade representative Barshefsky's assessment of Korea as "one of the toughest places in the world to do business."[20] Nor has Washington's view of Japan changed. Despite the Tokyo government's free market rhetoric, it is seen as a market that is hard to penetrate owing to "structural impediments" like tight conglomerate relationships cutting across industries and a continuing hand-in-glove relationship between the bureaucracy and Japanese business. As for the Southeast Asian countries, the assessment in Washington is that while they may have liberalized their capital accounts and financial sectors, they remain highly protected when it comes to trade and are dangerously flirting with "trade distorting" exercises in industrial policy like Malaysia's national car project, the Proton Saga, or Indonesia's drive to set up a passenger aircraft industry.

A golden opportunity to push the US agenda opened up with the financial crisis, and Washington exploited it to the hilt, advancing its interests behind the banner of free market reform. The rollback of protectionism and activist state intervention was incorporated into the stabilization programs negotiated by the Fund with Thailand, Indonesia, and Korea.

Thai authorities agreed to remove all limitations on foreign ownership of Thai financial firms and pushed ahead with even more liberal foreign investment legislation that would allow foreigners to own land, a practice that has long been taboo in that country. As US trade representative Barshefsky saw it, "commitments to restructure public enterprises and accelerate privatization of certain key sectors—including energy, transportation, utilities, and communications—which will enhance market-driven competition and deregulation [are expected] to create new business opportunities for US firms."[21]

> In Indonesia, Barshefsky emphasized that the IMF's conditionalities address practices that have long been the subject of this administration's bilateral trade policy.... Most notable in this respect is the commitment by Indonesia to eliminate the tax, tariff, and credit privileges, provided to the national car project. We have challenged the tax, tariff, and credit privileges provided to the national car project. Additionally, the IMF program seeks broad reform of Indonesian trade and investment policy, like the aircraft project, monopolies, and domestic trade restrictive practices, that stifle competition by limiting access for foreign goods and services.[22]

The national car project and the plan to set up a passenger jet aircraft industry are efforts at industrial policy that have elicited the strong disapproval of Detroit and Boeing, respectively.

In the case of Korea, as pointed out earlier, the US Treasury and the IMF did not conceal their close working relationship, with the Fund in a clearly subordinate position. Not surprisingly, the concessions made by the Koreans—including raising the limit on foreign ownership of corporate stocks to 55 percent, permitting the establishment of foreign financial institutions, full liberalization of the financial and capital market, abolition of the car classification system, and agreement to end government-directed lending for industrial policy goals—have a one-to-one correspondence with US bilateral policy towards Korea over the last decade.

Summing up Washington's strategic goal without having to use the euphemisms of his colleagues in the administration, Jeff Carten, undersecretary of commerce during President Clinton's first term said, "Most of these countries are going to go through a deep and dark tunnel.... But on the other end there is going to be a significantly different

Asia in which American firms have achieved much deeper market penetration, much greater access."[23]

JAPAN MISSES THE BOAT

While Washington did not hesitate to exploit the situation for its own ends, Japan missed a golden opportunity to move decisively into the role of Asia's economic leader by withdrawing its proposal for the establishment of an "Asian monetary fund" (AMF). The fund, with a possible capitalization of $100 billion, was proposed by Japan in August 1997, when Southeast Asian currencies were in free fall, as a multipurpose fund that would assist Asian economies in defending their currencies against speculators, provide emergency balance-of-payments financing, and make available long-term funding for economic adjustment purposes. As outlined by Japanese foreign ministry officials, notably the influential ministry of finance official Eisuke Sakakibara, the fund would have been a quick-disbursing mechanism that would be more flexible than the IMF, by requiring "a less uniform, perhaps less stringent set of required policy reforms as conditions for receiving help."[24] Not surprisingly, the AMF proposal drew strong support from Southeast Asian governments.

Just as predictably, the AMF aroused the strong opposition of both the IMF and the US. At the IMF-World Bank annual meeting in Hong Kong in September 1997, IMF managing director Michel Camdessus and his American deputy Stanley Fischer argued that by serving as an alternative source of financing, the AMF would subvert the IMF's ability to secure tough economic reforms from Asian countries in financial trouble. Washington's vehement response stemmed from the fact that increasing congressional constraints on the president's power to commit us bilateral funds to international initiatives have made the US "more dependent on its power in the IMF to exercise influence on financial matters in Asia. In this context, an Asian monetary fund in which Japan was the major player would be a blow to the US role in the region."[25] Analyst Eric Altbach claims that "[s]ome Treasury officials accordingly saw the AMF as more than just a bad idea; they interpreted it as a threat to America's influence in Asia. Not surprisingly, Washington made considerable efforts to kill Tokyo's proposal.[26]

Unwilling to lead an Asian coalition against US wishes, Japan back-tracked and eventually allowed the AMF to be watered down during a meeting of Asian finance ministers in Manila in mid-November 1997 into a vaguely defined mechanism to supplement the IMF, whose central role in stabilizing the region financially was affirmed. The results were interpreted as a defeat for Japan, which was seen throughout the region as having failed to break with the "occupation psychology" in its relationship with Washington.

The Japanese retreat left the regions' elites with little choice but to accede to IMF conditions. In Korea, newly inaugurated president Kim Dae-Jung promised full compliance with the IMF program, with some of his advisers reportedly offering to better the IMF demand of a minimum of 55 percent foreign ownership of Korean firms to 100 percent.[27] In Indonesia, President Suharto clashed with the IMF, but strangely enough not on the question of loosening the stringent IMF conditions, but on Suharto's insistence on an "IMF-plus" proposal of pegging the rupiah to the dollar and tying the amount of rupiah in circulation to the amount of the country's dollar reserves. In Thailand, compliance with a deflationary IMF program that was expected to produce a negative growth rate of -3.5 percent in 1998 won the new government of Prime Minister Chuan Leekpai the compliment of having "turned the corner" in the effort to restructure the economy.[28]

ASIANS DEBATE THE "ASIAN MODEL"

In the view of many, not only did Japan lose the battle for the AMF, but the financial crisis dealt a severe setback to the Japanese model of state-assisted capitalism that had been emulated in varying degrees by many of the East Asian countries during their ascent from underdevelopment, The central characteristics of this model were an activist, interventionist state, strong government discipline of the market and of the private sector, preferential access of domestic firms to the local market, and industrial targeting.

Washington's free market agenda is not without its partisans among Asia's elites. Even before the crisis, these people were already vocal in their view that the close state–business partnership at the core of

'"Asia, Inc." was the main cause of stagnation in Japan and increasing economic instability in Korea. In their view, it was the US corporate sector's embrace of radical downsizing and other reforms in the face of severe market penalties in the early 1990s that accounted for the United State's marked edge over the Japanese and the Europeans in everything from labor productivity to technological innovation. According to this school, state-assisted capitalism in Japan—the model for Korea and the Southeast Asian economies—may have worked in achieving high growth rates in the early phases of industrialization, but had become dysfunctional in an era of globalized markets, which rewards corporate structures that can respond swiftly, innovatively and profitably.

Moreover, they argued, state management spawned corrupt government–business relationships that both deprived local and foreign investors of accurate data on which to make sound market decisions and significantly added to the costs of doing business through the payment of "rent" to strategically placed groups like the Suharto family and cronies in Indonesia. In short, the old state–business partnership was a dinosaur, and only radical free market reform, along the lines of the still-to-be-implemented "big bang" financial reforms in Japan, could create the conditions for Asian firms to emerge as competitive enterprises.

To others, however, radical free market reform is a prescription for disaster. Asia's bureaucrats are very much aware that there is another, disturbing side to the newly competitive US capitalism. What the US economic managers have brought about in their pursuit of a lean and mean corporate strike force for global competition is one of the most unequal distributions of income among advanced industrial countries, the re-emergence of poverty on a significant scale, and tremendous alienation among the lower income groups. If this volatile discontent, which finds expression in inflamed anti-immigrant sentiment, is also the price that will be exacted by the dismantling of the institutions of Asian capitalism, such as the lifetime employment of the core industrial labor force that is one of the central pillars of Japan, Inc., or pre-IMF Korea, then the hesitations of Asia's economic managers are understandable.

An equally significant objection is that radical free market reform may lead, not to the transformation of Asian capitalism, but to its unraveling. In contrast to the development of capitalism in the United States, an activist state has always been a central component in the birth and development of capitalism in Asia. Neoliberal reform will simply recreate the international economy in the image of the US economy, thus setting up a global playing field in which the economic actors that emerged in one particular historical road to advanced capitalism, the free market/minimal state path, will have an unparalleled competitive edge.

In this view, the solution is not to throw out the baby—the activist state—with the bath water, but radically to reform the state–private sector relationship. Certainly, this would be along the lines of more transparency, more accountability to the public, and more democratic surveillance of both government and corporations. It would also be along the lines of greater government discipline of the private sector: one of the key lessons of the current crisis is not too much state intervention but lack of it. In the case of Korea, they point out that it was the loosening of state surveillance of the private sector in the 1980s that encouraged the *chaebol* to pour their profits, not into research and development, but into gambling in the stock market and in real estate. In the 1990s, notes analyst Ha-Joon Chang, growing *chaebol* power forced the state to give up activist investment coordination of the private sector altogether, leading to "over-capacity, which resulted in falling export prices, falling profitability due to low capacity utilization, and the accumulation of non-performing loans in a number of leading industries, including semiconductors, automobile, petrochemicals, and shipbuilding."[29]

Similarly, in the case of Southeast Asia, it was lack of state intervention in financial markets that allowed over-investment in the property sector. In fact, it was not until 1997 that central banks in Malaysia and the Philippines issued rulings limiting real estate loans to 20 percent of commercial banks' total exposure—by which time their real estate bubbles had already burst, as in Thailand.

From this perspective, the crying need is hardly deregulation or less state intervention but more effective regulation of the private sector and, in particular, the breaking up of corrupt particularistic patronage networks linking the public and private sectors. In order words, get rid of the monopolies of Suharto and his cronies, but do not allow this enterprise to be used by the IMF and the US as a smoke screen for their strategic goal of getting rid of activist government. Clean up government, so it can serve as a more effective partner and regulator of the private sector.

CRISIS ... AND OPPORTUNITY?

Free market ideology has become so dominant in international elite discourse that even its opponents in government and business—with the singular exception of Prime Minister Mahathir of Malaysia—mouth its platitudes while opposing it in practice. It is mainly reformers outside governing circles in academia or in non-governmental organizations who are voicing alternatives to the free market transformation of their societies that is now entering a more advanced stage. Although not yet "operationalized" in a hardheaded fashion, their agenda is getting an increasingly sympathetic hearing from the public, especially at a time when the US-IMF reform is associated with rocketing inflation and mass unemployment that hit over ten percent of the workforce in Korea, Indonesia, and Thailand.

In addition to reform of the state-business relations suggested above, what are some of the key themes of this alternative program?

First of all, one of the prime causes of the Asian financial crisis has been the indiscriminate globalization of financial markets. Controls are badly needed on capital inflows and outflows since they are proving to be highly destabilizing to developing economies. The call for controls is, of course, hardly unconventional these days, when even Alan Greenspan, chairman of the US Federal Reserve Board, suggested that the world financial system must be "reviewed and altered as necessary to fit the needs of the new global environment."[30]

From the perspective of Asia's reformers, however, capital controls are needed not just for purposes of stability but to steer the development process in a healthy direction, as a way of discriminating against the entry of speculative capital. Singapore's *Business Times,* a paper which is not exactly noted for radicalism, has pointed out that one of the key lessons of the crisis is that "short-term capital inflows are of highly dubious benefit when all they do is to finance asset inflation (stocks and real estate) and a nation is arguably better off without them."[31]

Very popular among reformers in the region is some version of the so-called Tobin tax (named after its proponent, the US economist James Tobin), a transactions tax imposed on all cross-border flows of capital that are not clearly earmarked as direct investment. Such a measure, it is claimed, would help slow down the frenzied and increasingly irrational movements of finance capital. A slowing down of the movements of speculative capital would also be accomplished by a device used by the Chileans and increasingly advocated by a number of Southeast Asian experts: require foreign portfolio investors and local enterprises contracting foreign loans to make an interest-free deposit in the central bank of an amount equal to 30 percent of their investment that they would not be able to withdraw for one or more years. This would make them think twice before pulling out at the scent of higher yields elsewhere.

The aim is not to discourage foreign direct investment. Such measures will create a strong disincentive for speculative capital to enter and exit arbitrarily, with all the destabilizing consequences of these movements, but will not penalize direct investors who are making more strategic commitments of their capital.

Second, while foreign investment of the right kind is important, growth must be financed principally from domestic savings and investment. This means good, progressive taxation systems. One of the key reasons for the reliance on foreign capital for fast track development was that the elites of Southeast Asia did not want to tax themselves to produce the needed investment capital. Regressive taxation systems are the norm in the region, where income tax payers are but a handful and indirect taxes that cut deeply into the resources of lower income groups are the principal source of income for government expenditures.

But progressive taxation would just be the start. Democratic management of national investment policies is also essential if local savings are not to be hijacked by financial elites and channeled to speculative gambles.

A third theme is that while export markets are important, development must be reoriented around the centrality of the domestic market as the main stimulus of development. Together with the pitfalls of excessive reliance on foreign capital, the lessons of the crisis include the negative consequences of the tremendous dependence of the regions' economics on export markets. In the view of reformers, this has only led to extreme vulnerability to the vagaries of the global market and sparked a regional and international race to the bottom that has beggared significant sectors of the labor force while only really benefiting foreign investors and the small domestic manufacturing elite.

A "Keynesian" strategy of enlarging the domestic market to generate growth must include a more comprehensive program of asset and income reform, including effective land reform. There is in this, of course, the unfinished social justice agenda of the progressive movement in Asia—an agenda marginalized by the dominant ideology of growth during the "miracle." Vast numbers of people remain marginalized because of grinding poverty, particularly in the countryside. Land and asset reform would simultaneously bring them into the market, empower them economically and politically, and create the conditions for social and political stability. Achieving economic sustainability based on a dynamic domestic market can no longer be divorced from issues of equity.

A fourth theme addresses the very central issue of what would serve as the organizing principle of the economy. The fundamental mechanism of production, distribution, and exchange will have to be something more sensible and rational than the "invisible hand" of the market. Yet neither the interventionist hand of the East Asian state nor the heavy hand of the socialist state is a good substitute. Certainly, the state is essential to curb the market for the common good, but in East Asia the state and the private sector have traditionally worked in nontransparent fashion to advance the interests of the upper classes and foreign capital. While not denying that market and state can play an important and subsidiary role in the allocation of resources, the emerging view is that the fundamental economic mechanism must be democratic decision making by communities, civic organizations, and people's movements. The challenge is how to make operational such institutions of economic democracy. This search for the "third way" is associated with the increasing importance of non-governmental organizations (NGOs) in society, and the way they are perceived and perceive themselves as a "fiscalizer" of both government and the market in an evolving system of checks and balances.

There are other elements in the alternative development thinking taking place in the region, but one universal theme is "sustainable development." The centrality of ecological sustainability is also said to be one of the hard lessons of the crisis. For the model of foreign capital-fueled high-speed growth is leaving behind little that is of positive value and much that is negative. In the case of Thailand, it is hard to dispute this contention by the reformers. As any visitor to Bangkok these days would testify, twelve years of fast track capitalism are leaving behind few traces except industrial plants that will be antiquated in a few more years, hundreds of unoccupied high-rises, a horrendous traffic problem that is only slightly mitigated by the repossession of thousands of late model cars from bankrupt owners, a rapid rundown in the country's natural capital, and an environment that has been irreversibly, if not mortally, impaired, to the detriment of future generations.

In place of eight to ten percent growth rates, many environmentalists in the region are now talking of rates of three to four percent. This links the social agenda with the environmental agenda; one reason for the push for high growth rates was so that elites could corner a significant part of economic growth while still allowing some growth to trickle down to the lower classes for the sake of social peace. The alternative—redistribution of wealth—is clearly less acceptable to the ruling groups, but it is the key to a pattern of development that combines economic growth, political stability, and ecological sustainability.

These ideas and others remain to be welded together into a coherent strategy, and that strategy in turn awaits a mass movement to carry it. The importance of such a movement must not be underestimated. One clear lesson of the crisis is that the region's elite are anachronistic. They will fight their displacement, but the drastic loss of legitimacy stemming from their economic mismanagement provides a window of opportunity for progressive movements, like Thailand's Forum of the

Poor—a unique alliance of environmentalists, farmers, and workers—to translate their ideas into effective political strategies for change. Frozen during the years of the long boom, mass politics with a class edge is about to return to center stage.

NOTES

1. "IMF reports plan backfired, worsening Indonesia woes," *The New York Times*, January 14, 1998.
2. Sachs, Jeffrey. "The IMF and the Asian flu," *American Prospect*, March–April 1998.
3. Charoonsantikul, Vatchara and Thanong Khantong. "Is the IMF mistreating its Thai patient?" *The Nation* (Bangkok), November 11, 1997.
4. Testimony of US trade representative Charlene Barshefsky, before the House Ways and Means Trade Subcommittee, US Congress, February 24, 1998.
5. Wolf, Martin. "Flow and blows," *The Financial Times*, March 3, 1997.
6. Fischer, Stanley. "Capital account liberalization and the role of the IMF," paper presented at the Asia and the IMF seminar, Hong Kong, September 19, 1997.
7. "Blaming Soros is no solution to currency woes," *The Nation* [Bangkok], July 1997.
8. Japan Ministry of Finance figures.
9. Tang, Min and James Villafuerte. *Capital Flows to Asia and Pacific Developing Countries: Recent Trends and Future Prospects* (Manila: Asian Development Bank, 1995), pg. 10.
10. HG (Hoare Govett) Asia. "Philippine figures hide a thing or two," *Communique: Philippines* (Hong Kong: HG Asia, 1996).
11. Chote, Robert. "Thai crisis highlights lessons of Mexico," *The Financial Times*, September 19, 1997.
12. Baker, Gill. "Why the big mango stayed on the tree," *Euromoney*, December 3, 1996.
13. Losses on the spot market refer to actual losses incurred by the Bank of Thailand in the sale of foreign exchange to prop up the value of the baht on a daily basis. Forward swap obligations refer to agreements to honor currency exchange transactions maturing at a certain date at a certain rate of exchange. These transactions are said to be "hedged," that is, the rate agreed upon is a less favorable rate of exchange (from the perspective of the weaker currency) than the present rate to protect the holders of the weaker currency from a possibly even more unfavorable rate of exchange dictated by market developments.
14. Yi Kyong-Tae, industrial director of Korea Institute of Economics and Technology, quoted in *Kyongje Sinmun*, November 24, 1989, pg. 17.

15. Naisbitt, John and Pat Aburdene. *Megatrends 2000* (New York: William Morrow, 1990), pg. 200.

16. Suh, Ki-Sun "Failure to restructure industry at root of economic woes," *Business Korea* 43, February 1991.

17. The evolution of the US trade war against Korea is documented in Bello and Chavez-Malaluan's *APEC: Four Adjectives in Search of a Noun* (Manila: Manila People's Forum on APEC, 1996), pp. 89–93.

18. Manguno, Joseph. "Korea: VCR firms face critical test in US market," *Asian Wall Street Journal Weekly,* April 3, 1989.

19. Lee, Keun-Sik. "The Korean economic crisis: causes and solutions," *Civil Society 1*:4, 1998.

20. Testimony of US trade representative Charlene Barshefsky.

21. Ibid.

22. Ibid.

23. "Worsening financial flu lowers immunity to US business," *The New York Times,* February 1, 1998.

24. Altbach, Eric. "The Asian Monetary Fund proposal: a case study of Japanese regional leadership," *Japan Economic Institute Report* No. 477A, 1997, pp. 8–9.

25 Testimony of US trade representative Charlene Barshefsky.

26. Ibid.

27. "The battle for Kim's economic soul," *Business Week,* January 16, 1998.

28. Neiss, Herbert. "Discipline must be maintained despite breathing space: Supachai," *Bangkok Post,* February 14, 1998.

29. Chang, Ha-Joon. "Korea: the misunderstood crisis," paper presented at the Conference on the Asian Crisis, University of Oslo, January 23–24, 1998.

30. "Monetary net needs rethink, says Japanese finance envoy," *The Financial Times,* March 3 ,1998.

31. "Time for less hectic growth," *Business Times,* August 20, 1997.

8

NOTES ON THE ASCENDANCY AND
REGULATION OF SPECULATIVE CAPITAL

with Kamal Malhotra, Nicola Bullard and Marco Mezzera

From *Global Finance: New Thinking on Regulating Speculative Capital Markets* (London, UK: Zed Books and Focus on the Global South, 2000)

Since the outbreak of the Asian financial crisis in July 1997, people have been divided over the question of what was the fundamental cause of the debacle. To the powerful US Treasury undersecretary Larry Summers, it was the witches brew known as "crony capitalism" that was "at the heart of the crisis."[1] Many of the policies that have been formulated to contain the crisis, in particular those of the International Monetary Fund (IMF), have stemmed from this line of thinking. As a result, the programs for the troubled economies contain not only short-term monetary and fiscal measures, but also stricter criteria for non-performing loans, more transparency in terms of ownership and accounting, tighter bankruptcy laws, prudential regulation, and the opening up of the financial sector to foreign investment.

Stanley Fischer, the American deputy director of the IMF, sums up the orthodoxy in this fashion: "Making sure that the financial sector pursues sound lending policies, making sure that banks have strong and adequate capital and that lending is based on economic criteria and not political or other criteria—this is the key to resolving the crisis in Asian markets."[2]

But another perspective, expressed very early on in the crisis, saw the focus on cleaning up domestic financial systems as flawed, stemming from a misdiagnosis of the problem.[3] One should be looking instead at the supply side of things, at the massive flow of foreign funds

into these economies in the form of bank credit, speculative investment, and currency speculation. The very same Stanley Fischer, in a
statement at the World Bank-IMF annual meeting in Hong Kong in
September 1997, appeared to put as much emphasis on the volatility of
external capital as on the poor state of local financial regulation.
"[M]arkets are not always right. Sometimes inflows are excessive, and
sometimes they may be sustained too long. Markets tend to act fast,
sometimes excessively."4 Another orthodox source, *The Economist*, had
an equally surprising comment on the causes of the crisis:

> The problem is that all financial markets, from currencies to shares,
> are subject to waves of excessive optimism followed by excessive pes-
> simism. In theory, speculation should be stabilizing: to make
> money, investors need to buy when the price is low and sell when it
> is high. However, in a bubble it is profitable to buy even when the
> price of an asset is high, as long as it is expected to rise further—
> until the bubble bursts. An investor will lose money if he does not
> go with the crowd.5

From this perspective, "the economic pain being imposed [by global
capital markets] on the ex-tigers is out of all proportion to the policy
errors of their governments."6

With the crisis moving from East Asia to Russia and Brazil, the
casino capitalism thesis became increasingly convincing. Even US
Treasury secretary Robert Rubin had to admit that part of the problem
stemmed from volatile capital movements that were "exacerbated by
modern technology, which increases the size and speed of the mistakes
people can make."7 At the IMF, Fischer was becoming even more critical of capital flows, saying that "international capital flows are not
only extremely volatile but also contagious, exhibiting the classic signs
of financial panics."8 Thus, while international capital mobility "is
potentially beneficial for the world economy, including the emerging
market and developing countries," this potential "can only be realized
if the frequency and scale of capital account crises can be reduced."9 By
early 1998, although the official posture at the US Federal Reserve, the

Treasury and the Fund continued to be one of heaping the blame on Asian crony capitalism, the highest officials in these agencies could no longer avoid responding to demands for reforming the "global financial architecture," if only to preemptively kill expectations of substantive change.[10]

FINANCE CAPITAL UNBOUND

For students of the global capitalist system, there is a world of difference between the international economy of the 1960s–1970s and that of the 1990s. This largely lies in the way that global finance "drives" the world economy today. Whether it was called the social democratic economy, the Keynesian economy, or state-assisted capitalism, the following features marked most key economies in both the North and the South during the "Bretton Woods Era," which extended from 1945 to around the mid-1970s. A state-managed *modus vivendi* between labor and capital limited capital flows, managed trade, dependence of corporations on retained earnings for investment, strong regulation of banks and the financial sector, fine-tuning of the economy through the use of monetary and fiscal mechanisms, and fixed exchange rates. From today's perspective, the US economy under Republican president Richard Nixon seems highly regulated.

In the financial sector, as a World Bank study noted, "as recently as the early 1970s, few countries, whether industrial or developing, were without restrictions on capital movements."[11] Capital controls were maintained in Europe well into the 1970s, with the IMF's articles of agreement (article VI, section 3) allowing members "to exercise such controls as are necessary to regulate international capital movements."[12]

Several factors, however, led to the liberalization of financial flows. The first of these were the massive surplus dollars that found their way abroad in international transactions made by the US as it financed the war in Vietnam. These dollars formed the basis of the eurodollar or eurocurrency market centered in London which the big commercial banks and other financial institutions tapped to expand their international and domestic activities—an option that freed them from their dependence on domestic retail banking.[13]

Second, eurocurrency liquidity was massively increased by the recycling of OPEC money following the oil price rises of the 1970s. Up to 1981, OPEC piled up a total of $475 billion investable surplus, and $400 billion of this was placed in the industrial countries.[14] This was an enormous supply of funds seeking profitable investment, and pressure for greater global financial liberalization came from the big commercial banks, which sought to recycle a lot of these funds via cross-border lending. Much of this lending went into the Third World because of the relatively unattractive opportunities in the industrial North during that decade. This preference for offshore lending also contributed to greater domestic deregulation as governments "started to make tax and other concessions to entice [capital] back onshore."[15]

A third key factor was the rise to hegemony of the free market, neoliberal ideology, which gathered steam with increasing difficulties, including "stagflation," encountered by the Keynesian state. Liberalization of trade and the capital account were the twin drives of neoliberalism's international program. Capital account liberalization received a great boost on Margaret Thatcher's assumption of power with her removal of foreign exchange controls in Britain. With London and Wall Street leading the way, the trinity of deregulation, globalization, and technological revolution combined to transform banking and finance.[16]

"Global bang" is what *The Financial Times* called the avalanche sweeping away geographic, institutional, and regulatory boundaries within the financial services industry. The technology of financial services has undergone an electronic revolution, and governments for reasons of necessity have scrapped, rewritten, or ignored the rules that have controlled and compartmentalized the industry since the Great Depression of the 1930s. In most countries, banks, savings associations, insurance companies, and investment houses can now do what used to be each other's business. The lines of demarcation that distinguished the international eurocurrency markets from national domestic financial markets have also become blurred or are disappearing altogether. Liberalization and globalization proceeded exponentially "in a reflexive fashion," as Soros put it. "Most regulations are national in scope, so the globalization of markets meant less regulation and vice versa."[17]

KEY FEATURES OF FINANCE CAPITALISM

The wave of liberalization in the 1980s exhibited several very important traits. First, having become overexposed in the Third World in the 1970s and early 1980s, the commercial banks pulled back from international lending. At the same time, other major players were emerging as key conduits for cross-border flows of capital. The most important of these were investment banks like Goldman Sachs and Merrill Lynch, mutual funds, pension funds, and hedge funds.

Related to this was a second development: the role of banks and conventional lending for raising funds was eclipsed by "securitization," or the transfer of capital via the sale of stocks or bonds. While loans accounted for $59.4 billion of lending on international capital markets and securities for $36.2 billion in 1976–1980, by 1993 the reverse was true, with securities accounting for $521.7 billion and loans for $136.7 billion.[18]

Third, there was an explosion of both old and new activities and instruments such as arbitrage and derivatives. Arbitrage is taking advantage of foreign exchange or interest rate differentials to turn a profit, while trading in derivatives refers to buying and selling "all the risk of an underlying asset without trading the asset itself."[19] Derivatives are, as one description had it, "very esoteric instruments, which are difficult to understand, monitor, or control."[20] They include such instruments as futures, forward contracts, swaps, and options.

Fourth, a great many transactions, including those involving derivatives, were increasingly hard to monitor because they were made "over the counter," not via the floor of an exchange but among a few parties by telephone and computers. Monitoring was made all the more difficult by the fact that many of these transactions, such as forward contracts, were "off-balance-sheet" or exchanges that were not reflected in the assets and liabilities statement, making the actual financial condition of many institutions very hard to ascertain.

GLOBALIZATION'S VOLATILE ENGINE

The globalization of finance meant that its dynamics increasingly serve as the engine of the global capitalist system. The unbalanced relationship of the financial sector to trade was captured in the fact that by the mid-1990s, the volume of transactions per day in foreign exchange markets came to over $1.2 trillion. This is equal to the value of world trade in goods and services in an entire quarter.[21]

With respect to production, the United Nations Conference on Trade and Development's (UNCTAD) Trade and Development Report in 1991 warned of the "ascendancy of finance over industry."[22] One dimension of this was the increasing role of financial operators with access to large amounts of finance capital working with large stockholders in skewing the behavior of corporations away from long-term growth, significant research and development spending, and limited returns on shares and towards short-term profitability and rising dividends. A spectacular manifestation of this trend was the "leveraged buyout" (LBO) phenomenon. Pioneered by Michael Milken of Drexel Burnham Lambert, firms with "undervalued shares" were targeted for hostile takeovers, management was ousted, and firms were downsized and restructured for greater short-term profits and higher dividends.

While the LBO phenomenon has subsided, fund managers, especially those of increasingly assertive pension funds invested in key corporations, continue to greatly determine corporate performance. As the former chair of the US firm Contel saw it,

> In sum, we have a group of people with increasing control of the Fortune 500 who have no proven skills in management, no experience at selecting directors, no believable judgment in how much should be spent for research or marketing—in fact, no experience except that which they have accumulated controlling other people's money.[23]

Another dimension of the skewed finance-production relationship is perhaps even more worrying: the ascendancy of finance may be related to the crisis of dwindling growth or even deflation, which has increasingly overtaken the real sectors of the global economy. This crisis has its roots in over-capacity or under-consumption, which today marks global industries from automobiles to energy to capital goods.

One manifestation of this is the 40 percent excess capacity of the manufacturing sector in China. Another is the 30 percent over-capacity of the automobile industry worldwide,[24] which has been the spark behind the recent wave of mergers that saw, among other things, Chrysler hook up with Daimler Benz and Ford with Volvo. Another key measure indicating this trend is the so-called "output gap" or the difference between actual output and output at full capacity. The estimated output gap of the European Union (EU) has been running, according to an estimate in *The Economist,* at two percent of the gross domestic product (GDP) for the last few years and is expected to widen. Japan's is a record seven percent.

Diminishing, if not vanishing, returns to key industries have led to capital being shifted from the real economy to squeezing "value" out of the financial sector. The result is essentially a game of global arbitrage, where capital moves from one financial market to another seeking to turn a profit from the exploitation of the imperfections of globalized markets. This is done via arbitrage between interest-rate differentials, targeting gaps between nominal currency values and "real" currency values, or short-selling in stocks, that is, borrowing shares to artificially inflate share values then selling. Not surprisingly, volatility, being central to global finance, has become the driving force of the global capitalist system as a whole.

Since differences in exchange rates, interest rates, and stock prices are much less among the more integrated developed country markets, movements of capital from the North to the so-called "big emerging markets" of Asia, and other countries of the South, have been much more volatile. While crises are endemic to the finance-driven global capitalist system, the crises of the last few years have been concentrated in the emerging markets.

The ascendancy of finance has been coupled with its almost absolute lack of regulation by the authorities. Deregulation at the national level has not been replaced by re-regulation at the global level, so that, as Randall Kroszner has written,

International financial transactions are carried out in a realm that is close to anarchy. Numerous committees and organizations attempt to coordinate domestic regulatory policies and negotiate international standards but they have no enforcement powers. The Cayman Islands and Bermuda offer not only beautiful beaches but also harbors that are safe from most financial regulation and international agreements.[25]

One of the reasons for this lack of regulation is finance capital's accumulation of tremendous political clout. Efforts to throw even the minimum of regulation—such as the Tobin tax—has been opposed by a strong lobby in key Northern governments, especially in Washington. This lobby draws its power not only from interests but from the reigning free market ideology, which it interprets (wrongly, according to free trade proponent Jagdish Bhagwati) as applying not only to trade in goods but to capital mobility.[26]

Recently christened the "Wall Street-Treasury complex," the lobby has been personified by key people such as former US Treasury secretary Robert Rubin, who was one of the mainstays of the investment bank Goldman Sachs, and Federal Reserve Board chairman Alan Greenspan, who ran a consulting firm in Wall Street for 30 years.[27] While finance capital was liberated from the straitjacket of the Keynesian economy by the Republican administrations of Ronald Reagan and George Bush, it has been under the Democratic administration of Bill Clinton that financial interests have become paramount in the foreign economic policy of the United States. As *The New York Times* put it, "Clinton and Rubin…took the American passion for free trade and carried it further to press for freer movement of capital. Along the way they pushed harder to win opportunities for American banks, brokerages, and insurance companies."[28]

FINANCE CAPITAL AND THE SOUTH

The integration of the South into global capital markets began in the nineteenth century, but the process was slowed down considerably by the Great Depression and WW II. After the war and up until the 1970s, the main conduits of capital flowing into the South were direct foreign investment and multilateral assistance provided by the World Bank, the IMF, and the regional development banks. Integration speeded up, however, with the massive recycling of Organization of Petroleum Exporting Countries (OPEC) money to the South following the oil price hikes of the 1970s.

The changing pattern of capital flows was illustrated sharply in the case of Latin America. Official sources supplied 59.8 percent of the average annual external resource inflow in 1961–1965, then dropped to 40.4 percent in 1966–1970, 25.3 percent in 1971–1975, and to only 12.1 percent in 1976–1978. Foreign investment as a percentage of foreign capital inflow likewise dropped from 33.7 percent in the second half of the 1960s to 15.9 percent in the second half of the 1970s. On the other hand, the share of foreign bank and bond finance rose sharply from 7.2 percent in the early 1960s to 46 percent in the early 1970s, and to 64.6 percent in the late 1970s.[29]

Just as "irresponsible" Asian banks and companies are now being made the scapegoat for the East Asian crisis, so were "profligate" governments the whipping posts of the crisis that broke out in 1982, which led to Latin America losing a decade of growth. But then as now, the capital flow to the South was more supply than demand driven. The hundreds of billions of dollars deposited in international commercial bank coffers by the OPEC countries was a massive amount seeking profitable investment, and the rationale for this movement of capital was provided by Citibank chairman Walter Wriston, who formulated the famous principle of sovereign lending: "Countries don't go bankrupt."[30]

The supply-driven dynamics of commercial bank lending was underlined by author Karin Lissakers' comprehensive account of the process. Commercial bank lending to developing country governments had, for all intents and purposes, stopped during the Great Depression. But,

[a]wash in oil money, with credit demand depressed in the home market, commercial banks resumed large-scale lending to developing countries and their governments. For US banks, international borrowing and lending was transformed from a limited adjunct of domestic business to an activity that dominated the balance sheet.

While their domestic businesses languished, international activities exploded, accounting for 95 percent of the earnings growth of the nation's ten largest banks during the first half of the decade and probably more than half their total earnings in the late 1970s.[31]

While long lines of New York bank senior managers trooped to the suites of developing country finance ministers during the annual World Bank-IMF meetings in Washington, their field representatives in those countries "competed for the nod from the same cluster of state corporations and agencies."[32]

On the eve of the Mexican default in 1982, some $400 billion in OPEC money had found its way to the coffers of Northern banks. The bulk of it had been recycled to Third World and Eastern European governments, who by the alchemy of finance, collectively owed the banks some $500 billion.

The IMF and World Bank structural adjustment programs that were supposed to discipline profligate governments paradoxically made the developing countries even more open to capital inflows from the Northern financial centers that had brought about the crash in the first place. While tight fiscal and monetary policies were imposed on the state, foreign exchange controls were lifted and capital account liberalization was promoted with the objective of freeing the market from the straitjacket of state regulation. The upshot was a dramatically reduced role for the state as a mediator between the domestic private sector and foreign capital.

The continuing swift accumulation of finance capital and the limited absorptive capacity in the North continued to be a problem in the early 1980s, when US Federal Reserve chairman Paul Volcker's anti-inflationary high interest rate policy dampened economic activity, not only in the US, but in the rest of the now financially integrated Group of Seven (G-7) economies as well. The ravaged state of the real economies in the Third World was not perceived as a critical barrier to further capital flows by Northern financial interests. This emerged clearly when (after squeezing nearly $220 billion from the region in 1982–1990) suddenly and in a spectacular fashion, to use Duncan Green's characterization, international capital markets started pouring money into Latin America. After years of net outflows, net capital inflow into the region came to $7 billion in 1991, then rose to $31 billion in 1992 and $32 billion in 1993.[33]

Mexico, in particular, was a star performer, attracting $4.5 billion in foreign investment in 1990, $15 billion in 1991, $18 billion in 1992, and $32 billion in 1993. Yet, to show the lack of correlation between the state of the real economy and the attractiveness of the financial sector, GDP declined from 4.5 percent in 1990 to 3.6 percent in 1991, to 2.8 percent in 1992, to 0.4 percent in 1993.[34] When broken down into categories of foreign investment, the figures indicate the inverse relationship between the attractiveness of the financial sector and that of the real economy. As Timothy Kessler points out, "The vast majority of foreign capital was invested in Mexico for the unambiguous purpose of extracting financial rents, while a decreasing proportion went to direct investment."[35]

If Mexico and Latin America suddenly became the darlings of foreign investors in the early 1990s, it was due in no small part to the IMF and the World Bank. As noted previously, both institutions pushed capital account liberalization, and this was motivated by the desire to encourage the creation of other conduits of capital to replace what had proven to be the dangerous sovereign lending channel. The Bank, in particular, came to the conclusion that portfolio investing might be a better way of channeling capital into the developing countries. This led to the public relations transformation of Latin American countries from economies deep in debt into "big merging markets"—a phrase coined by a World Bank staffer.[36]

Beyond this, the Bank, via its private investment arm, the International Finance Corporation (IFC), set up closed-end country funds in a selected number of countries, then in 1986 put up seed money, according to Justin Fox, for the first "emerging markets" fund.[37] The Capital Group, a money management giant based in Los Angeles, ran this fund. The fund did "exceptionally well," with total returns to investors of 24 percent in 1987, 42 percent in 1988, and 94 percent in 1989. "Those numbers," according to Fox, "drew in more and more money managers, which set the stage for the mad rush of 1993…"[38]

When one realizes that in the advanced economies, "a humdrum 15 percent a year return is all one can realistically afford to achieve,"[39] the mad rush was understandable. Or as the Asian Development Bank put it, "the declining returns in the stock markets of industrial countries and the low real interest rates compelled investors to seek higher returns on their capital elsewhere."[40] In any event, 1993 saw a rush of foreign capital to the Third World whose likes had not been seen since the late 1970s (though instead of being loans to governments, the capital came in as credit to the private sector or as purchases of stocks and bonds). The dynamics of the lending bonanza of 1993–1994 were brilliantly captured by Bernice Cohen in her 1997 book *The Edge of Chaos:*

The herd instinct of the mighty US mutual fund managers came to the world's attention during the massive exodus of investment dollars that was poured into the emerging markets between 1993 and December 1994. This bubble was borne along a tidal wave of loose money, searching restlessly for a super-profitable home. A watershed was reached in September 1993 when some Morgan Stanley analysts visited China with a group of fund managers, who collectively managed $400 billion of clients' funds. After this visit, the positive views of the world-renowned Barton Biggs, chief investment strategist at Morgan Stanley and Company at that time sent Southeast Asian shares soaring. The Hong Kong Hang Seng index rose 20 percent in five weeks. When Morgan Stanley had a change of heart shortly after this rise, these same markets were sent plunging, as investors *en masse,* rushed to respond to the updated advice. Quixotically, and in market-shaking quantities, they withdrew their cash. In 1993, almost $40 billion went into stock markets outside the industrialized world. Around $106 billion of emerging market shares were held by foreigners at the end of the year. During December 1993 and January 1994, net new sales of American mutual funds investing overseas totaled $11.5 billion. The proportion of money that found its way into Latin America during the second quarter of 1994 rose to 77 percent, up from 14 percent in the first three months of the year. Seven years earlier, the figure was only $2.4 billion. In five years, from 1988 to 1993, emerging market share prices had doubled. In

1992, the average return to investors was 67 percent, compared to a pedestrian level of around 15 percent from the funds held in the shares of the major industrial countries.[41]

SPECULATIVE CRISIS: TWO CASE STUDIES

Crises are endemic to this system of global finance, and they have their root in the volatility of the movements of capital seeking to exploit evanescent differences in interest rates, currency values, and stock prices. Since the early 1970s, there have been at least eight crises triggered by speculative capital movements, and these have been largely concentrated in the emerging markets. The Southern Cone financial crisis in the late seventies; the Third World debt crisis of the early 1980s; the savings and loan debacle in the US in the late 1980s; the so-called ERM (exchange rate mechanism of the European monetary system) crisis in 1992; the Mexican crisis of 1994–1995 and its follow-on crisis in Latin America (the so-called "tequila effect"); the East Asian crisis of 1997; the Russian meltdown of 1998 and the collapse of the Brazilian real and its impact in the rest of Latin America.[42]

A close study of two cases, the Mexican and East Asian crises, would reveal some common dynamics of what UNCTAD has called the "post-Bretton Woods financial crisis."

MEXICO: A SUPPLY-DRIVEN CRISIS

There are two striking things about the Mexican example. First was the rapid and massive buildup in foreign capital inflows into the region, with the country receiving $91 billion in just four years, a figure that amounted to 20 percent of all net capital inflows to developing countries.[43] Second, this surge was mainly a supply-driven phenomenon, with little basis in the actual prospects of the real economy, which experienced a decline in the GDP growth rate during the financial boom years, a continuing high unemployment rate that stood at around 40 percent of the work force, and poverty that engulfed around half of the population—all of which were a legacy of the structural adjustment imposed on the economy after the debt debacle of the 1980s.[44] This lack of correlation between the sorry prospects for the real economy and the rosy view of investors was captured in the World Bank's observation that the "rapidity and magnitude of the resurgence of private flows [to Mexico and other highly indebted countries] in the 1990s surprised many observers," demonstrating that "the spate of commercial lending in the 1970s, however misguided, made the developing countries an object of continuing interest for international financiers."[45]

But the process was not only supply driven, since the country's technocrats formulated financial measures that would attract the money into the country, though it is hard to claim that these measures were purely domestic in inspiration. Interest rates were maintained at a much higher rate than in the Northern money centers, so that an investor borrowing in New York's money market "could capture the spread between returns of five to six percent in America and twelve to 14 percent in Mexico."[46] Informally fixing the rate of exchange between the dollar and the peso via government buying and selling in the currency market was a policy calculated to assure foreign investors that they would not be blindsided by devaluations that would reduce the value of their investments.

As Jeffrey Sachs has pointed out, the role of external actors in promoting this policy was not insignificant: financial authorities "fell under the influence of money managers who championed the cause of pegged exchange rates" by arguing that "only a stable exchange rate could underpin the confidence needed for large capital inflows."[47] Finally, there was the policy of financial and capital account liberalization, and here again, the role of external institutions was central. The structural adjustment programs imposed by the IMF and the World Bank in the 1980s targeted not only liberalization of the trade account but also of the capital account. However, it was the country's entry into the Organization for Economic Cooperation and Development (OECD) in 1993 that was decisive, for this required the full elimination of all restrictions on capital movements.[48]

These moves were especially significant since a great deal of foreign investment was channeled into the purchase of government securities.

Such sales had been restricted prior to 1990, but the IMF and OECD liberalization made them wide-open targets for foreign speculation.[49] Cetes were peso-denominated Federal Treasury certificates and Tesebonos were dollar-denominated Treasury bonds. On the eve of the financial crisis, Cetes issues totaled $7.5 billion and Tesebonos came to $17.8 billion.[50] In 1993, foreign investors possessed 60 percent of short-term Cetes, 87 percent of Tesebonos, and 57 percent of the inflation-indexed bonds or ajustabonos.[51] So popular were these government debt instruments that their purchase by foreigners grew by 756 percent between 1991 and August 1994.[52]

The inflow of such a huge mass of foreign capital into the country caused a real appreciation of the currency, resulting in Mexico's exports becoming less competitive in world markets. It also resulted in a consumption boom that drove up the country's imports, since the de-industrialization that had occurred in the country as a consequence of structural adjustment ensured that much of domestic demand for light and durable consumer goods could no longer be met by domestic industry. The upshot was a current account deficit that stood at eight to 8.5 percent of GDP by 1994, a development that began to get foreign investors worried. This underlined the paradox of the situation brought about by capital inflows. As Ariel Buira notes,

> As inflows eventually translate into a growing current account deficit, the very same investors who were eager to bring in their capital will look at the size of the deficit and become nervous. Investors may overreact to any unfavorable development by withdrawing their funds and in this way may contribute to the emergence of a payments crisis. Thus, as capital inflows—a symbol of success—give rise to a current account deficit, ironically, they become the country's weakness.[53]

Worried about an unstable macroeconomic situation that they had collectively contributed to, individual investors began pulling out in 1994. The yawning current account gap served as another source of instability as currency speculators, local investors, and foreign investors, expecting or betting on a government "correction" (that is, devaluation) that would reduce the deficit, subjected the peso to a massive assault that began in mid-November 1994 and subsided only when the peso was floated in late December and promptly lost half of its nominal value. This combined attack by speculators and panicky investors seeking to change their pesos for dollars and get the hell out before the expected devaluation was simply too strong for the government to repel. On December 21, the Central Bank spent $4.5 billion of its already depleted reserves in a futile defense of the peso.[54] A massive devaluation was inevitable, and Mexico was plunged into its second financial crisis in 13 years.

SOUTHEAST ASIA: VOLATILITY SINKS
A DEVELOPMENT MODEL

In the case of Southeast Asia, the surge in the inflow of portfolio investment and short-term private bank credit in the early 1990s followed an earlier surge of foreign direct investment beginning in the mid-1980s. This sudden inflow of investment lifted the region from the recession of the mid-1980s and from the effects of the pullback of commercial bank lending to the Third World following the debt crisis of the early 1980s. A significant portion of these inflows came from Japan and was a direct consequence of the Plaza Accord of 1985, which drastically revalued the yen relative to the dollar and other major currencies, forcing Japanese manufacturers to relocate a significant part of their labor-intensive operations out of Japan into Southeast Asia.

Between 1985 and 1990, some $15 billion worth of Japanese direct investment flowed into the region in one of the largest and swiftest movements of capital to the developing world in recent history.[55] Japanese direct investment brought with it billions of dollars more in Japanese bilateral aid and bank loans, and provoked an ancillary flow of billions of dollars in foreign direct investment from the first generation newly industrializing economies of Taiwan, Hong Kong, and South Korea.

It was this prosperity that attracted portfolio investors and banks and, with the collapse of Mexico in 1995, fund managers. After a moment of uncertainty that saw them briefly cut their exposure in

Asia, fund managers channeled the biggest chunk of their investments and loans for developing country markets to the East Asian region. The interests of speculative investors seeking better climes than the then low-yield capital markets of the North and the overly risky markets of Latin America coincided with the search of Asian technocrats for alternative sources of foreign capital to take up the slack caused by the leveling off of Japanese capital by the early 1990s.

With the advice of fund managers and the IMF, Thailand followed Mexico's example and formulated a three-pronged strategy of liberalizing the capital account and the financial sector as a whole; maintaining high domestic interest rates relative to interest rates in Northern money centers in order to suck in portfolio investment and bank capital; and fixing the local currency at a stable rate relative to the dollar in order to insure foreign investors against currency risk.

Portfolio flows to both equities and bonds rose, and so did credit from international banks to Thai financial institutions and enterprises, which sought to take advantage of the large differential between the relatively low rates at which they borrowed from Northern money-center banks and the high rates at which they would re-lend the funds to local borrowers. The dynamics of this activity were described succinctly by one investment analyst:

> Since 1987 the Thai authorities have kept their currency locked to the US dollar in a band of [baht] 25–26 while maintaining domestic rates 500–600 points higher than US rates and keeping their borders open to capital flows. Thai borrowers naturally gravitated towards US dollar borrowings and the commercial banks accommodated them, with the result that the Thai banks have a foreign liability position equivalent to 20 percent of GDP. The borrowers converted to baht with the Bank of Thailand the ultimate purchaser of their foreign currency. Fuelled by cheap easy money, the Thai economy grew rapidly, inflation rose, and the current account deficit ballooned.[56]

In the short term, the formula was wildly successful in attracting foreign capital. Net portfolio investment came to around $24 billion in the three years before the crisis broke in 1997, while at least another $50 billion entered in the form of loans to Thai banks and enterprises. These results encouraged finance ministries and central banks in Kuala Lumpur, Jakarta, and Manila to copy the Thai formula, with equally spectacular results. According to Washington's Institute of International Finance, net private capital flows to Indonesia, Malaysia, the Philippines, Thailand, and Korea shot up from $37.9 billion in 1994 to $79.2 billion in 1995 to $97.1 billion in 1996.[57]

In retrospect, Thailand illustrated the fatal flaws of a development model based on huge and rapid infusions of foreign capital. First, just as in Mexico, there was a basic contradiction between encouraging foreign capital inflows and keeping an exchange rate that would make the country's exports competitive in world markets. The former demanded a currency pegged to the dollar at a stable rate in order to draw in foreign investors. With the dollar appreciating in 1995 and 1996, so did the pegged Southeast Asian currencies and so did the international prices of Southeast Asian exports. This process cut deeply into the competitiveness of economies that had staked their growth on ever-increasing exports.

The second problem was that the bulk of the funds coming in consisted of speculative capital seeking high and quick returns. With little regulation of its movements by governments that had bought into the IMF's *laissez-faire* ideology and had little experience in handling such massive inflows, foreign capital did not gravitate to the domestic manufacturing sector or to agriculture. These were considered low yield sectors that would provide a decent rate of return only after a long gestation period of huge blocks of capital. The high yield sectors with a quick turnaround time which foreign investment and foreign credit inevitably gravitated to were the stock market, consumer financing, and, in particular, real estate development. In Bangkok, at the height of the real estate boom in the early 1990s, land values were higher than in urban California.

Not surprisingly, a glut in real estate developed quite rapidly, with Bangkok leading the way with $20 billion worth of new commercial and residential space unsold by 1996. Foreign banks had competed to push loans on to Thai banks, finance companies, and enterprises in the boom years of the early 1990s. In 1996, it began to sink in that their borrowers were loaded with non-performing loans.

At the same time, alarm bells began to be sounded by the flat export growth rates for 1996 (an astonishing zero growth in the case of both Malaysia and Thailand) and burgeoning current account deficits. Since a foreign exchange surplus gained through consistently rising exports of goods and services was the ultimate guarantee that the massive foreign debt contracted by the private sector would be repaid, this was a massive blow to investor confidence. What the investors failed to realize was that the very policy of maintaining a strong currency that was calculated to draw them in was also the cause of the export collapse. And what many also failed to realize was that the upgrading of the quality of exports, which could have counteracted the rise in export prices, had been undermined by the easy flow of foreign money into the speculative sectors of the economy. Manufacturers chose to channel their investments there to quick profits, instead of pouring them into the hard slog of research and development and upgrading the skills of the work force.[58]

By 1997, it was time to get out. Because of the liberalization of the capital account, there were no mechanisms to slow down the exit of funds. With hundreds of billions of baht chasing a limited amount of dollars, the outflow of capital could be highly destabilizing. Many big institutional players and banks began to leave, but what converted a nervous departure into a catastrophic stampede was the speculative activity of the hedge funds and other arbitrageurs who, gambling on the authorities' eventual devaluation of the overvalued baht to contain the yawning current account deficit, accelerated it by unloading huge quantities of baht in search of dollars.

Hedge funds were particularly salient in the Thai debacle. These funds are essentially investment partnerships, which are limited to the very wealthy, are oftentimes based offshore, and are little regulated. They specialize in combining short and long positions in different currencies, bonds, and stocks in order to net a profit. These funds had been attacking the Thai baht occasionally since 1995. But the most spectacular assault occurred on May 10, 1997, when in just one day, hedge funds are said to have "bet US $10 billion against the baht in a global attack."[59] Of the Bank of Thailand's $28 billion forward book at the end of July 1997, approximately $7 billion, according to an IMF report,

> ...is thought by market participants to represent transactions taken directly with hedge funds. Hedge funds may have also sold the baht forward through offshore counterparties, onshore foreign banks, and onshore domestic banks, which then off-loaded their positions to the central bank.[60]

Under such massive attacks, the Bank of Thailand went on to lose practically all of its $38.7 billion of foreign exchange reserves at the end of 1996 in mid-1997. On July 2, the decade-long peg of 25 baht to the dollar was abandoned, and the Thai currency went on to lose over 50 percent of its value in a few months.

In Jakarta and Kuala Lumpur, there occurred the same conjunction of massive capital flow, the property glut, and a rise in the current account deficit. The same nervousness existed, but it was the baht collapse that triggered the panic among foreign investors. The deadly dynamics of capital flows that had been liberated from capital and foreign exchange controls were captured by Jeffrey Winters' account of the mass panic among a set of strategic actors in the portfolio investment scene: the so-called "emerging market fund managers" (EMFMs):

> Suddenly, you receive disturbing news that Thailand is in serious trouble, and you must decide immediately what to do with your Malaysian investments. It is in this moment that the escape psychology and syndrome begins. First, you immediately wonder if the disturbing new information leaking out about Thailand applies to Malaysia as well. You think it does not, but you are not sure. Second, you must instantly begin to think strategically about how other EMFMs and independent investors are going to react, and of course they are thinking simultaneously about how you are going to react. And third, you are fully aware, as are all the other managers, that the first ones to sell as a market turns negative will be hurt the least, and the ones in the middle and at the end will lose the most

value for their portfolio—and likely to be fired from their position as an EFFM as well. In a situation of low systemic transparency, the sensible reaction will be to sell and escape. Notice that even if you use your good connections in the Malaysian government and business community to receive highly reliable information that the country is healthy and not suffering from the same problems as Thailand, you will still sell and escape. Why? Because you cannot ignore the likely behavior of all the other investors. And since they do not have access to the reliable information you have, there is a high probability that their uncertainty will lead them to choose escape. If you hesitate while they rush to sell their shares, the market will drop rapidly, and the value of your portfolio will start to evaporate before your eyes.[61]

Winters comes to a radically different conclusion from Adam Smith, who believed that the invisible hand of the market is supposed to bring about the greatest good for the greatest number. Winters says, "The chain reaction was set in motion by currency traders and managers of large pools of portfolio capital who operate under intense competitive pressures that cause them to behave in a manner that is objectively irrational and destructive for the whole system, especially for the countries involved, but subjectively both rational and necessary for any hope of individual survival."[62]

THE THREE SCHOOLS OF GLOBAL FINANCIAL REFORM

In response to the thousand and one situations like the above, there are now a thousand and one proposals for world financial reform, ranging from suggestions for preemptive crisis mechanisms, to recommendations for the reform of the IMF, to several proposals for establishment of a "world financial authority" (WFA).[63] Rather than take them up one by one in technical fashion, let us go into the heart of the matter, that is the interests and ideologies served by the different proposals, and group the most important recommendations into three approaches. Of course, some proposals resist being easily pigeonholed and some are eclectic in terms of their technical measures. However, it is the thrust of a set of recommendations that we are seeking to capture.

We will call the first "it's the wiring, not the architecture" approach. The second might be termed the "back to Bretton Woods" system. And we might christen the third approach as "it's the development model, stupid!" strategy.

"IT'S THE WIRING, NOT THE ARCHITECTURE"[64]

One might say that this is basically the US position, although it is shared to some degree by many of the G-7 members, with probably the notable exception of Japan. The basic idea is that the current architecture is sound, there is no need for major reforms, and it's simply a question of improving the wiring of the system.

This school assigns primacy to "reforming" the financial sectors of the crisis economies through increased transparency, tougher bankruptcy laws to eliminate moral hazard, prudential regulation using the "core principles" drafted by the Basle committee on banking supervision, and greater inflow of foreign capital not only to re-capitalize shattered banks, but also to "stabilize" the local financial system by making foreign interests integral to it.

When it comes to the supply-side actors in the North, this perspective would leave them to voluntarily comply with the Basle principles. Although, government intervention might be needed periodically to catch free falling casino players whose collapse might bring down the whole global financial structure (as was the case in late 1998 when a consortium of New York banks—lead by the Reserve Bank of New York—organized a rescue of the hedge fund Long-Term Capital Management after the latter was unraveled by Russia's financial crisis).[65] The farthest the G-7 has gone in terms of dealing with the controversial hedge fund question was to issue a declaration in October 1998 commenting on the need to examine "the implications arising from the operations of leveraged international financial organizations including hedge funds and offshore institutions" and "to encourage offshore centers to comply with internationally agreed standards."[66]

Finally, when it comes to the existing multilateral structure, this view supports the expansion of the powers of the IMF, proposing not only greater funding but also new credit lines, such as the "contingency credit line" that would be made available to countries that are about to be subjected to speculative attack. Access to these funds would be dependent on a country's track record in terms of observing good macroeconomic fundamentals, as traditionally stipulated by the Fund.

While much has been made of the conflict between the US and the other members of the G-7 countries in the world press, the articulated differences appear to be marginal. France and Germany (at least before the resignation of Germany's Oskar Lafontaine as finance minister), with some support from Japan, have proposed the establishment of "target zones" that would reduce the fluctuations among the yen, dollar, and eurodollar. There are virtually no suggestions from the European Union on controlling capital flows on the supply side.

Japan has made additional proposals on the IMF, but these are variants of the position of either the US government or some US think tanks. The proposals include more IMF monitoring of hedge funds, getting the IMF to push private creditors and investors to participate in rescue programs (or "bailing them in" instead of bailing them out) and providing a "certified" line of credit to countries that follow good economic policies which are under speculative attack, something similar to Clinton's contingency credit line.[67]

In sum, it seems fairly obvious that, especially given its priority of transforming developing country financial systems using Northern standards, one of the key objectives of this approach is to extend the reach and deepen the global hold of Northern finance capital in developing economies under the guise of reforming the global financial architecture and stabilizing global financial flows.

THE "BACK TO THE BRETTON WOODS" SYSTEM

The second school of thought would put tougher controls at the global level, in the form of the Tobin tax or variants of it.[68] The Tobin tax is a transactions tax on capital inflows and outflows at all key points of the world economy that would "throw sand in the wheels" of global capital movements. Controls at the international level may be supplemented by national level controls on capital inflows or outflows. A model of such a measure was the Chilean inflow measure that required portfolio investors to deposit up to 30 percent in an interest-free account at the Central Bank for a year, which was said to be successful in discouraging massive capital portfolio inflows.[69] Among some writers, there is an ill-concealed admiration for Prime Minister Mohamad Mahathir's tough set of outflow measures, which included the fixing of the exchange rate, the withdrawal of the local currency from international circulation, and a one-year lock-in period for capital already in the country.[70]

In addition to controls at the national and international level, proponents of this view also see regional controls as desirable and feasible. The Asian Monetary Fund (AMF) is regarded as an attractive, workable proposal that must be revived. The AMF was proposed by Japan at the height of the Asian financial crisis to serve as a pool of the foreign exchange reserves of the reserve-rich Asian countries that would repel speculative attacks on Asian currencies. Not surprisingly, Washington vetoed it.

The thrust of these international, national, and regional controls is partly to prevent destabilizing waves of capital entry and exit and to move investment inflow from short-term portfolio investment and short-term loans to long-term direct investment and long-term loans. For some, capital controls are not simply stabilizing measures but are strategic tools, like tariffs and quotas, that may justifiably be employed to influence a country's degree and mode of integration into the global economy. In other words, capital and trade controls are legitimate instruments for the pursuit of trade and industrial policies aimed at national industrial development.

When it comes to the World Bank, the IMF, and the WTO, the thrust of this school is to reform these institutions along the lines of greater accountability, less doctrinal push for free trade and capital account liberalization, and greater voting power for developing countries. Like the G-7, advocates of this approach view the IMF as a mechanism to infuse greater liquidity into economies in crisis, but unlike the G-7, they would have the Fund do this without the tight conditions that now accompany its emergency lending. Some people in this school recommend the establishment of a WFA. The WFA's main task, in one formulation, would be to develop and impose regulations on global capital flows and serve as "a forum within which the rules of international financial cooperation are developed and implemented...by effective coordination of the activities of national monetary authorities."[71]

In other words, the Fund, World Bank, and WTO continue to be seen as central institutions of a world regulatory regime, but they must be made to move away from imposing one common model of trade and investment on all countries. Instead, they must provide a framework for more discriminate global integration, that would allow greater trade and investment flows but also allow some space for national differences in the organization of global capitalism.

As formulated by Dani Rodrik, the current chief economic adviser to the G24 (a grouping of developing countries), the ideal multilateral system appears to be a throwback to the original Bretton Woods system devised by Keynes that reigned from 1945 to the mid-1970s, where "rules left enough space for national development efforts to proceed along successful but divergent paths."[72] In other words, a "regime of peaceful coexistence among national capitalisms."[73]

Not surprisingly, this "global Keynesian" perspective has resonated well with economists and technocrats from developing countries, the devastated Asian economies, and the UN system, which is well known as a refuge of Keynesians who fled the neoliberal revolution at the World Bank and academic institutions.

"IT'S THE DEVELOPMENT MODEL, STUPID!"

Let us proceed to the third perspective, the one that we call "it's the development model, stupid!" school. Those that we classify as belonging to this school regard the IMF and WTO, in particular, as Jurassic institutions that would be impossible to reform both owing to both their deep neoliberal indoctrination and the hegemonic influence within them of the United States. Indeed, the world would be better off without them since they serve as the lynchpin of a hegemonic international system that systematically marginalizes the South.

The same skepticism marks their view on the possibility of imposing global capital controls or prudential regulations on hedge funds and other big casino players, again because of the strength of neoliberal ideology and financial interests.

National capital controls are seen as much more promising, and the experiences of China and India in avoiding the financial crisis, of Chile in regulating capital flows, and Malaysia in stabilizing its economy, have convinced proponents of this view that this is the way to go. Like the global Keynesians, this school would also see regional arrangements such as the AMF as feasible and workable.

Where the proponents of this view differ from the global Keynesians is the fact that their advocacy of capital controls is accompanied by a more fundamental and thorough critique of the process of globalization that goes beyond its blasting away legitimate differences among national capitalisms. Buffering an economy from the volatility of speculative capital is an important rationale for capital controls. However, even more critical is the consideration that such measures would be a *sine qua non* for a fundamental reorientation of an economy toward a more inner-directed pattern of growth that would entail, in many ways, a process of de-globalization.

The main problem from this viewpoint lies not in the volatility of speculative capital, but in the way that the export sector and foreign capital have been institutionalized as the engines of these economies. The problem is the indiscriminate integration of the developing economies into the global economy and the over-reliance on foreign investment, whether direct or portfolio investment, for development. It is not surprising that Mexico and Thailand were the epicenters of the recent financial earthquakes, for these two economies are among those handful of developing economies that have gone furthest in terms of trade, investment, and financial integration into the global capitalist economies.

While the current crisis is wreaking havoc on peoples' lives throughout the South, it also gives us the best opportunity in years to fundamentally revise our model and strategy of development.

In this process it would be ideal to have a more congenial international financial architecture, but since that is not going to happen in the short and medium term, there are two overriding tasks in the area of international finance. The first is preventing the current efforts to reform the global financial architecture from becoming a project to more thoroughly servile, penetrate, and integrate the financial sectors of developing country economies into the global financial system controlled by the North. The second is to devise a set of effective capital controls, trade controls, and regional cooperative arrangements that would "hold the ring" to allow a process of internal economic transformation to take place with minimal disruption from external forces.

DE-GLOBALIZING THE DOMESTIC ECONOMY

What are some of the priorities of what me might call a model of limited de-globalization of the domestic economy? What makes it different not only from the neoliberal economy but also from the national capitalisms whose "peaceful coexistence" would be ensured by Dani Rodrik's proposed Keynesian international architecture?

First, allow us to focus our observations on the East Asian region. There are some ideas or proposals being actively discussed throughout East Asia that are increasingly attractive to the peoples in crisis. An inventory would place the following at the top:

1. While foreign investment of the right kind is important, growth must be financed principally from domestic savings and investment through progressive taxation systems. Even in the depths of crisis, conspicuous consumption continues to mark the behavior of Asia's elites, who also send much of their wealth abroad to safe havens in Geneva, Tokyo, or New York. Regressive taxation systems are the norm in the region, where income taxpayers are but a handful and indirect taxes that cut into the resources of lower income groups are the principal source of government expenditures.

2. While export markets are important, they are too volatile to serve as reliable engines of growth. Development must be reoriented around

the domestic market as the principal locomotive of growth. Tremendous dependence of the region's economies on export markets led to extreme vulnerability to the vagaries of the global market and sparked the current self-defeating race to "export one's way out of the crisis" through competitive devaluation of the currency. This move is but the latest and most desperate manifestation of the panacea of export-oriented development.

3. Making the domestic market the engine of development, to use a distinctly unfashionable but unavoidable term, brings up the linkage between sustained growth and equity. For a "Keynesian" strategy of enlarging the local market to stimulate growth means increasing effective demand or bringing more consumers (hopefully discriminating ones) into the market via a comprehensive program of asset and income distribution, including land reform and an unfinished social justice agenda. Land and asset reform would simultaneously empower the poor economically and politically, bring them into the market, and create the conditions for social and political stability.

4. Regionalism can become an invaluable adjunct to such a process of domestic market-driven growth. This can happen only if both processes are guided not by a perspective of neoliberal integration but by a vision of regional import substitution and protected market integration, giving the region's producers the first opportunity to serve the region's consumers.

5. While there are other elements in alternative development thinking taking place in the region, one universal theme is "sustainable development." The model of foreign capital fuelled high-speed growth for foreign markets has left behind little else but environmental destruction. Many environmentalists are now linking the social agenda with the environmental agenda, and talking of three to four percent instead of eight to ten percent growth.

These and similar ideas are already being discussed actively throughout the region. What is still unclear is how these elements will hang together. The new political economy may be embedded in religious or secular discourse and language. Its ultimate coherence is likely to rest less on considerations of narrow efficiency than on a stated ethical priority given to community solidarity and security. Moreover, the new economic order is unlikely to be imposed from above in Keynesian technocratic style, but is likely to be forged in social and political struggles.

This fire down below, to borrow a line from William Golding, is one that is likely to upset the best laid plans of the tiny global elite, which is currently seeking to salvage an increasingly unstable free market order by extending its reach even farther under the banner of "global financial reform."

If this project of limited de-globalization of national financial structures is one that we find desirable, then the relevant task for those of us who are grappling with issues of international financial reform is twofold. The first is a defensive one of repelling attempts to more fully subjugate and integrate domestic financial systems into the global system under the guise of improving the global financial architecture. The other is devising a set of capital and border trade controls at both the regional and national level that would allow this process of domestic economic reorientation to take place with minimum disruption from the forces that will be always waiting in the wings to suffocate such a project.

NOTES

1. Summers, Larry. "The global economic situation and what it means for the United States," remarks to the National Governors' Association, Milwaukee, Wisconsin, August 4, 1998.

2. Quoted in Richard Mann, *Economic Crisis in Indonesia* (Toronto, Canada: Gateway Books, 1998) pg. 42.

3. This view is most notably represented by Jeffrey Sachs. See, among others, his "The IMF and the Asian flu," in *American Prospect*, March/April. 1998.

4. Fischer, Stanley. "Capital account liberalization and the role of the IMF," paper presented at the Asia and the IMF Seminar, Hong Kong, September 19, 1997.

5. "Mahathir, Soros, and the currency markets," *The Economist*, September 27, 1997, pg. 93.

6. Ibid.

7. Ignatius, David. "Policing hedge funds: who's in charge here?," *International Herald Tribune,* February 22, 1999.

8. Fischer, Stanley "On the need for an international lender of last resort," paper prepared for joint luncheon of the American Economic Association and the American Finance Association, New York, January 3, 1999.

9. Ibid.

10. See, for instance, Robert Rubin's "Strengthening the architecture of the international financial system," speech at the Brookings Institution, Washington, DC, April 14, 1998.

11. World Bank. *Managing Capital Flows in East Asia* (Washington DC: World Bank, 1996), pg. 3.

12. Henwood, Doug. *Wall Street* (New York: Verso, 1997), pg. 107–108.

13. Lissakers, Karin. *Bankers, Borrowers, and the Establishment* (New York: Basic Books, 1991), pg. 254.

14. Ibid., pg. 36.

15. Soros, George. *The Crisis of Global Capitalism* (New York: Public Affairs, 1999), pg. 108.

16. *Bankers, Borrowers, and the Establishment,* pg. 8.

17. *The Crisis of Global Capitalism,* pg. 119.

18. Hirst, Paul and Grahame Thompson. *Globalization in Question* (Cambridge: Polity Press, 1996), pg. 40.

19. Cooper, Ian. "The world of futures, forwards, and swaps," in *Mastering Finance* (London, UK: Financial Times, 1998), pg. 335.

20. *Globalization in Question,* pg. 41.

21. Buira, Ariel. "Key financial issues in capital flows to emerging markets," in *International Finance in a Year of Crisis* (Tokyo: United Nations University, 1998) pg. 68.

22. Quoted in UNCTAD *Trade and Development Report 1998* (Geneva: UNCTAD, 1998).

23. Quoted in *Wall Street,* pg. 292.

24. "Bavarians at the gates," *The Economist,* February 13, 1999, pg. 22.

25. Kroszner, Randall. "The market as international regulator," in *Mastering Finance,* pg. 399.

26. Bhagwati, Jagdish. "The capital myth: the difference between trade in widgets and dollars," in *Foreign Affairs,* Vol. 77, No. 3, May 1998, pg. 7–12.

27. "The three marketeers," *Time,* February 15, 1999, pg. 39; see also *Foreign Affairs,* pg. 12.

28. "How US wooed Asia to let cash flow in," *The New York Times,* February 16, 1999.

29. *Bankers, Borrowers, and the Establishment,* pg. 59.

30. Quoted in *Wall Street*, pg. 224.

31. *Bankers, Borrowers, and the Establishment*, pg. 45.

32. *Bankers, Borrowers, and the Establishment*, pg. 104

33. Green, Duncan. *Silent Revolution: The Rise of Market Economics in Latin America* (London, UK: Cassel, 1995), pg. 70.

34. Cameron, Maxwell and Vinoc Aggarwal. "Mexican meltdown: markets and post-NAFTA financial turmoil," *Third World Quarterly,* Vol. 17, No. 5, 1996, pg. 977.

35. Kessler, Timothy. "Political capital: Mexican policy under Salinas," *World Politics,* Vol. 51, October 1998, pg. 57.

36. Fox, Justin. "The great emerging markets rip-off," *Fortune,* May 11, 1998 (downloaded from Internet).

37. Ibid.

38. Ibid.

39. Cohen, Bernice. *The Edge of Chaos* (New York: John Wiley, 1997), pg. 348.

40. Tang, Min and James Villafuerte. *Capital Flows to Asian and Pacific Developing Countries: Recent Trends and Future Prospects* (Manila: Asian Development Bank, 1995), pg. 10.

41. *The Edge of Chaos*, pp. 347–348.

42. This list is based on a number of sources, including UNCTAD's *Trade and Development Report 1998*; and Barry Eichengreen and Donald Mathieson, *Hedge Funds and Financial Market Dynamics*, Occasional Paper 166 (Washington, DC: International Monetary Fund, 1998).

43. Fanelli, Jose Maria. "Financial liberalization and capital account regime: notes on the experience of developing countries," in *International Monetary and Financial Issues for the 1990s* (Geneva: UNCTAD, 1998), pg. 8.

44. For an account of this, see Walden Bello, *Dark Victory: The United States and Global Poverty* (Oakland, CA: Food First Books, 1994), pg. 37–42.

45. World Bank. *Managing Capital Flows in East Asia* (Washington, DC: World Bank, 1996), pg. 5–6.

46. Greider, William. *One World, Ready or Not: The Manic Logic of Global Capitalism* (New York: Simon and Schuster, 1997), pg. 260.

47. Sachs, Jeffrey. "Personal view," *The Financial Times,* July 30, 1997.

48. "Key financial issues in capital flows," pg. 7.

49. Ibid.

50. Cameron and Aggarwal, pg. 977.

51. Kessler, pg. 57.

52. Ibid.

53. Ibid., pg. 62.

54. "Mexican meltdown: markets," pp. 977–978.

55. Japan ministry of finance figures.

56. *Communique: Philippines,* op. cit.

57. Institute of International Finance. *Capital Flows to Emerging Market Economies* (Washington, DC: Institute of International Finance, 1998), pg. 3.

58. See HG (Hoare Govett) Asia, "Thailand—worth a nibble perhaps but not a bite," in *Communique: Thailand* (Hong Kong: HG Asia, 1996) (downloaded from the Internet).

59. Khantong, Thanong. "The currency war is the information war," talk presented at the seminar-workshop on "Improving the flow of information in a time of crisis: The challenge to the Southeast Asian media," Subic, Philippines, October 29–31, 1998.

60. *Hedge Funds and Financial Market Dynamics,* pg. 17

61. Winters, Jeffrey. "The financial crisis in Southeast Asia," paper delivered at the conference on the Asian crisis, Murdoch University, Fremantle, Western Australia, August 1998.

62. Ibid.

63. A list of the more significant proposals are found in Barry Eichengreen's *Toward a New Financial Architecture* (Washington, DC: Institute for International Economics, 1999).

64. Among the documents that broadly share this view are the following: Group of 22, "Reports on the international financial architecture, working groups on transparency and accountability, strengthening the financial system, and international financial crises," October 1998; Morris Goldstein, *The Asian Financial Crises: Causes, Cures, and Systemic Implications* (Washington, DC: Institute for International Economics, 1998); Robert Rubin, "Strengthening the architecture of the international financial system," speech at the Brookings Institution, Washington, DC, April 14, 1998 (downloaded from Internet); Stanley Fischer, "On the need for an international lender of last resort," paper prepared for the joint luncheon of the American Economic Association and the American Finance Association, New York, January 3, 1999; and Barry Eichengreen's *Toward a New International Financial Architecture.*

65. The Federal Reserve chairman explicitly opposed regulation of hedge funds during hearings at the US Congress in October 1998, when the LTCM fiasco occurred. See "Policing hedge funds."

66. Quoted in United Nations, *Toward a New Financial Architecture: A Report of the Task Force of the Executive Committee on Economic and Social Affairs of the United Nations* (New York: UNCTAD, 1999).

67. As summarized by David de Rosa, "Miyazawa's big ideas on how to run the IMF," Bloomberg News column, reproduced in *Manila Times,* March 3, 1999, pg.13.

68. Among the documents that might be said to broadly belong to this viewpoint are the

following: *Towards a New Financial Architecture: A Report of the Task Force,* pp. 83–110; UNCTAD, "The management and prevention of financial crises," *Trade and Development Report 1998*; Dani Rodrik, "The global fix," in *New Republic,* November 2, 1998 (downloaded from Internet); John Eatwell and Lance Taylor, "International capital markets and the future of economic policy," *CEPA Working Paper No. 9,* Center for Economic Policy Analysis (CEPA), (New York: New School for Social Research, 1998); Roy Culpeper, "New economic architecture: getting the right specs," remarks at the conference, "The Asian Crisis and Beyond: Prospects for the 21st Century," Carleton University, Ottawa, January 29, 1999.

69. The reserve requirement was brought down to zero percent in October 1998, allegedly because speculative inflows had dropped considerably owing to the crisis.

70. See, for instance, "New economic architecture: getting the right specs."

71. "International capital markets and the future of economic policy," pg. 14.

72. Ibid.

73. Ibid.

9

BREAKING WITH THE FAITH

Focus on Trade, September 1998
This column originally appeared in the September 17, 1998 issue
of the *Far Eastern Economic Review.*

Malaysia's moves in 1998 to impose fairly stringent capital controls elicited the predictable cries of dismay from the usual suspects: the International Monetary Fund (IMF), US Treasury undersecretary Larry Summers, *The Wall Street Journal,* and Philippine Central Bank governor Gabriel Singson.

But what was interesting about the global response this time was the way it revealed widening cracks in the establishment consensus. Prime Minister Mahathir's move had the effect of separating diehard ideologues from pragmatists, whose growing ranks include Massachusetts Institute of Technology hotshot Paul Krugman and *The Financial Times*, which editorialized that "under certain conditions, [capital controls] could prove the way forward for the Asian crisis economies."

There was a widespread sense that however one judged them, Malaysia's moves were understandable. While editorializing against the measures, even *The Economist* conceded that "the economic pain being imposed [by global capital markets] on the ex-tigers is out of all proportion to the policy errors of their governments."

Also palpable was a sense that neoclassical orthodox approaches had been given a chance to stabilize the situation for over a year and found severely wanting. The so-called "Washington consensus" solution had been to give even more freedom for speculative capital to enter and exit economies, coupled with a dose of the IMF deflationary medicine of high interest rates and tight fiscal policies. The cure proved worse than the disease, turning a serious crisis into a descent into hell.

So discredited is the Fund that it has been unable to resist its ward, the Thai government's recent adoption of a Keynesian recovery program consisting of government deficit spending to the tune of three percent of gross domestic product (GDP), bringing down interest rates, and *de facto* nationalization of the banking system—all no-no's in the IMF orthodoxy.

But the key to the increased willingness of the pragmatists to break with the neoclassical church is fear—fear that the madcap activities of unregulated global speculative capital are now threatening to sink not just Asia but the rest of the world as well, including the US economy. There is nothing like terror to make the blind see, even if like another prominent defector, Columbia University professor Jagdish Bhagwati, one who has made a living preaching the virtues of the market.

Welcome to reality, we say to them, but we must also point out that they are merely catching up with the rest of the world, with the truths that ordinary people experience when they are run over by this process called "globalization."

The Asian financial crisis has simply served to underline the fact that the theory about the net benefits of globalization via the engine of free markets in goods and capital has had little or no empirical backing. As with all ideologies, it was faith parading as science.

History, cunning as usual, appeared to derive a perverse pleasure from contradicting at almost every turn the Benthamite pronouncements of people like Larry Summers that free markets and the free flow of capital would result in the greatest good for the greatest number. The dissonant data ranged from the common net welfare losses for the US, Canada, and Mexico in NAFTA, to the pervasive stagnation imposed by free market structural adjustment programs imposed by the IMF on most Latin American and Third World economies, to the environmental devastation wrought by unregulated local and transnational firms in East Asia, to the spawning of Mafia capitalism by the radical free market reforms in Russia and Eastern Europe, courtesy of the Fund, Washington, and, yes, Harvard's Jeffrey Sachs, yet another luminary that has recently seen the light.

The question is no longer whether the world will move away from the rule of the invisible hand but how fast it will do so. While the former ideologues are paralyzed with doubts about the old and fears of the new, others have already moved or are moving toward a new order. Some of the contours of that order may not be discernible at this point, and the process leading to it might be fraught with unpredictability and uncertainty. What are some of these trends that are likely to gain momentum over the next few months and years?

One should expect tremendous pressures from civil society, governments, and even sections of international capital itself (George Soros) are likely to lead either to more Malaysia-type unilateral measures. Or the pressures could lead to the eventual adoption of the Tobin tax or one of its variants, which would be levied on capital movements across borders in an effort to throw sand in the wheels of speculative investors and currency speculators.

In Asia, the financial crisis is likely to lead away from the failed Philippine strategy of distancing oneself from the rest of the pack in an invidious effort to draw investors fleeing one's neighbors, to regional coordination in the setting of exchange rates, trade policy, and debt repayment policy. Now burdened with having to pay off the debts of their irresponsible private sectors with public funds—debts which come to 80 percent of total external debt in the case of Thailand and Indonesia—many Asian governments are beginning to realize that unless they get together to formulate a common stand to write off part of the debt, write down much of the rest, and reschedule the remainder, they risk repeating the experience of the Third World in the 1980s, when the creditors, united behind the IMF, took advantage of debtor disunity to pick the debtors off one by one and imposed draconian debt repayment policies on all of them.

Within societies in the region, we are likely to see a move away from dependence of foreign investment and export orientation and toward economic strategies based principally on domestic financial resources and the local market. This means greater pressures for asset and income redistribution to create the dynamic domestic market that can serve, in place of the roller coaster that is the global economy, as the engine of growth.

The Economist bewailed the emergence of the "sentiment that it is not merely the international capital market but the basic principles of capitalist economics that need to be questioned." But institutions like The Economist have only themselves to blame for the rising revolt against the irrationalities of free market capitalism. The revolt has been provoked to a large extent by hubris, by the arrogance of its partisans and their lack of connection to real people with real troubles and real fears.

10

POWER, TIMIDITY, AND IRRESPONSIBILITY IN GLOBAL FINANCE

Focus on Trade, August 1999

Asia's stock markets are soaring again. To some, this portends real economic recovery. To others, it is an ominous sign that the "electronic herd, " as *The New York Times* columnist Thomas Friedman calls it, is back in its Asian grazing grounds, happily snapping up promising stocks and high interest bonds now, but ready to move out tomorrow, perhaps in another furious stampede triggered by God knows what.

The herd began moving in Manila the day after President Joseph Estrada's State of the Nation address on July 26, 1999. The foreign funds that had been pouring into the country over the last few months reversed course, forcing the Philippine stock market index to drop 113 points to a three-month low. Some asked, was the Philippine chief executive looking more besotted than usual?

One would have expected that two years after the outbreak of the Asian financial crisis, there would be institutions in place to prevent a repeat of the massive and rapid exit of $100 billion that triggered the collapse of the region's economies. After all, even the US Treasury chief, Larry Summers, who held the view that "crony capitalism" was the main reason for Asia's troubles, later admitted that "a strong case can be made that excessive capital inflows may have contributed importantly to the recent problems in emerging markets."

A quick look around shows that Chile has lifted its controls on foreign capital inflows, while Malaysia has withdrawn the controversial restrictions on foreign capital outflows that it imposed last year. These moves certainly do not stem from the fact that mechanisms on the national level have been rendered superfluous by the erection of serious capital controls at the international level. For all its brave talk about creating a "new global financial architecture," the Group of Seven (G-7) at its summit in Cologne in mid-June, 1999 gave birth to a mouse—a program that put the emphasis on voluntary disclosure of financial information by hedge funds and other financial mechanisms, and voluntary risk management by the private sector.

Cologne also produced another ironic result—a stronger International Monetary Fund (IMF) to exact economic reforms from emerging economies, but without the organizational reforms in terms of greater transparency, greater accountability, greater consultation, and a more self critical approach to its programs that the Fund's many critics have long demanded.

The Cologne program bears the stamp of Summers and his predecessor, Robert Rubin. Alternative proposals within the G-7, such as "target zones" to reduce fluctuations among the euro, dollar, and yen, practically vanished when the controversial Keynesian Oskar Lafontaine resigned as Germany's finance minister in March 1999. The remaining potential counterweight to US domination of the financial agenda is Japan, but it has refused to play the role of Washington's fiscalizer.

Japan proved to be a very big disappointment to many people and governments in Asia when it backed down and submitted to pressure from the US. Since then, Japan has largely danced to the American tune. No concrete proposals have come from Tokyo on global capital controls, though minister of finance Kiichi Miyazawa and other finance ministry officials have rhetorically targeted hedge funds on occasion. Tokyo has also made critical noises about the IMF, but has not followed these up with actual proposals for institutional reform.

The vaunted Miyazawa Plan has, in fact, elicited US approval, largely because it provides aid that is conditioned on advancing Washington's agenda for Asia—that is, rapid liberalization, deregulation, and privatization. In the Philippines, Miyazawa money has been made contingent on Manila's implementing two things: the privatization of the National Power Corporation, which has been a longstanding demand of the World Bank and the IMF, and the opening up of retail trade to foreign participation, of which the American Chamber of Commerce has been a prime advocate.

It is not that Japan lacks the clout to stand up for an alternative paradigm of global financial stabilization. When it comes to issues that bear on its domestic economy, Japan has not hesitated to take decisions that Washington protested but could do nothing about, like Tokyo's refusal to open up its forestry and fisheries sector and its move to restrict the short-selling of stocks. What Japan has studiously avoided is filling a leadership role for Asian interests.

Unchallenged by Europe and Japan, the US has dominated the global financial agenda. This agenda has been fairly consistent. The reason that Washington has felt uncomfortable about attaching urgency to controlling global flows of speculative capital is that, as a *The New York Times* series in 1999 revealed, US Treasury's push for rapid, indiscriminate liberalization of the capital accounts of the Asian economies was a central cause of the crisis. As the crisis developed, Washington's agenda, as former governor of the Federal Reserve Lawrence Lindsey has pointed out, has been to take advantage of the situation to push its longstanding bilateral agenda of opening up trade and financial markets.

Now it is true that Larry Summers talks about "properly paced liberalization," but it remains the case that capital account and trade liberalization in the emerging markets continues to be the central thrust of its program for global financial reform. Washington's main antidote against global financial instability is not international measures to throw sand in the wheels of speculative capital but more liberalization at the national level. Summers revealed the logic behind this approach in his comments on Argentina in a speech: "Today, fully 50 percent of the banking sector, 70 percent of private banks, in Argentina are foreign-controlled, up from 30 percent in 1994. The result is a deeper, more efficient market, and external investors with a greater stake in staying put." To put it in the curious algebra of the US Treasury, financial liberalization equals financial stability equals the global interest.

In sum, five years after the Mexican financial crisis and two years after outbreak of the Asian financial crisis, Washington's single-minded pursuit of its financial agenda and European and Japanese timidity have ensured that the world remains without a serious system of defense against the periodic stampedes of the electronic herd. This is irresponsibility of the highest order.

PART THREE

The US Globalization, Geopolitics, and Unilateralism

11

THE US ECONOMIC EXPANSION:
BOON OR BANE FOR ASIA?

On February 26, 2000, the Japanese newspaper *Asahi Shimbun*
carried an interview with the author on the US economic
boom's impact on Asia. This article is an expansion
of the points made by the author in that interview,
in a question-and-answer format.

What is behind the US economic expansion?

As the US enters its ninth year of expansion, there is a lot of triumphalist talk among many American economists and officials about
a "new economy" where the business cycle has been abolished. There
are reasons to be skeptical about this claim, and one major reason is
that the expansion has been driven largely by hyperactivity on Wall
Street. And this hyperactivity is largely due to frenzied trading in
Internet shares, which has led to a tremendous overvaluation of
Internet stocks. The economic boom is now being fuelled largely by
the financial, speculative sector, and within that sector by just one
group of firms.

There is, in fact, a contrast between the performance of "new" technology and "high" technology firms, with a widening gap between the

skyrocketing share values in the former and the increasingly stagnant situation in the latter. Now, there is simply no way one can defy the laws of gravity, even in economics. What goes up must come down, or, if you prefer, the higher they go, the harder they fall. Once Wall Street values go too far ahead of the real economy, then the stage is set for the fall. There is evidence, according to Larry Elliot, the economic analyst of *The Guardian,* that the American boom is being sustained by artificial means, with the rise in the Nasdaq index being underpinned by Internet firms borrowing money to buy each other's shares—the equivalent, he notes, "of taking in each other's washing."

You mean the expansion is less a sign of health than a symptom of disease?

If you put it that way, yes, in the same way Wall Street's exuberance in the 1920s was the advanced state of a disease. If the financial sector is marked by frenzied activity, that's because the real sectors of the economy, especially manufacturing, are under-performing in terms of profitability. Despite brutal downsizing *cum* wage repression of the US labor force, it was only in 1995–1996, according to Robert Brenner, that the rate of profit in the manufacturing sector exceeded its 1973 level. Yet this figure was still 30 percent below its level in the late 1960s!

A sure sign of stagnation of the traditional sectors of the US economy is the recent wave of mergers and acquisitions (M & A's). Giant mergers have shaken up the automobile industry, the energy industry, and all other key sectors of the economy. Monopolistic moves such as Microsoft's predatory moves, and America Online's takeover of Netscape and swallowing of the already bloated Time Warner Corporation, indicate that the Internet economy is moving quickly from its competitive, "creative destruction" phase, where medium-sized agile upstarts can thrive, to its monopolistic phase, where conglomerate T-Rexes are completely in control. Mergers are to a great extent a response to crises of profitability, with monopolistic control being instituted in an industry to prevent the market from further eroding profit margins.

So what is the fundamental problem?

There is tremendous over-capacity all the way around, and this is what led to the Daimler Benz-Chrysler union, the Renault takeover of Nissan, the Mobil-Exxon merger, the BP-Amoco-Arco deal, and increased monopolistic coordination in the global airline industry— pace the "Star Alliance." US computer industry's capacity is rising at 40 percent annually, far above expected increases in demand. In the auto industry, worldwide supply is expected to reach 80 million in the period 1998–2002, while demand will rise to only 75 percent of the total. This estimate in the increase in demand is likely to be an overestimate since it was made before the Asian financial crisis! Overproduction is responsible for the buyout by foreign interests of our key cement producers in the Philippines. The drive is to consolidate the cement industry globally so as to control global output. As economist Gary Shilling puts it, there are "excessive supplies of almost everything."

Over-capacity is another way of saying there is overproduction or that there is under-consumption. Overproduction is relative to demand. Demand is dependent on consumer purchasing power, which is another way of saying that it is greatly a function of the distribution of income. There is a lot of news about how tight the labor market is and unemployment is down to record levels in the US, but it was only around 1997 that real wages registered a slight rise after years of decline or stagnation. As Robert Brenner has pointed out, the massive restructuring to regain profitability that marked the 16-year period 1979–1995, forced the bottom 60 percent of the US labor force to work for progressive lower wages, so that by the end of the period, their wages were ten percent lower than they were in the beginning. The restructuring that is supposed to have made the US economy super-competitive has also burdened it with the worst distribution of income among the major advanced countries. And income distribution in the US is now worse than it was ten years ago.

But we need to look at this at a global scale, since US corporations operate with the global market in mind and they are at the cutting edge of the techno-economic revolution known as globalization. The gap between capitalism's tremendous productive capacity and the limited purchasing power of most of the participants in this system is even more stark at a global level. The number of people living below poverty level globally increased from 1.1 billion in 1985 to 1.2 billion in 1998, and is expected to reach 1.3 billion this year. If you exclude China, where statistics are not reliable, the proportion of the population of the developing world classified as poor had remained broadly constant since 1987, according to the United Nations University-World Institute for Development Economics Research survey. Based on the proportion of the population living in great poverty, there are now 48 countries classified as least developed countries (LDC)—three more than a decade ago.

If you move from poverty to income inequality as an indicator of purchasing power, the picture is even clearer. A study of 124 countries representing 94 percent of the world's population shows that the top 20 percent of the world's population raised its share of total global income from 69 to 83 percent. In 1998, the income of the world's top three billionaires—Bill Gates with $90 billion, Warren Buffet with $36 billion, and Microsoft co-founder Paul Allen with $30 billion—was greater than the combined income of the 600 million that live in the 48 least developed countries. Tremendous wealth among the few at the top, tremendous poverty among the billions at the bottom, and a middle stratum whose incomes are eroding or are stagnant—this is the contradiction that is responsible for the overproduction, over-capacity, and under-consumption that is wracking the US-dominated global economy.

But doesn't Asia benefit from the US economic expansion?

This is the conventional explanation. That is, US demand for Asian goods is said to be the factor pulling East Asia out of the financial crisis. The reality is more complex. If you look at the Asian financial crisis from a historical perspective, it becomes clear that its origins were linked to the dynamics of the US economy. During the 1980s and 1990s, a large part of the prosperity of top 20–25 percent of the US population was funneled into mutual funds, hedge funds, and other investment juggernauts. Owing to the low levels of profitability, American industry was overall not an attractive investment area, and the Internet revolution had not yet occurred. Looking for higher rates of return with a quick turnaround time, these funds, in the form of bank credit or portfolio investment, went first to Mexico and Latin America, then when the Mexican economy collapsed in 1995, to East Asia. US funds fuelled the stock market and property boom from Seoul to Bangkok to Jakarta.

Over-investment was the natural result. When the current account, exchange rate, and other macroeconomic indicators started going hay-wire, US funds led the pullout from the region, a panic that was deliberately exacerbated by George Soros and other hedge fund artists in order to profit from exchange rate differentials triggered by rush for dollars as investors dumped the peso, rupiah, baht, and ringgit. The herd behavior of US fund managers was—and there is now a consensus on this—central to the Asian financial debacle.

The Asian financial crisis, in fact, stems from natural dynamics of a global economy which is driven mainly by the dynamics of the US financial sector. Diminishing returns to key industries have led to capital increasingly being shifted from the real economy to squeezing "value" out of already created value in the financial sector. The result is essentially a game of global arbitrage led by US financial operators: capital moves from one financial market to another seeking to turn a profit from the exploitation of imperfections of globalized markets via arbitrage between interest rate differentials. Gaps are targeted between nominal currency values and "real" currency values, or short-selling in stocks, that is, borrowing shares to artificially inflate share values then selling. Not surprisingly, volatility, being central to global finance, has become the driving force of the global capitalist system as a whole.

Since differences in exchange rates, interest rates, and stock prices are much less among the more integrated developed country markets, movements of capital from the North to the so-called "big emerging markets" of the South and Asia have been much more volatile. While crises are endemic to the finance-driven global capitalist system, the crises of the last few years have been concentrated in emerging markets like those in Asia.

But hasn't the US economy been largely a positive factor in the Asian recovery?

I have doubts about the strength of this so-called recovery. But assuming there is a recovery, I would say that the US has played a positive role only in the very restricted sense of being a market for Asian exports. But if you survey the situation more broadly, it is hard to contend that the US role is, on balance, positive. Using the International Monetary Fund (IMF) as a battering ram for trade and investment liberalization in the industrial and financial sectors, US transnational industrial and financial interests have been leading the takeover of Asian industrial and financial assets from Seoul to Bangkok.

Sure, foreign investment has been pouring into some economies, but the greater part of this is not "greenfield" investments that add new capacity to an economy like Japanese investment, but American and to some extent European investment that is directed at acquiring radically depreciated Asian assets. Much of the industrial and financial structure built up over a generation by Asian entrepreneurs is passing to Northern transnational corporations (TNCs) at fire sale prices. In many cases, the objective of the buyer is not to add to productive capacity but simply to strip firms of their assets or reduce their capacity in line with a global production plan to up profitability by bringing down supply to meet stagnant global demand.

It's time to stop mouthing the stock phrases about how the US economy is a rising tide that is raising Asian boats. The reality of the US-Asia economic relationship during the crisis has been best expressed by none other than Jeff Garten, President Bill Clinton's former undersecretary of commerce, who said: "Most of these countries are going to go through a deep and dark tunnel.... But on the other end there is going to be a significantly different Asia in which American firms have achieved much greater market penetration, much greater access."

I 2

THE "SHRIMP-TURTLE CONTROVERSY" AND
THE RISE OF GREEN UNILATERALISM

Focus on Trade, July 1997

Thailand and other Asian countries were central actors in a dispute that shaped up as a landmark battle in the volatile area of trade and the environment: the so-called shrimp-turtle controversy.

The World Trade Organization (WTO) in 1997 agreed to a request to convoke a dispute settlement panel to rule on the compatibility with WTO trading rules of a US ban on the import of shrimps caught in the wild with nets that are not equipped with "turtle excluding" devices. The move, which also covered products from shrimps caught in such a fashion, was meant to protect an internationally recognized endangered species, the sea turtle, and was based on the US endangered species act that required US shrimp fishermen to equip their nets with such devices.

ROUND TWO

The shrimp-turtle issue is widely regarded as round two of the trade-environment dispute, the first round being the tuna-dolphin case that played out in the early 1990s, which was instigated by the US ban, based on that country's marine mammal protection act, on the import of tuna caught with purse seine nets, which were supposed to entrap large numbers of dolphins. A General Agreement on Tariffs and Trade (GATT) dispute resolution panel ruled against Washington, but the decision was never adopted by GATT (the precursor of the WTO), leaving the US technically unconstrained by the ruling.

The shrimp-turtle move affects shrimp exports to the US from an estimated 40 countries, the most significantly affected being Asian countries. While Thailand, Malaysia, and Pakistan were the formal complainants, some 25 other countries reserved their rights as "interested parties."

Although Washington lifted the ban on shrimps from Thailand because it equipped its fishing fleet with turtle-excluding devices, Bangkok joined Malaysia and Pakistan as a complainant "out of principle." Most likely it was from self-interest, since the Thais wanted to preempt the application of the US law to shrimp that are raised in aquaculture farms, which account for 75 percent of Thailand's shrimp production. This is not an unreasonable fear since environmentalists also contend that shrimp farms are extremely damaging to mangrove ecosystems.

The Philippines came on as an interested party for the same reason. As one Geneva-based Filipino diplomat told us, "We're not affected now. But if the Americans extend the ban to aquaculture products, then we will really be hit hard since most of our shrimp exports are produced in aquaculture farms."

NORTHERN VERSUS SOUTHERN ENVIRONMENTALISTS

Like Asian trade officials, though for more complex reasons, Asian environmentalists have also been drawn to the dispute, which has split the global environmental community.

Many Northern environmental organizations either explicitly or tacitly support the US move. For them, the issue is not unilateralism, but the principle that trade restrictions can be placed on imports not only on the basis of the nature of a product per se but also on the basis of how it is produced—that is, governments ought to be able to restrict imports if they are produced with unsustainable production processes and methods (PPMs). Their big worry is that the WTO dispute resolution panel will rule as the old GATT did in the tuna-dolphin case: that the US move is unjustified because it is not based on product characteristics but on PPMs, which is said to go against current international trading rules.

Asian and other Southern environmentalists are caught in a

dilemma. On the one hand, they are concerned that the sea turtle is in danger of extinction and deep-sea shrimp fishing without turtle-excluding devices contributes seriously to their decimation. On the other hand, they are bothered greatly by the US move to apply its domestic law to activities that take place outside US jurisdiction. The US ban, to them, seeks to achieve a fine objective with the wrong approach—unilateralism.

For them, restrictions ought to be applied not only to shrimps harvested in the wild, but also to those that are produced in environmentally damaging aquaculture farms, but this should be done according to clear cut rules of multilateral environmental agreements (MEAs) that are negotiated among countries. Moreover, trade restrictions should be parallel with positive moves to compensate the affected producers and provide for technology transfer that would assist them to shift to more sustainable PPMs.

The tendency among Southern environmental non-governmental organizations (NGOs) to line up against the US ban is more pronounced than during the tuna-dolphin conflict. Perhaps one reason is that the shrimp ban took place in the context of a US trade strategy that has become more unilateralist and more aggressive towards the South, especially toward Asian countries. This trend has accelerated despite the founding of the WTO, which was supposed to strengthen and expand a "rule-based" multilateral system of international trade governance.

THE MARCH OF UNILATERALISM

Since the WTO came into being in January 1995, the US has threatened to impose special 301 sanctions on China twice for alleged intellectual property rights (IPR) violations, and threatened super 301 sanctions against Japan and Korea for restrictions on the imports of automobiles and automobile parts. Washington has also placed practically all of its other partners in the Asia Pacific Economic Cooperation (APEC) on the "priority watch list" or "watch list" of IPR "violators," a move which makes them candidates for sanctions under the special 301 section of the US Trade Act.

Moreover, the US has used the WTO in fairly blatant ways to push its trade interests. For instance, it set itself up as the key arbiter of whether or not China is able to join the WTO. And Washington shamelessly used key WTO gatherings, such as the first ministerial meeting in Singapore in December 1996, to push through initiatives which principally benefit US corporations, like the landmark Information Technology Agreement (ITA) to reduce tariffs on IT products to zero by the year 2000 among the countries that control over 95 percent of IT trade.

Despite pleas from the WTO secretariat and other WTO members that it disavow Super 301 and Special 301, Washington affirmed their use and explicitly confirmed unilateralism as the main prong of US trade strategy. Shortly after the ratification of the GATT-WTO Agreement, then US trade representative Mickey Kantor told the US Senate Finance Committee in April 1995: "We will continue to use every tool at our disposal—301, Super 301, Title VII, general system of preferences (GSP), the Telecommunications Trade Act, or WTO accession—to open markets around the globe." This stance was reaffirmed by Kantor's successor, Charlene Barshefsky, who told a US House of Representatives committee on March 18, 1997:

> There are some who believe that simply opening markets on a global scale is the be-all and end-all, no matter how it is done or no matter who benefits. I subscribe to a different view. It is imperative that we open markets in a manner consistent with the rules of the WTO, but we must make sure Americans benefit directly from the process, and to do that Americans must drive the rules of the new global landscape and the opening of markets.

It is in this context of accelerating American unilateralism that many Southern environmental NGOs are staking their positions in shrimp-turtle debate. For them, it is unfortunate that it is on the shrimp-turtle issue that the lines are being drawn in the struggle against unilateralism, but to make an exception of this case would tantamount to conciliating unilateralism, with all the potential perils this would pose to the wellbeing of Southern societies and environments.

THE THREAT OF GREEN PROTECTIONISM

Many Southern environmentalists seek a harmonious relationship between environment and development, and they see a serious threat to sustainable development emanating not only from unilateral trade measures like the shrimp ban but also from a whole set of environmental measures that, while taken for a good cause, become *de facto* a form of "green protectionism."

In the North, environmental product standards are going up, with detrimental effects on Third World producers. A study on the impact of such measures on Indian industry done by the UN Conference on Trade and Development (UNCTAD) found that in the leather tanning and textile industries, which are key export earners, the costs of eco-friendly dyes required to meet international standards in the leather tanning industry are approximately three times higher than the costs of the dyes currently being used.

Also likely to have a negative impact are new packaging laws which are meant to reduce the quantity of packaging and promote its recovery and recycling. Simply getting information on and understanding packaging requirements in different Northern markets is difficult and costly. Meeting new rules on recycled or recyclable content for packaging often adds significant costs, especially when Southern producers have to import green packaging material to be able to export their goods to certain markets.

The reduction of market access posed by packaging requirements is already very real for some countries. In Thailand, exports of frozen fishery products have been negatively affected, and other sectors dependent on significant quantities of plastic and non-biodegradable matter for packaging are likely to suffer as well.

"Eco-labeling" or specifying the environmentally relevant contents or production method of a product is also perceived as posing new threats to market access, although most significant eco-labeling programs in the North are still voluntary. This is especially the case in premium markets made up of environmentally discriminating middle class consumers. To compete, Southern producers find that they must invest significant amounts in raw materials, new chemicals, new production processes, and testing and certification. For Indian leather products, the cost of testing and certification alone is said to be as high as 33 percent of the current export price.

Thailand and other Asian countries need to take the trend toward higher environmental product standards and eco-labeling in the North seriously since according to UNCTAD, 60 percent of Asia's manufacturing exports originate in areas where the new environmental requirements are emerging.

Governments have to pay special attention to the needs of their small and medium entrepreneurs. As a study of the secretariat of the WTO's Committee on Trade and the Environment has underlined, while the big Southern manufacturers might have the capital and technological capabilities to adjust to higher environmental standards, the small and medium enterprises who have neither the cash nor technological sophistication will face difficulties.

NEEDED: AN ENVIRONMENTAL MARSHALL PLAN

Most Southern environmentalists do not oppose the raising of environmental product standards in the North. In fact, they support it. But in order to prevent this trend from turning into a situation of *de facto* green protectionism that discriminates against developing country producers, they underline the importance of positive measures, such as technology transfer aimed at upgrading and rendering more environmentally friendly the production processes in the South.

This would include loosening patent and copyright rules so as to facilitate the adoption, at low or reasonable prices, of Northern-owned eco-friendly technology—something that Northern corporations may loathe to do. But support may not only be in the form of the transfer of packaged technology but also in that of financial assistance for indigenous research and development activities in the South meant to come up with appropriate technology that meet higher environmental standards.

Such measures would not only benefit developing country

exporters, say Southern environmentalists, but they would have the effect of generalizing higher environmental industrial standards and production processes in Southern countries, where old industrial technologies have contributed significantly to making cities like Bangkok, Sao Paulo, and Manila ecological disaster areas.

The problem is: Are the Northern countries willing to come up with the resources to facilitate this environmental upgrading of industry in the South? Many Southern environmentalists are skeptical, pointing to the fact that at the UN Conference on Environment and Development in Rio in 1992, the North promised billions of dollars in environmental aid for the South, part of which was meant to support the spread of environmentally friendly industrial technology. Very little, if any, of this aid has materialized, they emphasize.

Very little, too, has come as a result of the Montreal Protocol of 1987, which promised assistance to Southern countries to ease their transition from the production and use of chlorofluorocarbons (CFCs) and other ozone-depleting substances.

It is clear, however, that without the equivalent of an environmental "Marshall Plan," higher environmental product standards in the North will, in fact, result in *de facto* green protectionism, with tremendous negative consequences for the well being of developing countries that are increasingly following export-oriented development strategies.

13

DANGEROUS LIAISONS: PROGRESSIVES, THE RIGHT, AND THE ANTI-CHINA TRADE CAMPAIGN

with Anuradha Mittal
Food First Backgrounder, Spring 2000

Like the United States, China is a country that is full of contradictions. It is certainly not a country that can be summed as "a rogue nation that decorates itself with human rights abuses as if they were medals of honor."[1] This characterization by AFL-CIO chief John Sweeney joins environmentalist Lester Brown's Cassandra-like warnings against the Chinese people in hitting a new low in the rhetoric of the "Yellow Peril" tradition in American populist politics. Brown accuses the Chinese of being the biggest threat to the world's food supply because they are climbing up the food chain by becoming meat-eaters.[2]

These claims are disconcerting. At other times, we may choose not to engage their proponents. But not today, when they are being bandied about with studied irresponsibility to reshape the future of relations between the world's most populous nation and the world's most powerful one.

A coalition of forces seeks to deprive China of permanent normal trading relations (PNTR) as a means of obstructing that country's entry into the World Trade Organization (WTO). We do not approve of the free trade paradigm that underpins PNTR status. We do not support the WTO; we believe, in fact, that it would be a mistake for China to join it. But the real issue in the China debate is neither the desirability nor undesirability of free trade and the WTO. The real issue is whether the United States has the right to serve as the gatekeeper to international organizations such as the WTO. More broadly, it is whether the United States government can arrogate to itself the right to determine who is and who is not a legitimate member of the international community. The issue is unilateralism—the destabilizing approach that is Washington's oldest foreign policy tradition.

The unilateralist anti-China trade campaign enmeshes many progressive groups in the US in an unholy alliance with the right wing that, among other things, advances the Pentagon's grand strategy to contain China. It splits a progressive movement that was in the process of coming together in its most solid alliance in years. It is, to borrow Omar Bradley's characterization of the Korean War, "the wrong war at the wrong place at the wrong time."

THE REAL CHINA

To justify US unilateralism vis-a-vis China, opponents of PNTR for China have constructed an image of China that could easily have come from the pen of Joseph McCarthy.

But what really is China? Since the anti-China lobby has done such a good job telling us about China's bad side, it might be appropriate to begin by showing the other side.

Many in the developing world admire China for being one of the world's most dynamic economies, growing between seven and ten percent a year over the past decade. Its ability to push a majority of the population living in abject poverty during its Civil War period in the late 1940s into decent living conditions in five decades is no mean achievement. That economic dynamism cannot be separated from an event that most countries in the global South missed out on: a social revolution in the late 1940s and early 1950s that eliminated the worst inequalities in the distribution of land and income and prepared the country for economic takeoff when market reforms were introduced into the agricultural sector in the late 1970s.

China likewise underlines a reality that many in the North, who are used to living under powerful states that push the rest of the world around, fail to appreciate: this is the critical contribution of a liberation movement that decisively wrests control of the national economy from foreign interests. China is a strong state, born in revolution and steeled in several decades of wars hot and cold. Its history of state formation accounts for the difference between China and other countries of the South, like Thailand, Brazil, Nigeria, and South Korea. In this it is similar to that other country forged in revolution: Vietnam.

Foreign investors can force many other governments to dilute their investment rules to accommodate them. That is something they find difficult to do in China and Vietnam, which are prepared to impose a thousand and one restrictions to make sure that foreign capital indeed contributes to development, from creating jobs to actually transferring technology.

The Pentagon can get its way in the Philippines, Korea, and even Japan. These are, in many ways, vassal states. In contrast, it is very careful when it comes to dealing with China and Vietnam, both of whom taught the US that bullying doesn't pay during the Korean War and the Vietnam War.

Respect is what China and Vietnam gets from transnational corporations and Northern governments. Respect is what most of our governnments in the global South don't have. When it comes to pursuing national interests, what separates China and Vietnam from most of our countries are successful revolutionary nationalist movements that got institutionalized into no-nonsense states.

WHAT IS THE "CASE" AGAINST CHINA?

Of course, China has problems when it comes to issues such as its development model, the environment, workers rights, human rights, and democracy. But here the record is much more complex than the picture painted by many US non-governmental organizations (NGOs).

The model of development of outward-oriented growth built on exports to developed country markets of labor-intensive products is no scheme to destroy organized labor thought up by an evil regime.

This is the model that has been prescribed for over two decades by the World Bank and other Western-dominated development institutions for the developing countries. When China joined the World

Bank in the early 1980s, this was the path to development recommended by the officials and experts of that institution.

Through the strategic manipulation of aid, loans, and the granting of the stamp of approval for entry into world capital markets, the Bank pushed export- oriented, labor-intensive manufacturing and discouraged countries from following domestic market-oriented growth based on rising wages and incomes. In this connection, it must be pointed out that World Bank policies vis-a-vis China and the Third World were simply extensions of policies in the US, Britain, and other countries in the North, where the Keynesian or social democratic path based on rising wages and incomes was foreclosed by the anti-labor, pro-capital, neoliberal policies of Ronald Reagan, Margaret Thatcher, and their ideological allies.

Development in China has been accompanied by much environmental destruction and must be criticized. But what many American environmentalists forget is that the model of double-digit gross domestic product (GDP) growth based on ever rising consumption levels is one that China and other developing countries have been encouraged to copy from the North, where it continues to be the dominant paradigm.

Again, the World Bank and the whole Western neoclassical economics establishment, which has equated development with unchecked levels of consumption, must bear the central part of the blame.

Northern environmentalists love to portray China as representing the biggest future threat to the global environment. They assume that China will simply emulate the unrestrained consumer-is-king model of the US and the rest of the developed countries, which is questionable. What they forget to mention is that per capita consumption in China is currently just one tenth of that of developed countries.[3] What they decline to point out is that the US, with five percent of the world's population, is currently the biggest single source of global climate change, accounting as it does for a quarter of global greenhouse gas emissions. As the Center for Science and Environment (CSE) points out, the carbon emission level of one US citizen in 1996 was equal to that of 19 Indians, 30 Pakistanis, 17 Maldivians, 49 Sri Lankans, 107 Bangladeshis, 134 Bhutanese, or 269 Nepalis.[4]

When it comes to food consumption, Lester Brown's picture of Chinese meat-eaters and milk drinkers being the main destabilizers of the world food supply is simply ethnocentric, racist, and wrong. According to UN Food and Agriculture Organization (FAO) data, China's consumption of meat in 1992–1994 was 33 kg per capita, and this is expected to rise to 60 kg per capita in 2020. In contrast, the comparable figures for developed countries were 76 kg per capita in 1992–1994, rising to 83 kg in 2020. When it comes to milk, China's consumption was 7 kg per capita in 1992–1994, and expected to rise marginally to 12 kg in 2020. Per capita consumption in developed countries, in contrast, was 195 kg and predicted to decline only marginally to 189 kg in 2020.[5]

The message of these two sets of figures is unambiguous: the unchecked consumption levels in the United States and other Northern countries continue to be the main destabilizer of the global environment.

China is no workers' paradise. It has serious problems when it comes to workers' rights, just like the United States. Yet it is simplistic to say that workers have no rights, or that the government has, in the manner of a pimp, delivered its workers to the transnational corporations to exploit.

There *are* unions. China has the biggest trade union confederation in the world, with 100 million members. Granted, this confederation is closely linked with the government. But this is also the case in Malaysia, Singapore, Mexico, South Africa, Zimbabwe, and many other countries. The Chinese trade unions are not independent from government, but they ensure that workers' demands and concerns are not ignored by government. If the Chinese government were anti-worker, as AFL-CIO propaganda would have it, it would have dramatically reduced its state enterprise sector by now. It is precisely concern about the future of the hundreds of millions of workers in state enterprises that has made the government resist the prescription of Chinese neoliberal economists, foreign investors, and the US government to radically dismantle the state enterprise sector—all of whom are guided by narrow efficiency/profitability criteria, and are completely insensitive to the employment issue.

The fact is, workers in China probably have greater protection and access to government than industrial workers who live in right-to-work states (where non-union shops are encouraged by law) in the United States. As Daniel Lazare, author of the acclaimed *The Frozen Republic,* reminds us:

> The state of American labor law is scandalous. Entire categories of workers, often the most vulnerable and exploited, are effectively barred from unionizing: domestic servants, agricultural workers, temporaries, free lancers, and so on. Six decades after the great organizing battles of the 1930s, thousands of workers are still fired each year for union organizing, supposedly a federally-protected activity. According one survey, 71 percent of employees believe that workers who dare to organize will lose their jobs. Massive corporate law-breaking like this is the chief reason why unions lose more than 50 percent of government-supervised recognition elections in the private sector. Yet federal authorities rarely give corporate law-breakers more than a slap on the wrist.[6]

If there is a government that must be targeted by the AFL-CIO for being anti-labor, it must be its own government, which, in collusion with business, has stripped labor of so much of its protections and rights that the proportion of US workers unionized is down to only 13 percent!

There is much to be done in terms of bringing genuine democracy and greater respect for human rights in China. And certainly, actions like the Tienanmen massacre and the repression of political dissidents must be condemned, in much the same way that Amnesty International criticizes the United States for relying on mass incarceration as a principal mechanism of social control.[7] But this is not a repressive regime devoid of legitimacy like the Burmese military junta.

As in the United States and other countries, there is a lot of grumbling about government, but this cannot be said to indicate lack of legitimacy on the part of the government. Foreign observers in China note that while there might be disaffection, there is widespread acceptance of the legitimacy of the government. Monopolization of decision making by the Communist Party at the regional and national level is still the case, but relatively free elections now take place in many of the country's rural villages in an effort to de-concentrate power from Beijing to better deal with rural economic problems, according to Thomas Friedman, who is otherwise quite critical of the Chinese leadership.[8]

Lack of Western-style multiparty systems and periodic competitive elections does not mean that the government is not responsive to people. The Communist Party is all too aware of the fact that its continuing in power is dependent on popular legitimacy. This legitimacy in turn depends on convincing the masses that it is doing an adequate job its fulfilling four goals: safeguarding national sovereignty, avoiding political instability, raising people's standard of living, and maintaining the rough tradition of equality inherited from the period of classical socialism. The drama of recent Chinese history has been the way the party has tried to stay in power by balancing these four concerns of the population. This balancing act has been achieved, as Asia expert Chalmers Johnson writes, via an "ideological shift from an all-embracing communism to an all-embracing nationalism [that has] helped to hold Chinese society together, giving it a certain intellectual and emotional energy and stability under the intense pressures of economic transformation."[9]

Demand for democratic participation is certainly growing and should be strongly supported by people outside China. But it is wishful thinking to claim that US-style forms of democratic expression have become the overwhelming demand of the population.

While one might not agree with all the points he makes, a more accurate portrayal of the state of things than that given by the anti-China lobby is provided by the English political philosopher John Gray in his classic work *False Dawn:*

China's current regime is undoubtedly transitional, but rather than moving towards "democratic capitalism," it is evolving from the western, Soviet institutions of the past into a modern state more suited to Chinese traditions, needs, and circumstances. Liberal democracy is not on the historical agenda for China. It is very doubtful if the one-child policy, which even at present is often circumvented, could survive a transition to liberal democracy. Yet, as China's present rulers rightly believe, an effective population policy is indispensable if scarcity of resources is not to lead to ecological catastrophe and political crisis. Popular memories of the collapse of the state and national defenselessness between the world wars are such that any experiment with political liberalization which appears to carry the risk of near-anarchy of post-Soviet Russia will be regarded with suspicion or horror by the majority of Chinese. Few view the break-up of the state other than a supreme evil. The present regime has a potent source of popular legitimacy in the fact that so far it has staved off that disaster.[10]

THE ANTI-CHINA TRADE CAMPAIGN: WRONG AND DANGEROUS

It is against this complex backdrop of a country struggling for development under a political system, which, while not democratic along Western lines, is nevertheless legitimate and which realizes that its continuing legitimacy depends on its ability to deliver economic growth that one must view the recent debate in the US over the granting of permanent normal trade relations to China.

PNTR is the standard tariff treatment that the United States gives nearly all its trading partners, with the exception of China, Afghanistan, Serbia-Montenegro, Cuba, Laos, North Korea, and Vietnam. Granting of PNTR is seen as a key step in China's full accession to the World Trade Organization since the 1994 Marrakech Agreement establishing the WTO requires members to extend PNTR to other WTO members mutually and without conditions. This is the reason that the fight over PNTR is so significant—it is linked to China's full accession to the WTO.

Organized labor is at the center of a motley coalition that is against granting PNTR to China. This coalition includes right wing groups and personalities like Pat Buchanan, the old anti-China lobby linked to the anti-communist Kuomintang Party in Taiwan, protectionist US business groups, and some environmentalist, human rights, and citizens' rights groups. The intention of this right-left coalition is to use trade sanctions to influence China's economic and political behavior, as well as to make it difficult for China to enter the WTO.

There are fundamental problems with the position of this alliance, many of whose members are, without doubt, acting out of the best intentions.

First of all, the anti-China trade campaign is essentially another manifestation of American unilateralism. Like many in the anti-China trade coalition, we do not uphold the free trade paradigm that underpins the PNTR. Like many of them, we do not think that China will benefit from WTO membership. But what is at issue here is not the desirability or non-desirability of the free trade paradigm and the WTO in advancing people's welfare. What is at issue here is Washington's unilateral moves to determine who is to be a legitimate member of the international economic community—in this case, who is qualified to join and enjoy full membership rights in the WTO.

This decision of whether or not China can join the WTO is one that must be determined by China and the 137 member-countries of the World Trade Organization, without one power exercising effective veto power over this process. To subject this process to a special bilateral agreement with the United States that is, moreover, highly conditional on the acceding country's future behavior, falls smack into the tradition of unilateralism.

One reason the anti-China trade campaign is particularly disturbing is that it comes on the heels of a series of recent unilateralist acts, the most prominent of which have been Washington's cruise missile attacks on alleged terrorist targets in the Sudan and Afghanistan in August 1998, its bombing of Iraq in December 1998, and the US-instigated NATO 12-week bombardment of Kosovo in 1999. In all three cases, the US refused to seek UN sanction or approval but chose to act without international legal restraints. Serving as the gatekeeper for China's integration into the global economic community is the economic correlate of Washington's military unilateralism.

Second, the anti-China trade campaign reeks of double standards. A great number of countries would be deprived of PNTR status were the same accusations leveled at them that are now being thrown at China, including Singapore (where government controls the labor movement), Mexico (where labor is also under the thumb of government), Saudi Arabia and the Gulf states (where women are systematically relegated by law and custom to second class status as citizens), Pakistan (where a military dictatorship reigns), Brunei (where democratic rights are non-existent), to name just a few US allies. What is the logic and moral basis for singling out China when there are scores of other regimes that are much more insensitive to the political, economic, and social needs of their citizenries?

Third, the campaign is marked by what the great Senator J. William Fulbright denounced as the dark side of the American spirit that led to the Vietnam debacle—that is, "the morality of absolute self-assurance fired by the crusading spirit."[11] It draws emotional energy not so much from genuine concerns for human and democratic rights in China, but from the knee-jerk emotional ensemble of anti-communism that continues to plague the US public despite the end of the Cold War. When one organizer says that non-passage of the PNTR would inflict defeat on "the brutal, arrogant, corrupt, autocratic, and oligarchic regime in Beijing," the strong language is not unintentional. It is meant to hit the old Cold War buttons to mobilize the old anti-communist, conservative constituency, in the hope of building a left-right populist base that could—somehow—be directed at "progressive" ends.

Fourth, the anti-China trade campaign is intensely hypocritical. As many critics of the campaign have pointed out, the moral right of the US to deny permanent normal trading rights to China on social and environmental grounds is simply nonexistent given its record. It is the United States that has the largest prison population in the world, the highest income disparities among industrialized countries, the world's biggest emitter of greenhouse gases, quasi-slavery conditions for farm workers, and the highest number of state-sponsored executions.[12] And one more note on the subject of executions, the US is currently executing people at the rate of one every five days and it is one of only six nations that execute people for crimes committed under the age of 18, the others being Iran, Nigeria, Pakistan, Saudi Arabia, and Yemen.[13]

Fifth, the anti-China trade campaign is intellectually flawed. The issue of labor control in China lies at the core of the campaign, which blames China's government for the low wages that produce the very competitively priced goods that are said to contribute to displacing US industries and workers. This is plain wrong: the relatively low wages in China stem less from wage repression than from the dynamics of economic development. Widespread poverty or low economic growth is the main reason for the low wages in developing countries. Were the state of unionism the central determinant of wage levels, as the AFL-CIO claims, labor costs in authoritarian China and democratic India, with its formally free trade union movement, would not be equal, as they, in fact, are. Similarly, it is mainly the process of economic growth—the growing productivity of labor, the reduction of the wage-depressing surplus of rural labor, rising profits—that triggers the rapid rise in wage levels in an economy, as shown in the case of Taiwan, Korea, and Singapore, which had no independent unions and where strikes were illegal during their periods of rapid development.[14] It is this process that is now at work in China itself, where real wages rose by an average 6.0 percent in the period 1991–1997,[15] making it likely that in a few years this country will outstrip many developing countries in terms of labor costs.

Saying that the dynamics of development rather than the state of labor organizing is by far the greatest determinant of wage levels is not to say that the organization of labor is unimportant. Successful organizing has gotten workers a higher level of wages than would be possible were it only the dynamics of economic development at work. It is not to argue that labor organizing is not desirable in developing economies. It is not only desirable but necessary, so that workers can keep more of the value of production for themselves, reduce their exploitation by capitalist elites, and gain more control over their conditions of work.

Sixth, the anti-China trade campaign is dishonest. It invokes concern about the rights of Chinese workers and the rights of the Chinese people, but its main objective is to protect American jobs against cheap imports from China. This is cloaking self-interest with altruistic rhetoric. What the campaign should be doing is openly acknowledging that its overriding goal is to protect jobs, which is a legitimate concern and goal. And what it should be working for is not invoking sanctions on human rights grounds, but working out solutions such as managed trade, which would seek to balance the need of American workers to protect their jobs while allowing the market access that allows workers in other countries to keep their jobs and their countries to sustain a certain level of growth while moving to change their development model.[16]

Instead, what the rhetoric of the anti-China trade campaign does is to debase human rights and democratic rights language with its hypocrisy while de-legitimizing the objective of protecting jobs—which is a central social and economic right—by concealing it.

Seventh, the anti-China trade campaign is a classic case of blaming the victim. China is not the enemy. It is a prisoner of a global system of rules and institutions that allows transnational corporations to take advantage of the differential wage levels of counties at different levels of development to increase their profits, destabilize the global environment by generalizing an export-oriented, high-consumption model of development, and concentrate global income in fewer and fewer hands.

Not granting China PNTR will not affect the functioning of this global system. Not giving China normal trading and investment rights will not harm transnational corporations (TNCs); they will simply take more seriously the option of moving to Indonesia, Mauritius, or Mexico, where their ability to exact concessions is greater than in China, which can stand up to foreign interests far better than the weak governments of these countries. What the AFL-CIO and others should be doing is targeting this global system, instead of serving up China as a proxy for it.

A POSITIVE AGENDA

The anti-China trade campaign amounts to a Faustian bargain that seeks to buy some space for US organized labor at the expense of real solidarity with workers and progressive worker and environmental movements globally against transnational capital. But by buying into the traditional US imperial response of unilateralism, it will end up eventually eroding the position of progressive labor, environmental, and civil society movements both in the US and throughout the world.

What organized labor and American NGOs should be doing instead is articulating a positive agenda aimed at weakening the power of global corporations and multilateral agencies that promote TNC-led globalization. The first order of business is to not allow the progressive movement to be sandbagged in the pro-permanent normal trade relations, anti-permanent trade relations terms of engagement that now frames the debate. While progressives must for the time being oppose the more dangerous threat posed by the unilateralists, they should be developing a position on global economic relations that avoids both the free trade paradigm that underlies the PNTR and the unilateralist paradigm of the anti-PNTR forces. The model we propose is managed trade, which allows trading partners to negotiate bilateral treaties that address central issues in their relationship—among them, the need to preserve workers' jobs in the US with the developing countries' need for market access. Advocacy of managed trade must, however, be part of a broader campaign for progressive global economic governance. The strategic aim of such a campaign must be the tighter regulation, if not replacement, of the model of corporate-led free market development that seeks to do away with social and state restrictions on the mobility of capital at the expense of labor. In its place must be established a system of looser global economic cooperation and integration that allows countries to follow paths of national and regional development that make the domestic market and regional markets, rather than the global market, the engine of growth, development, and job creation.

This means support for measures of asset and income redistribution that would create the purchasing power to make domestic markets viable. It means support for trade measures and capital controls to give countries more control over their trade and finance so that commodity and capital flows become less disruptive and destabilizing. It means support for regional integration or regional economic union among the developing countries as an alternative to the damages of indiscriminate globalization.

A key element in this campaign for a new global economic governance is the abolition, radical transformation, or radical dis-empowerment of the International Monetary Fund (IMF), the World Bank, and the World Trade Organization that serve as the pillars of the system of corporate-led globalization and its replacement with a pluralistic system of institutions that complement but at the same time check and balance one another, giving the developing countries the space to pursue their chosen paths to development.

The IMF, World Bank, and WTO are currently experiencing a severe crisis of legitimacy, following the debacle in Seattle, the April protests in Washington, and the release of the report of the International Financial Institutions Advisory Commission appointed by the US Congress, which recommends the radical downsizing or transformation of the Bank and Fund.[17] Now is the time for the progressive movement to take the offensive and push for the elimination or radical transformation of these institutions. Yet here we are, being waylaid from this critical task at this key moment by an all-advised, divisive campaign to isolate the wrong enemy!

Another key thrust of a positive agenda is a coordinated drive by civil society groups in the North and the South to pressure the US, China, and all other governments to ratify and implement all conventions of the International Labor Organization (ILO) and give the ILO more effective authority to monitor, supervise, and adjudicate implementation of these conventions. This campaign must be part of a broader effort to support the formation of genuine labor unions in China, the American South, and elsewhere in a spirit of real workers' solidarity. This, instead of relying on government trade sanctions that are really self-serving rather than meant to support Third World workers, is the route to the creation of really firm ties of solidarity across North-South lines.

This social and economic program must be tied to a strategy for protecting the global environment that also eschews sanctions as an approach and puts the emphasis on promoting sustainable development models in place of the export-led, high-consumption development model; pushes the adoption of common environmental codes that prevent transnational firms from pitting one country against another in their search for zero-cost environmental regimes; and promotes an environmental Marshall Plan aimed at transferring appropriate green process and production technology to China and other developing countries. Above all, this approach must focus not on attacking China and the South, but on changing the production and consumption behavior and levels in the North that are by far the biggest source of environmental destabilization.

Finally, a positive agenda must have as central element civil society groups in the North working constructively with people's movements in China, the United States, and other countries experiencing democratic deficits to support the expansion of democratic space. While the campaign must be uncompromising in denouncing acts of repression like the Tienanmen Square massacre and Washington's use of mass incarceration as a tool of social control, it must avoid imposing the forms of Western procedural democracy on others and hew to the principle that it is the people in these countries themselves that must take the lead in building democracy according to their rhythm, traditions, and cultures.

ABANDONING UNILATERALISM

The anti-China trade coalition is an alliance born of opportunism. In its effort to block imports from China, the AFL-CIO is courting the more conservative sectors of the US population, including the Buchanan right wing, by stirring the old Cold War rhetoric. Nothing could be a more disconcerting image of this questionable project than James Hoffa, head of the Teamsters, and Pat Buchanan holding hands during the anti-China trade rally in mid-April, with Buchanan promising to make Hoffa his top trade negotiator if he won the race for president.

Most serious human rights and environmental advocates, both within China and outside, have refused to be part of the anti-China trade campaign, largely because they have seen through its narrow, self-serving agenda.[18] But there are some environmental groups and citizens groups, which have long unsuccessfully courted labor, that support the campaign because they see it as the perfect opportunity to build bridges to the AFL-CIO. As a result, what we have is an alliance built on the assertion of US unilateralism rather than on the cornerstone of fundamental shared goals of solidarity, equity, and environmental integrity.

This is not a progressive alliance but a right-wing populist alliance in the tradition of the anti-communist Big Government-Big Capital-Big Labor alliance during the Cold War, the labor-capital alliance in the West that produced the Exclusion and Anti-Miscegenation Acts against Chinese, Japanese, and Filipino workers in the late nineteenth and early twentieth centuries, and, more recently, the populist movement that has supported the tightening of racist immigration laws by emphasizing the divide between workers who are citizens and workers who are not, with the latter being deprived of basic political rights.

It is a policy that will, moreover, feed global instability by lending support to the efforts of the US right and the Pentagon to demonize China as The Enemy and resurrect containment as America's Grand Strategy, this time with China instead of the Soviet Union as the enemy in a paradigm designed to advance American strategic hegemony. As in every other instance of unprincipled unity between the right and some sectors of the progressive movement, progressives will find that it will be the right that will walk away with the movement while they will be left with not even their principles.

It is time to move away from this terribly misguided effort to derail the progressive movement by demonizing China, and to bring us all back to the original spirit of Seattle as a movement of the citizens of the world against corporate-led globalization and for genuine international cooperation.

NOTES

1. Quoted in John Gershman, "How to Debate the China Issue without China Bashing," *Progressive Response,* Vol. 4, No. 17, April 20, 2000.

2. Brown, Lester. *Who Will Feed China?* (New York: Norton, 1995).

3. Agarwal, Anil, Sunita Narain and Anju Sharma, eds. *Green Politics* (New Delhi: Center for Science and Environment, 2000), pg. 108.

4. Ibid., pg. 16.

5. FAO and IMPACT data cited in Simeon Ehui, "Trade and Food Systems in the Developing World," presentation at the Salzburg seminar, Salzburg, Austria, May 11, 2000.

6. Lazare, Daniel. "America the Undemocratic," *New Left Review*, No. 232 (November–December 1998), pg. 7.

7. Amnesty International. *United States of America: Rights for All* (London: Amnesty International Publications, 1998).

8. Friedman, Thomas. *The Lexus and the Olive Tree* (New York: Farrar, Straus Giroux, 1999), pg. 50.

9. Johnson, Chalmers. *Blowback: The Costs and Consequences of American Empire* (New York: Metropolitan Books, 2000), pg. 50.

10. Gray, John. *False Dawn* (New York: New Press, 1998), pp. 189–190.

11. J. William Fulbright, quoted in Walter McDougall, *Promised Land, Crusader State* (Boston: Houghton Mifflin, 1997), p. 206.

12. See Anuradha Mittal and Peter Rosset, "The Real Enemy is the WTO, not China," *Peaceworks*, March 1, 2000; and Jim Smith, "The China Syndrome—or, How to Hijack a Movement," *LA Labor News*, April 2, 2000.

13. "America the Undemocratic," pg. 6.

14. For the state of the labor movement in these societies in the period of rapid growth, see Walden Bello and Stephanie Rosenfeld, *Dragons in Distress: Asia's Miracle Economies in Crisis* (Oakland, CA: Food First Books, 1990).

15. Bowles, Paul and Xiao-yuan Dong. "Globalization, 'Chinese Walls,' and Industrial Labor," *IDS Bulletin*, Vol. 30, No. 4 (1999), pg. 99.

16. See *Blowback*, pg. 174.

17. *Report of the US Congressional International Financial Institution Advisory Commission* (Washington: DC, US Congress, Feb. 2000).

18. Human Rights Watch, for instance, has refused to endorse the campaign. For reactions within China, see "China's Dissidents Urge US to Back Normal Trade Relations with Beijing," *International Herald Tribune*, May 12, 2000.

14

WHY LAND REFORM IS NO LONGER POSSIBLE
WITHOUT REVOLUTION

with Marissa de Guzman
Business World, June 19-20, 2000

As we mark another year in the inglorious history of agrarian reform, it might be instructive to explore the elements that spelled the difference between continuing failure of land redistribution in the Philippines and its striking success in places like Korea, Taiwan, and Japan. Perhaps the decisive factor were the contrasting roles played by critical external actors, in particular the United States.

WHY THE US BACKED REFORM

In Korea, agrarian reform was a case of military exigency. In their drive down the peninsula in 1950, the North Koreans distributed the lands of the fleeing rural elite among the South Korean peasants. When it was their turn to march up the peninsula as the North Koreans retreated, the Americans were faced with the choice of maintaining the *de facto* reform or undoing it and reinstating the South Korean landlords as property holders. Faced with the prospect a provoking a full-scale peasant revolution on their rear, the Americans let the North Korean reforms stand, and later pressed the reactionary government of Rhee Syngman to legalize them in order to create a conservative anti-communist political base in the countryside.

In the case of Taiwan, local landlords were expropriated—many of them massacred—by the Kuomintang government of Chiang Kai-Shek that had been evicted from the mainland by the Communists in 1949. The Kuomintang saw land reform in terms of realpolitik: they did not want Taiwan's local landed class around as a competing power center and saw agrarian reform as a means to eliminate them as well as build a pro-Kuomintang constituency among the peasants. Eager to stabilize the island as a bastion against Mao's revolution that threatened across the Taiwan Straits, the US vigorously backed the Kuomintang reform program with large doses of technical advice and aid that established, among other things, an effective system of support services.

In Japan, General Douglas MacArthur saw land reform as an essential part of the comprehensive program of demilitarization of Japanese society that was essential if a Western-style liberal democracy was to flourish in occupied Japan.

In all three cases, the US did not have any compunctions about sacrificing rural elites since, in the case of Japan, the gentry had been the social base of Japanese militarism. In the case of Taiwan and Korea, the landowning class had served as the local base of Japanese colonial rule from the turn of the century to 1945.

CONTOURS OF RADICAL LAND REFORM

Backed by American policy and aid—not to mention firepower—the results of the land reform programs in these countries were impressive. In Japan, rigorous limitation of landownership to three hectares in densely irrigated areas resulted in the redistribution of two-fifths of the country's land to 4.5 million tenants, or over half of the agricultural population.

The ambitious land-to-the-tiller program in Taiwan, which also limited ownership to three hectares, transferred 250,000 hectares of Taiwan's cultivated lands to tenants. Owner-cultivators rose from 61 to 88 percent of farm families, and tenant farmers plunged from 39 to two percent.

In Korea, a ceiling of three hectares for land ownership was also adopted, resulting in the redistribution of 470,000 hectares. Owner cultivators as a percentage of farm families rose from 14 percent to 70 percent and tenant farmers dropped from 83 to 30 percent. The South Korean reform was, however, less thorough than in Taiwan and Japan. Much of the land scheduled for land redistribution was not transferred to tenants because landlords were able to disguise themselves as tillers or register land titles under their sons or other relatives. Systems for the delivery of credit, fertilizers, and extension services were not in place, leading many recipients to lose their land. Despite these limitations, the Korean land reform, like the Taiwanese and Japanese reforms, broke the back of landlord power and made small owner-cultivators the dominant class in the countryside.

REFORM'S CONSEQUENCES

Aside from promoting rural equality and stabilizing the countryside socially, land reform in all three societies had profound economic consequences. Most important was the elimination of a backward and grossly inequitable system of land tenure that restricted the development of a domestic market, siphoned off to unproductive consumption resources that would otherwise have gone into investment in industry, and served as a social base for authoritarianism.

Land reform created a vibrant domestic market that stimulated vigorous industrial growth. This is most evident in the case of Taiwan, where the income of owner-cultivators rose 62 percent in the 15 years following the reform. This rural purchasing power triggered the growth of a variety of industries, including food processing, light manufacturing, agri-chemicals, machine industries, and metalworking enterprises. Farmers' purchases of goods from outside the agricultural sector rose 56 percent from 1950 to 1955. Underlining this link between rural demand and industrial vigor was the birth of the light machine sector: there were only seven power tillers in the whole of Taiwan in 1954; six years later there were over 3,000, of which about half were manufactured locally.

WASHINGTON'S PROTEGES

The role of external actors in the Philippines was different. Not surprisingly, land reform measures went in a different direction: nowhere. One would have expected that on its coming to the Philippines, the country that had known no feudalism in land—that had been "born bourgeois," to use Louis Hartz' words—would have broken up large estate agriculture. The sale of excess church lands ordered by the colonial government in the first years of the new century should have provided the wedge for the transformation of Philippine agriculture into a system based on small owner-cultivators. Instead, the friar lands were sold to the gentry—a move that was not merely an adjunct to military pacification, but part of an evolving strategy to forge the regional rural elites into a national ruling class that would serve as the base of American colonial rule. The Americans, for instance, allowed their former foe, General Emilio Aguinaldo, to acquire a 2,540 acre ex-friar estate in Cavite.

US colonial viceroys like General Douglas MacArthur not only forged intimate political links with the landed class, but also close personal ties. This served the elite well after WW II, when MacArthur saw to it that charges of collaboration with the Japanese were dropped against most of the rural elite families. No event captures the US government's double standards in dealing with Asian landed elites more than MacArthur's absolving his landlord friend Manuel Roxas of the sin of collaborating with the Japanese to enable him to run for president of the new republic, at the same time that he was preparing to radically expropriate Roxas' class counterparts in conquered Japan.

The last chance the US had of significantly influencing the course of agrarian development in the Philippines was probably during the Huk insurgency in the early 1950s, when peasant alienation fueled a full-blown communist insurrection in a country regarded as a key bastion of the US forward defense system against expansive Asian communism. But primordial loyalty to its local elite proteges emasculated the US government's feeble support for reform, a point underlined by Washington's recalling Robert Hardie, a US adviser whose proposal for land reform was bitterly denounced by local landed families in 1953.

Instead of land reform, US advisers sought to defuse agrarian unrest by promoting land resettlement. Working with the populist Defense Secretary Ramon Magsaysay, Colonel Edward Landsdale, the CIA's point man in the Philippines, formulated the Economic Development Corporation (EDCOR) project, which sought to resettle Huk surrenderees in Mindanao, then portrayed as "virgin territory." This strategy did help defuse the insurgency in Central Luzon, but it did nothing to alleviate the land problem there or anywhere else. Indeed, it was a significant step in promoting the uncontrolled Christian migration to Muslim and Lumad territory that has led to the unending crisis in Mindanao.

WASHINGTON AND MARCOS' LAND REFORM

When Marcos declared land reform a cornerstone of the "new society" in 1972, US support for land reform was, surprisingly, lukewarm. Apparently, this attitude stemmed from the US Agency for International Development's (USAID) experience of land reform in Vietnam, where it was seen as having been disruptive and destabilizing. More important than USAID as an influence on Marcos was the US-dominated World Bank. But the Bank, then led by Robert McNamara, deliberately shied away from promoting land reform, with its rural development strategy paper asserting that the Bank would "put primary emphasis not on the redistribution of income and wealth—as justified as that may be in many of our member countries—but rather on improving the productivity of the poor."

When the Marcos land reform program ground to a halt in 1975, owing to Marcos' realization that the small and medium landlords owning 7–24 hectares were actually an important base of his rule, there was little protest from Washington, except for loud denunciations by the CIA land reform expert Roy Prosterman. By the end of the Marcos era, only 126,000 hectares out of an originally projected 1,767,000 hectares of tenanted rice and corn land had been transferred to owner-cultivators.

POST-MARCOS LAND REFORM

Corazon Aquino, like Marcos, also promised to make land reform a cornerstone of her government. Washington, which helped bring Aquino to power, was again lukewarm when it came to support for land reform, perhaps feeling that the matter was no longer urgent with the marginalization of the National Democratic Front and the New People's Army as significant political actors. Lacking both external and internal stimuli and ridden with a myriad loopholes, the Comprehensive Agrarian Reform Program (CARP) floundered. The real test of a land reform program is the compulsory acquisition of private lands: towards the end of Aquino's term, CARP could boast of having acquired and distributed only 10,467 hectares of private land via compulsory acquisition.

Unlike the case with his predecessors, agrarian reform was not articulated as a centerpiece program by President Fidel Ramos, who explicitly placed the so-called social agenda behind "preparing the Philippines for global competition" by an ambitious program of trade and investment liberalization. Not surprisingly, by the end of one decade of CARP in December 1998, only 60 percent of the total land targeted for transfer had actually been distributed.

The marginalization of agrarian reform continued under the administration of President Joseph Estrada, notwithstanding the president's pro-poor rhetoric. By the end of 1999, only 27 percent of targeted land in estates that were 50 hectares or larger in size had been successfully acquired and distributed. For targeted land in estates in the 24–50 hectare range and 5–24 hectare range, the figures were only five and four percent, respectively.

During the last years of Ramos and under Estrada, what might be described as a process of aggressive counter-reform has been gathering steam. The landlord-dominated Congress allocated the Department of Agrarian Reform only P600 million for land acquisition and distribution in 1999, or half the budget for 1998. Cancellations of emancipation patents (EPs) and certificates of land ownership awards (CLOAs), owing to successful legal action by landlords, have increased at an alarming rate, with 17,534 EPs and CLOAs covering 40,677 hectares nullified during the last four years of Ramos and 15,0644 EPs and CLOAs covering 36,315 hectares cancelled during Estrada's first two years.

REFORM'S DISMAL RECORD ELSEWHERE

The Philippines is not alone in experiencing the failure of a reformist land redistribution program without aggressive foreign backing. In the case of Thailand, of 2.7 million hectares subject to reform under the Land Reform Law of 1975, only 47,619 hectares had been distributed to tenants as of 1993. Nothing captures the sorry state of land reform in Thailand better than the fact that after over 17 years of land reform in the mid-1990s, only 43 families had received full land ownership rights to a total area that came to only 126 hectares!

The Thai and Philippine experiences with reformist land redistribution programs that lacked vigorous US sponsorship were paralleled in Latin America. In Bolivia, Guatemala, Venezuela, Chile, Brazil, Colombia, Ecuador, Peru, and El Salvador, land reforms were initiated but none could be labeled successful in terms of making smallholders the dominant force in agriculture. The US government was not a disinterested actor in all this. As Solon Barraclough notes, "The United States government's position in respect to land reform in the region was very interesting, if inconsistent. It intervened to reverse the Guatemalan reform when United Fruit Company lands were taken. It supported reform 15 years later in Peru, however, in spite of the expropriation of some US investors. It did not intervene in Bolivia except to help the new government with aid. It mildly supported reform in Venezuela. In Cuba it did everything possible to overthrow Castro. In Chile, it strongly supported the Alessandri and Frei reforms but intervened to help overthrow the Allende government that was executing the same land reform law. It pushed for reform in El Salvador but opposed it in Nicaragua... Obviously land reform itself was of little concern. What mattered was the political orientation of the regime concerned."

Even where it intervened, as in Chile and El Salvador, the US pressure on local elites was mild compared to the heavy-handed supervision it exercised in the reforms in Korea, Japan, and Taiwan. Probably the reason is that, although Latin American countries were wracked by insurgencies, they were not on the political and military frontlines of the Cold War, as the Northeast Asian countries were. Nevertheless, as the case of El Salvador illustrated, without Washington's determined ground level support, land reform could be successfully stalemated by recalcitrant elites.

AGRARIAN REVOLUTION

Ironically enough, aside from US-sponsored land reform, the only other kind of land distribution that has a fair chance of success in really transforming the rural order is that which takes place as part of a larger revolutionary process. The most successful land reform effort before the twentieth century was the late eighteenth century agrarian revolution in France that literally decapitated the landed aristocracy and gave birth to a vigorous smallholder-based capitalist agriculture. Over 130 years later, it took only a few months after the outbreak of the February Revolution in St. Petersburg in 1917 for the Russian peasantry to almost totally dispossess most of the country's landed gentry and assert traditional village communal control of lands.

Cuba's agrarian reform was the most profound and far-reaching in Latin America, with the expropriation of over three-fourths of the country's land in the few months after Castro's 1959 ascent to power. It was also one of the most successful, with overall agricultural output increasing by three percent annually from the mid-1960s to the mid-1980s and bringing in its wake improvements in the nutrition and health of the rural population.

In China, land reform from 1949 to 1952 redistributed ownership rights among the peasantry and collectivization in 1955–1956 abolished private land ownership. Despite the changes in the control and use of land with the adoption of the market-oriented contract system in the 1980s, the dynamism of the agricultural sector in the last two decades would not have been possible without the foundation of relative equality in access to land that had been laid by land reform and collectivization in the fifties.

To conclude, the most successful agrarian reforms appear to have been either those that were vigorously supported by an external power like the United States for anti-revolutionary reasons, or those that were part of a broader revolutionary conflagration. There are few, if any, instances of really successful efforts at reformist programs of land redistribution with no vigorous foreign backing. With the end of the Cold War, US interest in successful land reform in its client states has practically disappeared. Owing to this trend, reformist land distribution in the Philippines is heading nowhere, but to the demise of the peasantry and the deepening crisis of Philippine agriculture. It now seems quite evident that only an agrarian revolution that is part of a bigger radical project to restructure Philippine society can now save the peasantry and Philippine agriculture from this dismal future.

15

WASHINGTON AND THE DEMISE OF THE "THIRD WAVE" OF DEMOCRATIZATION

Business World, March 31, 2000

During a visit to Manila in 2000, Stanley Roth, the assistant secretary of state for Asia-Pacific Affairs, said that the chances of a coup attempt are "nearly zero." That was classic American diplomacy—a statement that served less as an assessment of the status of things than a calculated warning against restiveness in the barracks.

Roth doesn't like the military meddling in politics. A key aide to Rep. Stephen Solarz, head of the US House of Representatives' Asia-Pacific subcommittee, in the 1980s, Roth played a minor, though important, role in shifting US support from Ferdinand Marcos to Cory Aquino in the mid-1980s. With Bill Clinton's victory in 1992, he became a low profile but key figure in the Democratic foreign policy team headed by Secretary of State Warren Christopher and National Security Adviser Anthony Lake. It was this group that forged the line of "promoting democracy," that formed one of the pillars of the Clinton foreign policy towards the Third World, alongside containing Islamic fundamentalism and isolating "rogue regimes" like North Korea.

"Promoting democracy" was billed as a distinctive, idealistic foreign policy thrust that contrasted with the support for authoritarian allies that had been the key feature of US policy under Ronald Reagan and with the pragmatic adjustment to rising democracies that had marked the Bush administration's approach. In fact, the Clinton line was a continuation of the Bush line, but with a heavy dose of ideological rhetoric. It was part of Washington's protracted response to the spread of electoral democracies in Africa, Latin America and Asia from the early 1980s to the early 1990s.

THE "THIRD WAVE"

Labeled as the "third wave" of democratization globally, the move toward electoral democracy as a system of governance is documented in the statistics of Freedom House in New York: the number of free or liberal democratic states rose from 42 in 1972 to 56 in 1985 to 76 in 1995—or from 29 percent of all states in1972 to 33.5 percent in 1985 to 39.8 percent in 1995.

This movement toward freer political systems, it must be pointed out, largely took place in spite of, not because of US foreign policy. From the seventies to the mid-1980s, Washington had engaged in a foreign policy of supporting a string of repressive strongmen that were seen as serving US strategic objectives—from the Shah of Iran, Mobutu in Africa, Pinochet in Chile, to Marcos in the Philippines and Chun Doo-Hwan in Korea. The rationale for this policy was perhaps best articulated by Reagan's UN ambassador, Jeane Kirkpatrick, who wrote in a notorious *Commentary Magazine* article in 1981 that an autocrat ally like Somoza or Marcos deserved to be supported because "without him, the organized life of society will collapse, like an arch from which the keystone has been removed."

But even as these lines were being penned, dictatorships in the Third World were in an advanced state of decay. After 20 years in power, the Brazilian military was gradually forced out of power in the early 1980s by widespread popular disaffection and economic incompetence. After losing the Falklands War in 1982, the military junta in Argentina, stripped of all shreds of legitimacy, was hounded out of power by a vengeful civilian population. In South Asia, the death of the strongman General Muhammad Zia opened the doors to the restoration of civilian constitutional rule in Pakistan. In the Philippines, Ronald Reagan's visceral loyalty to the embattled Marcos was overridden by pragmatists at the State Department, who thought it the better part of wisdom to hitch the US to the democratic upsurge triggered by the Aquino assassination. Confronting a similar situation in Korea in 1987, the US lined up behind the student-led democratic revolution. A few years later, Washington quietly threw its weight behind the democracy movement that faced down the military strongman Suchinda in the streets of Bangkok in May 1992.

PROMOTING "POLYARCHY"

By the time Clinton and the Democrats came to power in 1993, the third wave of democratization was at its apogee, with the dismantling of the apartheid regime in South Africa and the erosion or collapse of several one party and personalist regimes in Sub Saharan Africa. Like so many other things in the Clinton presidency, "promoting democracy" was one-third substance and two-thirds public relations. Promoting democracy merely attached an attractive ideological rationale to a pragmatic shift in policy that had been going on for nearly a decade under the Republican administrations—it was, after all, Republican Party operators that had created the National Endowment for Democracy (NED), which was active in influencing democratic oppositions in the Third World in a conservative, pro-Washington direction.

Nonetheless, television images of US troops landing in Haiti in 1995 to drive out the military junta and restore President Aristide to his rightful place as the people's elected leader and Washington's strong rhetoric against the State Law and Order Restoration Council (SLORC) regime in Burma contributed to wiping out memories of Washington's sordid past of support for repressive regimes and endowed the Clinton administration with the aura of being a champion of democracy.

Promoting democracy in practice meant Washington's encouragement of free elections, political party competition, the rule of law, checks, and balances, judicial independence—all of which rested on the diffusion and institutionalization of a core of liberal values such as the freedom of speech and freedom of association. Such a regime was seen as providing the framework for the spread of market forces, the untrammeled operation of which was expected to spur economic growth as well as put an end to the unholy relationship between authoritarian government and monopoly businesses known as "crony capitalism." What democracy promotion was not about was creating institutions and pushing policies that would bring about more equality in access to wealth and resources as demanded by the poor majority.

In short, what emerged were liberal democratic systems along the lines of the Washington or Westminster model, along with this regime's fundamental flaw: the great influence exercised on the decision making process by the realities of severe economic and social inequality. Liberal democracy, as it developed in the Third World, prevented the monopoly over political power by one faction of the elite and provided an ideal avenue for opposing factions of the same class to deploy their resources to peacefully compete for votes and alternate in political office. This was not popular democracy but, according to political scientist William Robinson, "polyarchy," or "a system in which a small group actually rules and mass participation in decision making is confined to leadership choice in elections carefully managed by competing elites."

For elites the advantage of a system of formal democracy was that it married political legitimacy to a system of gross economic inequality.

POLYARCHY IN TROUBLE

As Clinton left office, the policy of promoting polyarchy or elite democracies ran into serious problems. Though there have been some dramatic recent instances of democratic transition as in Indonesia, the rate of increase of electoral democracies has sharply declined in recent years. More important, asserts political analyst Larry Diamond, the quality of democratic practice in the new democracies is deteriorating. This "end of the third wave of democratization" takes various forms—from actual coups, as in Pakistan, to greater military autonomy in internal security operations, as in Turkey, Sri Lanka, and Colombia, to widespread vote rigging as in Niger, Bangladesh, and Chad, to "strongman democracies" as in the case of Alberto Fujimori in Peru or Hugo Chavez in Venezuela.

Why are formal democracies or polyarchies in trouble? Of course, there is the problem of the difficulty of institutionalizing multiparty electoral systems in states that had experienced only military rule following colonial rule at independence. In many cases, as in Peru, Pakistan, and Zambia, fragile democracies have lost their legitimacy because they became the vehicles through which the IMF and the World Bank imposed budget-cutting structural adjustment programs that triggered or worsened economic stagnation and impoverishment.

But most of all, the erosion of legitimacy was created by the structural incapacity of a multiparty electoral system run by wealthy interests to produce less poverty and less inequality via serious social reform.

It is interesting to point out the striking parallels between the dynamics of the troubled polyarchies in the Third World and their model, US electoral democracy. Increasing numbers of Americans are troubled by the way elections, legislative decisions, and executive moves are increasingly determined by the deployment of vast amounts of wealth in the electoral system. Noting that "nothing on the scale of the American system of political expenditure and influence exists anywhere else," William Pfaff, the columnist of the *International Herald Tribune,* remarks that the US has become a "plutocracy," or a system governed by corporate wealth. Nevertheless, the political system is quite stable—at least in the near future—because inequality in access to political power is mitigated by the fact that the majority of Americans are materially comfortable. This cannot be said of Third World democracies like the Philippines, which are wracked by poverty and inequality.

DEMOCRATIC DEGENERATION?

With democracies stuck, are military regimes likely to experience a comeback in the next few years? Though there might be some successful military coups, it is unlikely that there will be a general trend showing a return to direct military or presidential-military rule. For one thing, many armies are reluctant to return to power and again risk incurring the blame for political failures. A second reason is that while people may be disaffected with many elite democracies, they are even more distrustful of military rule. A third reason is that once attractive authoritarian ideologies, such as "Asian values," are greatly discredited and seen as self-serving rationales for civilian or military elites.

What is more likely in the near or medium term is what Diamond describes as a situation in which "democracy, instead of expiring altogether, has been hollowed out, leaving a shell of multiparty electoralism, often with genuine competitiveness and uncertain outcomes, adequate to obtain international legitimacy and assistance." A number of political systems might move along the path of "strongman democracies" such as those in Peru or Venezuela, where executives expand their powers with the support of the military, temporarily suspend or change the constitution, dismiss and reorganize the legislature or judiciary, and, as Diamond puts it, "reshape to their advantage a constitutional system that subsequently retains the formal structure or appearance of democracy."

A more probable outcome in most countries might be a slowly degenerating liberal democracy in a context where the authoritarian left and the authoritarian right are not strong enough to seize power in the short term yet are powerful enough to destabilize it. Here the "democratic center" is held together by competing political elites which are passively committed to democratic constitutional rules but lack the vision or courage to legislate and implement the program of social and economic democracy that the masses demand.

This has been the scenario in the Philippines, and it became more of a reality with each day that Estrada remained as president. And in the Philippines and elsewhere, Washington will grit its teeth but it will stand by the elite democrats.

But nothing is predestined or predetermined. We can avoid this "death of democracy by a thousand cuts," to borrow a phrase from Larry Diamond. Democracy can be reinvigorated in this country but only if there are groups that are determined to expand the democracy agenda to include fundamental economic and social reform within a constitutional electoral order. That is a big challenge in this country of shortsighted, greedy elites. That is a tall order when Washington smells an anti-US agenda in every progressive political program. But it is not impossible.

PART FOUR

The Struggle for the Future

16

PRAGUE 2000:

TOWARD A DEGLOBALIZED WORLD

Focus Dossiers, September 2001

The historic Prague Spring of 1968 spelled the beginning of the end for the Soviet Empire. In the year 2000, Prague was the site of the World Bank-International Monetary Fund annual meetings, joining Seattle in December 1999 and Washington, DC, in April 2000, as one of the catalytic events ushering the beginning of the end of hegemony of corporate-driven globalization.

We came to a crossroads in Prague. For years we were told that globalization was benign, that it was a process that brought about the greatest good for the greatest number. Good citizenship lay in accepting the impersonal rule of the market and good governance meant governments getting out of the way of market forces and letting the most effective incarnation of market freedom, the transnational corporation (TNC), go about its task of bringing about the most efficient mix of capital, land, technology, and labor.

The unrestricted flow of goods and capital in a world without borders was said to be the best of all possible worlds, though when some observers pointed out that to be consistent with the precepts of their eighteenth century prophet, Adam Smith, proponents of the neoliberal doctrine would also have to allow the unrestricted flow of labor to create this best of all possible worlds, they were ignored. Such inconsistencies could be overlooked since for over two decades, neoliberalism or, as it was grandiosely styled, the "Washington consensus" had carried all before it. As one of its key partisans has nostalgically remarked recently, "the Washington consensus seemed to gain near-universal approval and provided a guiding ideology and underlying intellectual consensus for the world economy, which was quite new in modern history."[1]

GLOBALIZATION UNRAVELS I:
THE ASIAN FINANCIAL COLLAPSE

The unrestricted flow of speculative capital in accordance with the doctrine of the Washington consensus was what the governments in East Asia institutionalized in the early 1990s, under the strong urging of the International Monetary Fund (IMF) and the US Treasury. The result: the $100 billion that flowed in between 1993 and 1997 flowed out in the bat of an eyelash during the Great Panic of the summer of 1997, bringing about the collapse of Asian economies and spinning them into a mire of recession and massive unemployment from which most still have to recover. Since 1997, financial instability or the constant erosion of Asian currencies has become a way of life under IMF-imposed monetary regimes that leave the value of the money to be determined day-to-day by the changing whims, moods, and preferences of foreign investors and currency speculators.

GLOBALIZATION UNRAVELS II:
THE FAILURE OF STRUCTURAL ADJUSTMENT

The Asian financial crisis put the IMF on the hot seat, leading to a widespread popular reappraisal of its role in the Third World in the 1980s and early 1990s, when structural adjustment programs were imposed on over 70 developing countries. After over 15 years, there were hardly any cases of successful adjustment programs. What structural adjustment had done instead was to institutionalize stagnation in

Africa and Latin America, alongside rises in the levels of absolute poverty and income inequality.

Structural adjustment and related free market policies that were imposed beginning in the early 1980s were the central factor that triggered a sharp rise in global inequality. An authoritative UN Conference on Trade and Development (UNCTAD) study covering 124 countries showed that the income share of the richest 20 percent of the world's population rose from 69 to 83 percent between 1965 and 1990.[2] Adjustment policies were a central factor behind the rapid concentration of global income in recent years—a process which in 1998 saw Bill Gates with a net worth of $90 billion, Warren Buffet with $36 billion, and Microsoft co-founder Paul Allen with $30 billion. These three men achieved a combined income that was greater than the total combined income of the 600 million that live in the world's 48 least developed countries, a great number of whom had been subjected to adjustment programs.

Structural adjustment has also been a central cause of the lack of any progress in the campaign against poverty. The number of people globally living in poverty—that is, on less than a dollar a day—increased from 1.1 billion in 1985 to 1.2 billion in 1998, and was expected to reach 1.3 billion by 2000.[3] According to a recent World Bank study, the absolute number of people living in poverty rose in the 1990s in Eastern Europe, South Asia, Latin America and the Caribbean, and Sub Saharan Africa—all areas that came under the sway of structural adjustment programs.[4]

Confronted with this dismal record, James Wolfensohn of the World Bank had the sense to move the institution away from its identification with structural adjustment with public relations initiatives like the structural adjustment program review initiative (SAPRI), that it said would be jointly conducted with non-governmental organizations (NGOs). But the IMF under the doctrinaire Michel Camdessus refused to see the handwriting on the wall. It sought instead to embed adjustment policies permanently in the economic structure through the establishment of the extended structural adjustment facility (ESAF).

As a consequence of greater public scrutiny following its disastrous policies in East Asia, the Fund could no longer pretend that structural adjustment had not been a massive failure in Africa, Latin America, and South Asia. During the World Bank-IMF meetings in September 1999, the Fund conceded failure by renaming the extended structural adjustment facility (ESAF) the "poverty reduction and growth facility." However, there was no way the Fund could successfully whitewash the results of its policies. When the Group of Seven (G-7) proposed to make IMF certification a condition for eligibility in the now-defunct heavily indebted poor countries (HIPC) debt initiative, Rep. Maxine Walters of the US House of Representatives spoke for many liberal American lawmakers when she commented, "Do we have to involve the IMF at all? Because, as we have painfully discovered, the way the IMF works causes children to starve."[5]

So bereft of legitimacy was the Fund that US Treasury secretary Larry Summers, who in an earlier incarnation as chief economist of the World Bank was one of the chief backers of structural adjustment, told the US Congress that the "IMF-centered process" of macroeconomic policymaking would be replaced by "a new, more open and inclusive process that would involve multiple international organizations and give national policymakers and civil society groups a more central role."[6]

GLOBALIZATION UNRAVELS III: THE DEBACLE IN SEATTLE

Freedom, said Hegel, is the recognition of necessity. Freedom, the proponents of neoliberalism like Hegel's disciple Francis Fukuyama tell us, lies in the recognition of the inexorable irreversibility of free market globalization. Over 50,000 people who descended on Seattle in late November 1999 did not buy this Hegelian-Fukuyaman notion of freedom as submission and surrender to what seemed to be the ineluctable necessity of the World Trade Organization (WTO).

In the mid-1990s, the WTO was sold to the global public as the lynchpin of a multilateral system of economic governance that would provide the necessary rules to facilitate the growth of global trade and the spread of its beneficial effects. Nearly five years later, the implications and consequences of the founding of the WTO had become as clear to large numbers of people as a robbery carried out in broad daylight. What were some of these realizations?

By signing the Agreement on Trade Related Investment Measures (TRIMs), developing countries discovered that they had signed away their right to use trade policy as a means of industrialization.

By signing the Agreement on Trade-Related Intellectual Property Rights (TRIPs), countries realized that they had given high tech transnationals like Microsoft and Intel the right to monopolize innovation in the knowledge-intensive industries, and provided biotechnology firms like Novartis and Monsanto the go-signal to privatize the fruits of aeons of creative interaction between human communities and nature such as seeds, plants, and animal life.

By signing the Agreement on Agriculture (AOA), developing countries discovered that they had agreed to open up their markets while allowing the big agricultural superpowers to consolidate their system of subsidized agricultural production that was leading to the massive dumping of surpluses on those very markets, a process that was, in turn, destroying smallholder-based agriculture.

By setting up the WTO, countries and governments discovered that they had set up a legal system that enshrined the priority of free trade above every other good—above the environment, justice, equity, and community. They finally got the significance of consumer advocate Ralph Nader's warning a few years earlier that the WTO was a system of "trade *uber alles.*"

In joining the WTO, developing countries realized that they were not, in fact, joining a democratic organization. Decisions in the WTO were not made in formal plenaries, but in nontransparent backroom sessions, and where majority voting was dispensed with in favor of a process called "consensus"—a process in which a few big trading powers imposed their consensus on the majority of the member countries.

The Seattle ministerial brought together protesters from all over the world focusing on a wide variety of issues. Some of their stands on key issues, such as the incorporation of labor standards into the WTO, were sometimes contradictory, it is true. But most of them, whether they were in the streets or they were in meeting halls, were united by one thing: their opposition to the expansion of a system that promoted corporate-led globalization at the expense of justice, community, national sovereignty, cultural diversity, and ecological sustainability.

Seattle was a debacle created by corporate overreach, which is quite similar to Paul Kennedy's concept of "imperial over-stretch" that is said to be the central factor in the unraveling of empires.7 The collapse of the ministerial from the pressure of these multiple sources of opposition underlined the truth in Ralph Nader's prescient remark made four years earlier, that the creation of global trade pacts like the WTO was likely to be "the greatest blunder in the history of the modern global corporation." Previously corporations operated within a more or less "private penumbra" making it difficult to effectively crystallize opposition. Nader argued that "now that the global corporate strategic plan is out in print...gives us an opportunity."8

Truth is eternal, but it only makes a difference in human lives when it becomes power. In Seattle, truth was joined to the power of the people and became fact. Suddenly, facts that had previously been ignored or belittled were acknowledged even by the powers-that-be whose brazen confidence had been shaken. That the supreme institution of globalization was fundamentally undemocratic was recognized even by representatives of its most stout defenders: the United States and the United Kingdom.

Listen to US trade representative Charlene Barshfsky after the revolt of the representatives of developing countries that helped bring down the ministerial: "The process...was a rather exclusionary one," she admitted. "All meetings were held between 20 and 30 key countries...And that meant 100 countries, 100, were never in the room...[T]his led to an extraordinarily bad feeling that they were left out of the process and that the results...had been dictated to them by the 25 or 30 privileged countries who were in the room."9

Listen to Stephen Byers, the UK secretary for trade and industry, after the Seattle shock: "WTO will not be able to continue in its present form. There has to be fundamental and radical change in order for it to meet the needs and aspirations of all 134 of its members."10

GLOBALIZATION UNRAVELS IV:
MELTZER TORPEDOES THE BANK

The Asian financial crisis triggered the IMF's crisis of legitimacy. The Seattle ministerial collapse brought the WTO to a standstill. However, under Australian-turned-American Jim Wolfensohn's command, the World Bank seemed likely to escape the massive damage sustained by its sister institutions. But the torpedo in the form of the famous Meltzer Commission found its mark in February of 2000.

Formed as one of the conditions for the US Congress' voting for an increase of its quota in the IMF in 1998, the Commission was a bipartisan body set up to probe the record of the Bank and Fund, with the end in view of coming up with recommendations for the reform of the two institutions. Exhaustively examining documents and interviewing all kinds of experts, the Commission came to the devastating conclusion that with most of its resources going to the better off countries of the developing world and with the astounding 65–70 percent failure rate of its projects in the poorest countries, the World Bank was irrelevant to the achievement of its avowed mission of global poverty alleviation. And what to do with the Bank? The Commission urged that most of the Bank's lending activities be devolved to regional developing banks. It does not take much for readers of the report to realize that, as one of the Commission's members revealed, it "essentially wants to abolish the International Monetary Fund and the World Bank," a goal that had "significant pockets of support ... in our Congress."[11]

Much to the chagrin of Wolfensohn, few people came to the defense of the Bank. It was in a state of shock that the Bank held its joint spring meeting with the IMF in a Washington, DC that was shut down by some 40,000 protestors. The spirit of demoralization that gripped the Bank was conveyed in Wolfensohn's missive to Bank staffers before the meeting that "the next week will be a trying time for most of us."[12] That the April 2000 meeting of the Bretton Woods twins could take place only under heavy police protection, with the use of a system of decoys to breach protesters' lines in order to bring apprehensive delegates to the fortified bunkers at Pennsylvania and

19th NW in central DC, spoke volumes about the tattered legitimacy of the two institutions.

THE DAVOS PROCESS I: RE-LEGITIMIZING GLOBALIZATION

Why do I keep coming back to the question of legitimacy? Because, as the great Italian thinker Antonio Gramsci pointed out, when legitimacy has vanished and is not regained, it is only a matter of time before the structure collapses, no matter how seemingly solid it is. Many of the key advocates of globalization realized this in the wake of the joint crisis of the WTO and the Bretton Woods twins. They knew that the strategy of denial these three institutions deployed in the past would no longer work, and the aggressive approach of pro-globalization firebrands like Martin Wolf of *The Financial Times,* who accused NGOs of ignorance and being an "uncivil society," was likely to be counterproductive.

To the more sober-minded among the pro-globalization forces, the first thing to do was to recognize the facts. Fact number one, according to the influential free trader C. Fred Bergsten, head of Washington's Institute of International Economics, was that "the anti-globalization forces are now in the ascendancy."[13] And fact number two was that central to the response to these forces "has to be an honest recognition and admission that there are costs and losers," that "globalization does increase income and social disparities within countries" and "leave some countries and some groups behind."[14]

Here is where the Davos process—of which the current exercise of the World Economic Forum (WEF) is a part—has proven to be central to the project of re-legitimizing globalization. Davos, high up in the Swiss Alps, is not the center of a global capitalist conspiracy to divide up the world. Davos is where the global elite meets under the umbrella of the WEF to iron out a rough consensus on how to ideologically confront and defuse the challenges to the system. Meeting shortly after what many regarded as the cataclysm in Seattle, the Davos crew in January 2000 composed the politically correct line. Repeated like a mantra by personalities like Bill Clinton, Tony Blair, Bill Gates, Nike CEO Phil Knight, and WEF guru Klaus Schwab, the chorus went this way: "Globalization is the wave of the future. But globalization is leaving the majority behind. Those voices spoke out in Seattle. It's time to bring the fruits of globalization and free trade to the many."

It was the British prime minister Tony Blair who best articulated the vision and rhetoric of "compassionate globalization." Blair said: "Alongside the advance of global markets and technologies, we are seeing a new search for community, locally, nationally, and globally that is a response to change and insecurity, but also reflects the best of our nature and enduring values. With it is coming a new political agenda—one that is founded on mutual responsibility—both within nations and across the world."[15]

He continued: "We have the chance in this century to achieve an open world, an open economy, and an open economy with unprecedented opportunities for people and business. But we will succeed only if that open society and economy is underpinned by a strong ethos of mutual responsibility—by social inclusion within nations, and by a common commitment internationally to help those affected by genocide, debt, and environment."[16]

"I call it a third way," Blair declared with passion. "It provides a new alternative in politics—on the center and center-left, but on new terms. Supporting wealth creation. Tackling vested interests. Using market mechanisms. But always staying true to clear values—social justice, democracy, cooperation.... From Europe to North America, Brazil to New Zealand, two great strands of progressive thought are coming together. The liberal commitment to individual freedom in the market economy, and the social democratic commitment to social justice through the action of government, are being combined."[17]

One thing the British public has finally realized about Mr. Blair is that with him, there is a huge gap between rhetoric and substance. What actually does "globalization with a conscience" or the "third way" or "globalization with compassion" have to offer? To find out, one must turn from Blair to Bergsten, who, to his credit, dispenses with the soaring rhetoric and admits that the program is actually a system of "transitional safety nets...to help the adjustment to dislocation" and "enable people to take advantage of the phenomenon [of globalization] and roll with it rather than oppose it."[18] Instead of being run over by the globalization express, people will be asked to quietly and peacefully roll over and adjust to the constant and unpredictable change wrought by the TNC's search for profitability.

THE DAVOS PROCESS II:
CO-OPTING THE UNITED NATIONS

As important as the rhetoric in the Davos response is the process of bringing people on to the bandwagon. This would be achieved through dialogue, consultation, and the formation of "partnerships" between TNCs, governments, the United Nations, and civil society organizations.

The UN was a piece of cake. Discussions with the secretary general Kofi Annan produced the "Global Compact" that has become the centerpiece of the United Nations' millennial celebrations. Signed by 44 TNCs, the Compact has been promoted by Annan as a major step forward for it supposedly commits its signatories to respect human, labor, and environmental rights and provide positive examples of such behavior. On the other hand, to many NGOs the Global Compact is turning out to be one of the UN's biggest blunders for the following reasons:

> Despite a Compact provision that membership in the Compact will not be given to business entities complicit in human rights violations, the founding membership includes the worst corporate transgressors of human rights, environmental rights, and labor rights like Nike, Rio Tinto, Shell, Novartis, and BP Amoco.

> The Compact will provide a great public relations venue for these corporations to promote a clean image very different from the reality; compliance with the Compact will be self-monitored and no sanctions exist for violating the Compact's principles.

> The Corporations will be able to use the UN logo as a seal of corporate responsibility, thus appropriating the UN's image of international civil service "not only for short-term profit but also for the long-term business goal of positive brand image."[19]

THE DAVOS PROCESS III: MANAGING CIVIL SOCIETY

As for civil society organizations, they were not as naive as Annan and the UN, and neutralizing them demanded more sophisticated measures. As a first step, one had to divide their ranks by publicly defining some as "reasonable NGOs" that were interested in a "serious debate" about the problems of globalization, and others as "unreasonable NGOs" whose agenda was to "close down discussion."[20] Then towards those identified as "reasonable," one put into motion what one might call a strategy of "disarmament by dialogue," designed to integrate them into a "working partnership" for reform.

Here the model was the "NGO Committee on the World Bank" and other joint World Bank-NGO bodies set up by Wolfensohn and his lieutenants in the mid-1990s. While the NGOs that joined these bodies may have done so with the best of intentions, Wolfensohn knew that their membership in itself already helped to legitimize the Bank, and that over time these NGOs would develop a stake in maintaining the formal relationship with the Bank. Not only was Wolfensohn able to split the Washington NGO community, but he was able to harness the energies of a number of NGOs—many of them unwittingly—to project the image of a Bank that was serious about reforming itself and reorienting its approach to eliminating poverty before the Meltzer Commission was able to expose the hollowness of the Bank's claims.

Wolfensohn 's neutralization of a significant section of the Washington NGO community in the mid-1990s should serve as a warning to civil society of the mettle of the forces it is up against. The stakes are great, and how civil society responds at this historical moment to the aggressive courtship being mounted will make the difference in the future of the globalization project. Developments are so fluid in the correlation of forces in the struggle between the pro-globalization and anti-globalization camps that strategies that might have been realistic and appropriate pre-Seattle, when the multilateral institutions had more solidity and legitimacy, are timid and inappropriate if not counterproductive, now that the multilateral agencies are in a profound crisis of legitimacy. Let me be specific:

Will NGOs breathe life into a WTO process that is at standstill by pushing for the incorporation of labor and environmental clauses into the WTO agreements, instead of reducing the power and authority of this instrument of corporate rule by doing all in their power to prevent another trade round from ever taking place?

Will they throw a life saver to the Bretton Woods institutions by participating in the civil society-World Bank-IMF consultations that are to be the central element of the "comprehensive development framework" that Wolfensohn and the IMF leadership sees as the key to the re-legitimization of the Bretton Woods twins?

Will they allow themselves to be sucked into the Davos process of "reasonable dialogue" and "frank consultation" when the other side sees dialogue and consultation mainly as the first step to the disarmament of the other side?

REFORM OR DISEMPOWERMENT?

Our tactics will depend not only on the balance of forces but will turn even more fundamentally on our answer to the question: Should we seek to transform or to disable the main institutions of corporate-led globalization?

Institutions should be saved and reformed if their functioning, while defective, nevertheless can be reoriented to promote the interests of society and the environment. They should be abolished if they have become fundamentally dysfunctional. Can we really say that the IMF can be reformed to bring about global financial stability, the World Bank to reduce poverty, and the WTO to bring about fair trade? Are they not, in fact, imprisoned within paradigms and structures that create outcomes that contradict these objectives? Can we truly say that these institutions can be reengineered to handle the multiple problems that have been thrown up by the process of corporate-led globalization?

The dominant institutions of globalization can no longer handle the multiple problems thrown up by the process of corporate-led globalization. Instead of trying to reform the multilateral institutions, it would be more *realistic* and "cost-effective," to use a horrid neo-liberal term, to move to disempower, if not abolish them, and create totally new institutions that do not have the baggage of illegitimacy, institutional failure, and Jurassic mindsets that are attached to the IMF, World Bank, and WTO?

DISABLING THE CORPORATION

I would contend that the focus of our efforts these days is not to try to reform the multilateral agencies, but to deepen the crisis of legitimacy of the whole system. Gramsci once described the bureaucracy as but an "outer trench behind which lay a powerful system of fortresses and earthworks." We must no longer think simply in terms of neutralizing the multilateral agencies that form the outer trenches of the system, but of disabling the transnational corporations that are fortresses and the earthworks that constitute the core of the global economic system. I am talking about disabling not just the WTO, the IMF, and the World Bank but the transnational corporation itself. And I am not talking about a process of "re-regulating" the TNCs, but of eventually disabling or dismantling them as fundamental hazards to people, society, the environment, to everything we hold dear.

Is this off the wall? Only if we think that the shocking irresponsibility and secrecy with which the Monsantos and Novartises have foisted biotechnology on us is a departure from the corporate norm. Only if we also see as deviations from the normal Shell's systematic devastation of Ogoniland in Nigeria, the Seven Sisters' conspiracy to prevent the development of renewable energy sources in order to keep us slaves to a petroleum civilization, Rio Tinto and the mining giants' practice of poisoning rivers and communities, and Mitsubishi's recently exposed 20-year-cover up of a myriad of product-safety violations to prevent a recall that would cut into profitability. Only if we think that it is acceptable business practice and ethics to pull up stakes, lay off people, and destroy long-established communities in order to pursue ever cheaper labor around the globe—a process that most TNCs now engage in.

These are not departures from normal corporate behavior. They are *normal* corporate behavior. And corporate crimes against people and the environment has become a way of life because, as the British philosopher John Gray tells us, "Global market competition and technological innovation have interacted to give us an anarchic world economy." To such a world of anarchy, scarcity, and conflict created by global *laissez-faire,* Gray continues, "Thomas Hobbes and Thomas Malthus are better guides than Adam Smith or Friedrich von Hayek, with their Utopian vision of a humanity united by 'the benevolent harmonies of competition.'"[21] Smith's world of peacefully competing enterprises has, in the age of the TNC, degenerated into Hobbes' "war of all against all."

Gray goes on to say that "as it is presently organized, global capitalism is supremely ill-suited to cope with the risks of geo-political conflict that are endemic in a world of worsening scarcities. Yet a regulatory framework for coexistence and cooperation among the world's diverse economies figures on no historical or political agenda."[22] Recent events underline his point. When the ice cap on the North Pole is melting at an unprecedented rate and the ozone layer above the South Pole has declined by 30 percent, owing precisely to the dynamics of this corporate civilization's insatiable desire for growth and profits, the need for cooperation among peoples and societies is more stark than ever. We must do better than entrust production and exchange to entities that systematically and fundamentally work to erode solidarity, discourage cooperation, oppose regulation except profit-enhancing and monopoly-creating regulation, all in the name of the market and efficiency.

It is said that in the age of globalization, nation states have become obsolete forms of social organization. I disagree. It is the corporation that has become obsolete. It is the corporation that serves as a fetter to humanity's movement to new and necessary social arrangements to achieve the most quintessentially human values of justice, equity, democracy, and to achieve a new equilibrium between our species and the rest of the planet. Disabling, disempowering, or dismantling the transnational corporation should be high on our agenda as a strategic end. And when we say this, we do not equate the TNC with private enterprise, for there are benevolent and malevolent expressions of private enterprise. We must seek to disable or eliminate the malevolent ones, like the TNC.[23]

THE STRUGGLE FOR THE FUTURE I: DE-GLOBALIZATION

It is often said that we must not only know what we are against but what we are for. I agree—though it is very important to know very clearly what we want to terminate so we do not end up unwittingly fortifying it so that, like a WTO energized with social and environmental clauses, it is given a new lease on life.

Let me end, therefore, by giving you my idea of an alternative. It is, however, one that has been formulated for a Third World, and specifically Southeast Asian, context. Let me call this alternative route to the future "de-globalization."

What is de-globalization?

I am not talking about withdrawing from the international economy. I am speaking about reorienting our economies from production for export to production for the local market; about drawing most of our financial resources for development from within rather than becoming dependent on foreign investment and foreign financial markets; about carrying out the long-postponed measures of income redistribution and land redistribution to create a vibrant internal market that would be the anchor of the economy; about de-emphasizing growth and maximizing equity in order to radically reduce environmental dis-equilibrium; about not leaving strategic economic decisions to the market but making them subject to democratic choice; about subjecting the private sector and the state to constant monitoring by civil society; about creating a new production and exchange complex that includes community cooperatives, private enterprises, and state enterprises, and excludes TNCs; about enshrining the principle of subsidiaries in economic life by encouraging production of goods to take place at the community and national level if it can be done so at reasonable cost in order to preserve community.

We are talking about a strategy that consciously subordinates the logic of the market, the pursuit of cost efficiency to the values of security, equity, and social solidarity. We are speaking about re-embedding the economy in society, rather than have society driven by the economy.

THE STRUGGLE FOR THE FUTURE II: A PLURAL WORLD

De-globalization, or the re-empowerment of the local and national, can only succeed if it takes place within an alternative system of global economic governance. What are the contours of such a world economic order? The answer is contained in our critique of the Bretton Woods *cum* WTO system as a monolithic system of universal rules imposed by highly centralized institutions to further the interests of corporations—in particular, US corporations. To try to supplant this with another centralized global system of rules and institutions, though these may be premised on different principles, is likely to reproduce the same Jurassic trap that ensnared organizations as different as IBM, the IMF, and the Soviet state, and this is the inability to tolerate and profit from diversity.

Today's need is not another centralized global institution but the de-concentration and decentralization of institutional power and the creation of a pluralistic system of institutions and organizations interacting with one another, guided by broad and flexible agreements and understandings. We are not talking about something completely new. It was under such a more pluralistic system of global economic governance, where hegemonic power was still far from institutionalized in a set of all-encompassing and powerful multilateral organizations and institutions, that a number of Latin American and Asian countries were able to achieve a modicum of industrial development in the period from 1950 to 1970. It was under such a pluralistic system, under a General Agreement on Tariffs and Trade (GATT) that was limited in its power, flexible, and more sympathetic to the special status of developing countries, that the East and Southeast Asian countries were able to become newly industrializing countries through activist state trade and industrial policies that departed significantly from the free market biases enshrined in the WTO.

Of course, economic relations among countries prior to the attempt to institutionalize one global free market system beginning in the early 1980s were neither ideal, nor were the Third World economies. But these conditions and structures underline the fact that the alternative to an economic *Pax Romana* built around the World Bank-IMF-WTO system is not a Hobbesian state of nature. The reality of international relations in a world marked by a multiplicity of international and regional institutions that check one another is a far cry from the propaganda image of a "nasty" and "brutish" world. Of course, the threat of unilateral action by the powerful is ever present in such a system, but it is one that even the most powerful hesitate to take for fear of its consequences on their legitimacy as well as the reaction it would provoke in the form of opposing coalitions.

More space, more flexibility, more compromise—these should be the goals of the Southern agenda and the civil society effort to build a new system of global economic governance. It is in such a more fluid, less structured, more pluralistic world, with multiple checks and balances, that the nations and communities of the South—and the North—will be able to carve out the space to develop based on their values, their rhythms, and the strategies of their choice.

Let me quote John Gray one last time. "It is legitimate and indeed imperative that we seek a form of rootedness which is sheltered from overthrow by technologies and market processes which in achieving a global reach that is dis-embedded from any community or culture, cannot avoid desolating the earth's human settlements and its non-human environments." The role of international arrangements in a world where toleration of diversity is a central principle of economic organization would be "to express and protect local and national cultures by embodying and sheltering their distinctive practices."[24]

Let us put an end to this arrogant globalist project of making the world a synthetic unity of individual atoms shorn of culture and community. Instead, let us herald an internationalism that is built on, tolerates, respects, and enhances the diversity of human communities and the diversity of life.

NOTES

1. Bergsten, C. Fred. "The backlash against globalization," speech delivered at the 2000 meeting of the Trilateral Commission, Tokyo, April 2000 (downloaded from Internet).

2. Cited in Giovanni Andrea Cornia, "Inequality and poverty trends in the era of liberalization and globalization," paper delivered at the United Nations millennium conference, Tokyo, January 19–20, 2000.

3. Ibid. See also "Number of world's poor unchanged in the 1990s," *Reuters,* August 3, 2000.

4. "Inequality and poverty trends."

5. Quoted in Associated Press, reproduced in *Business World,* November 15, 1999.

6. Op-ed column, *Washington Post,* reproduced in *Today* (Manila), November 15, 1999.

7. Kennedy, Paul. *The Rise and Fall of the Great Powers* (New York: Vintage Books, 1989).

8. Nader, Ralph. Speech at International Forum on Globalization teach-in on "The social, ecological, cultural, and political costs of economic globalization," Riverside Church, New York, November 10, 1995; quoted in Joshua Karliner, *The Corporate Planet* (San Francisco: Sierra Club, 1997), pg. 207.

9. Press briefing, Seattle, Washington, December 2, 1999.

10. Quoted in "Deadline set for WTO reforms," *Guardian News Service,* January 10, 2000.

11. "The backlash against globalization."

12. Wolfensohn, James. Memo on "Disruptions at spring meetings," World Bank, Washington, DC, April 13, 2000.

13. "The backlash against globalization."

14. Ibid.

15. Prime Minister Anthony Blair, speech at the World Economic Forum, Davos, Switzerland, January 28, 2000.

16. Ibid.

17. Ibid.

18. "The backlash against globalization."

19. Letter of International Coalition against Global Compact, July 26, 2000.

20. The Wolfensohn memo, above, is an interesting exercise in this branding or categorizing of NGOs.

21. Gray, John. *False Dawn* (New York: New Press, 1998), pg. 207.

22. Ibid.

23. For excellent recent critiques of the corporation, see David Korten, *When Corporations Rule the World* (San Francisco: Kumarian Press/Beret-Koehler, 1995); Joshua Karliner, *The Corporate Planet* (San Francisco: Sierra Club Books, 1997); and Richard Barnet and John Cavanagh, *Global Dreams: Imperial Corporations and the New World Order* (New York: Simon and Shuster, 1994).

24. Gray, John. *Enlightenment's Wake* (London, UK: Routledge, 1995), pg. 181.

17

GLOBAL CIVIL SOCIETY:
PROBLEMS AND PROMISES

Hangyoreh Shimun (Seoul), July 2000

There is much talk about the emergence of non-governmental organizations (NGOs) or civil society organizations (CSOs) as major international actors. They have elicited criticism from some quarters. Martin Wolf, the columnist of *The Financial Times,* has called them "uncivil society" and attacked them for opposing the project of globalization advanced by the World Trade Organization (WTO), World Bank, and the International Monetary Fund (IMF), saying that that their stands on various issues stem from ignorance and simplistic interpretations of a complex world.

However, more liberal quarters have acknowledged that their criticisms have some justification, for example, on the issue of the dangers posed by genetically modified organisms (GMOs). Both corporations and governments have moved to initiate "dialogue" with NGOs, often with the purpose of co-opting them into corporate or government agendas by conceding some of their criticisms while rejecting others, particularly their more fundamental critiques of the processes of corporate globalization.

When we examine the problems and promises posed by civil society organizations, the first thing to remember is that they are not invariably a progressive phenomenon. While we are familiar with CSOs that belong to the left, the right also has its CSOs, such as business associations, trade groups, and the conservative religious formations—for instance, the formidable *Opus Dei* in Catholic countries. The CSOs on the right often exert a greater influence on political and economic actors.

This influence is sometimes not noticed because it is covertly exercised through the many different networks in which members of conservative CSOs participate. In contrast, progressive CSOs or NGOs are more public and transparent, so that the press has an easier time chronicling their activities. Despite this greater visibility, the civil society organization of the right is generally much more influential than the civil society organization of the left. They are, to borrow from Gramsci, more "organic" to the class structure.

While the plurality of progressive civil society actors or NGOs is often extolled, pluralism often masks tremendous factionalism. The competition and intrigues among CSOs are just as intense and destructive as conflicts in the political and business worlds. Among NGOs in the North and the South, a source of intense competition that can quickly make allies into adversaries is funding. Nothing has proven more problematic in terms of building common fronts and common programs among CSOs and NGOs than fights over funds.

Having pointed out these negative features of the CSO scene, one now turns to the promise of progressive CSOs in the creation of a more just and equitable order at home and abroad.

First of all, CSOs are quickly emerging as a third or fourth actor in the formulation and implementation of macro-political and macro-economic decisions. In many Asian countries, real decision making power used to be monopolized by politicians, technocrats, and the business elite. That is increasingly less and less possible in the face of the mass mobilization by labor groups, environmental groups, and human and social rights groups, often working in alliances. Coordination, even of a rough sort, among a variety of CSOs, has become more pronounced after the Asian financial crisis, which exposed the corruption of the old order and the necessity of monitoring and checking the old elites.

Second, CSOs are crucial not only as checks on elites, they are also the key to the evolution of the democracy. Representative democracy has always suffered from what Rousseau saw as its tendency to develop a "corporate will" separate from the general will, thus perverting the purposes of representation. The development of the American democratic system into a plutocratic system, where Republicans and Democrats in Congress have become common subjects of corporate money, is the best example of the Rousseauian dilemma of large-scale representative democracies.

With their constant pressure on bureaucrats and parliamentarians to be accountable, CSOs are a force for more democracy. By organizing the energies of millions of citizens to impinge on the daily political scene, CSOs are a force pushing the evolution of more direct forms of democratic rule. Combined with advanced applications of information technology that allow citizens and citizens' groups to instantaneously communicate with one another, CSO activity may be the key to the emergence of direct democracy in contemporary mass societies.

Finally, CSOs are a force for effective internationalism that can check the power of politically hegemonic forces like the US government and transnational corporations. The power of states and counter-hegemonic alliances among states has been eroded by corporate-led globalization. But the combination of citizens' resistance to globalization and communications technology has created global citizens' movements that can assemble and meet the enemy at a moment's notice. The "Battle of Seattle" in December 1999 and the "Battle of Washington," in April 2000 are examples of the new trans-border activist movements.

The development of civil society, in short, presents opportunities for democracy both vertically and horizontally. It is the route to a more humane, more participatory, and more equitable future. There are, of course, major obstacles that need to be surmounted if this vision is to become a reality.

First of all, there is the North-South divide among NGOs. Many Northern NGOs are often focussed on single issues, such as the environment or human rights, and carry agendas that are filtered through the lens of these particular issues. Southern NGOs, on the other hand, are more comprehensive in their concerns. They are concerned almost equally with the environment, social equity, development, national sovereignty, and democracy. While environmental NGOs in the North are sometimes solely concerned about bringing down the level of greenhouse gas emissions, Southern NGOs want to make sure that bringing down carbon dioxide levels in the South is done in a way that does not conflict with the legitimate aspirations to development of their countries. Similarly, they are concerned that labor and environmental standards in the North do not become a mechanism of protectionism against the entry of products from the Third World.

Second, there is the question of compromising with or fundamentally opposing corporate-led globalization. For some CSOs, both in the North and the South, corporate-led globalization is inevitable; the main task is to humanize it. Some labor and environmental NGOs seek only to attach "social" or "environmental" clauses to WTO agreements. Others see the WTO as fundamentally problematic and push for abolishing or radically reducing its powers.

Third, there is the question of working with governments. Some CSOs adopt a stand of maximizing cooperation with governments so as to get governments to adopt some of their agenda. Many environmental NGOs in the North worked with the US government to ban imports of tuna and shrimp to the US if they were not caught with methods specified in US government legislation. In the South, some NGOs have strongly supported the nationalist policies of certain governments, while muting their criticisms of other aspects of their governments, like the bad record of these governments in the area of human rights and democracy. In contrast, other NGOs in both the North and the South have made it a point to limit working relationships with governments to a minimum, while maximizing their critical stance.

Pluralism will continue to mark global civil society. This is its source of strength. But it can also be a source of fatal weakness, one which will prevent the emergence of a working unity of CSOs globally. The challenge is how to ensure that differences in strategies and tactics do not become the sources of permanent and bitter divisions. The challenge is how to keep dialogue going so that differences on some issues do not prevent coming together in solidarity on other issues.

Corporations, governments, and multilateral organizations that carry the pro-corporate globalization project are waiting to seize on divisions among CSOs and NGOs. With the deepening crisis of legitimacy of the globalization project after Seattle and the massive protests of 2000, "dialoguing with civil society" has become a key feature of the global establishment's effort to regain the initiative. It is important to make sure that even as we disagree among ourselves, we do not play into their hands.

18

2000: THE YEAR OF GLOBAL PROTEST AGAINST GLOBALIZATION

Yes! Magazine, Spring 2001

The year 2000 will probably go down as one of those defining moments in the history of the world economy, like 1929. The structures of global capitalism appear to be solid, with many in the global elite in Washington, Europe, and Asia congratulating themselves for containing the Asian financial crisis and trying to exude confidence about launching a new round of trade negotiations under the World Trade Organization (WTO). What we witnessed, nevertheless, was a dramatic series of events that might lead to that time when, as the poet says, "all that is solid melts into this air."

For global capitalism, the year began a month early, on November 30–December 1, 1999, when the third ministerial of the WTO collapsed in Seattle. It ended in 2000 with an equally momentous event: the unraveling of the Climate Change Conference in the Hague.

SEATTLE: THE TURNING POINT

The definitive history of the Seattle events still needs to be written, but they cannot be understood without the explosive interaction between the militant and unrelenting protests of some 50,000 people in the streets and the rebellion of developing country delegates inside the Seattle Convention Center. Much has been said about the different motivations of the street protestors and the Third World delegates, and the differences within the ranks of the demonstrators themselves. True, some of their stands on key issues, such as the incorporation of labor standards into the WTO, were sometimes contradictory. But most of them were united by one thing: their opposition to the expansion of a system that promoted corporate-led globalization at the expense of social goals like justice, community, national sovereignty, cultural diversity, and ecological sustainability.

Still, the Seattle debacle would not have occurred without another development: the inability of the European Union and the United States to bridge their differences on key issues, like what rules should govern their monopolistic competition for global agricultural markets. And the fallout from Seattle might have been less massive were it not for the brutal behavior of the Seattle police. The assaults on largely peaceful demonstrators by police in their Darth Vader-like uniforms in full view of television cameras made Seattle's mean streets the grand symbol of the crisis of globalization.

When it was established in 1995, the WTO was regarded as the crown jewel of capitalism in the era of globalization. However, with the Seattle collapse realities that had been ignored or belittled were acknowledged even by the powers-that-be, whose brazen confidence in their own creation had been shaken. That the supreme institution of globalization was fundamentally undemocratic and its processes non-transparent was recognized even by representatives of some of its stout defenders pre-Seattle. The global elite's crisis of confidence was evident in the words of Stephen Byers, the UK secretary for Trade and Industry: "The WTO will not be able to continue in its present form. There has to be fundamental and radical change in order for it to meet the needs and aspirations of all 134 of its members."

Seattle was no one-off event. Bitter criticism of the WTO and the Bretton Woods institutions was a not-so-subtle undercurrent of the tenth assembly of the UN Conference on Trade and Development (UNCTAD), held in Bangkok in February. What brought an otherwise uneventful international meeting to the front pages of the world press was the pie-splattered face of outgoing IMF managing director Michel Camdessus, who was on the receiving end of a perfect pitch from anti-IMF activist Robert Naiman.

FROM WASHINGTON TO MELBOURNE

Naiman's act helped set the stage for the first really big post-Seattle confrontation between pro-globalization and anti-globalization forces:

the spring meeting of the IMF and the World Bank in Washington, DC. Some 30,000 protestors descended on America's capital in the middle of April and found a large section of the northwest part of the city walled off by some 10,000 policemen. For four rain-swept days, the protestors tried unsuccessfully to breach the police phalanx to reach the IMF-World Bank complex at 19th and H Streets, NW, resulting in hundreds of arrests. The police claimed victory. But it was a case of the protestors losing the battle but winning the war. Just the mere fact that 30,000 people had come to protest the Bretton Woods twins was already a massive victory according to organizers who said that the most one could mobilize in previous protests were a few hundred people.

From Washington the struggle shifted to Chiang Mai in the highlands of Northern Thailand, where the Asian Development Bank (ADB), a multilateral body notorious for funding gargantuan projects that disrupted communities and destabilized the environment, held its thirty-third annual meeting in early May. So shaken was the ADB leadership by the sight of some 2,000 people asking it to leave town that soon after the conference, ADB president Tadao Chino established an vice presidential level "NGO task force" to deal with the civil society. Fearful of even more massive protests in 2001, the ADB also shifted the site of its next annual meeting from Seattle to Honolulu in the belief that latter would be a secure site.

Chiang Mai had significance beyond the ADB, however. With a majority of protestors being poor Thai farmers, the Chiang Mai demonstrations showed that the anti-globalization mass base went beyond middle class youth and organized labor in the advanced countries. Equally important, key organizers of the Chiang Mai actions, like Bamrung Kayotha, one of the leaders of the Forum of the Poor, had participated in the Seattle protest. They saw Chiang Mai not as a discrete event, but as a link in the chain of international protests against globalization.

The battle lines were next drawn Down Under to Melbourne, Australia, in early September. The glittering Crown Casino by Melbourne's upscale waterfront had been chosen as the site of the Asia-Pacific Summit of the World Economic Forum (Davos Forum), which had become a leading force in the effort to put a more liberal face to globalization. The casino, many activists felt, was a fitting symbol of finance-driven globalization. In nearly three days of street battles, some 5,000 protestors were at times able to seal off key entrances to the casino, forcing the organizers to bring some delegates in and out by helicopter, again in full view of television. And again, as in Seattle, rough handling of demonstrators by the police, many of them mounted, magnified the global controversy over the event.

THE BATTLE OF PRAGUE

Later that month came Europe's turn. Some 10,000 people came from all over the continent to Prague, prepared to engage in an apocalyptic confrontation with the Bretton Woods institutions during the latter's annual meeting in that beautiful Eastern European city in the most beautiful of seasons. Prague lived up to its billing. With demonstrations and street battles trapping delegates at the Congress Center or swirling around them as they tried to make their way back to their quarters in Prague's famed Old Town, the agenda of the meeting was, as one World Bank official put it, "effectively seized" by the anti-globalization protestors. When a large number of delegates refused to go to the Congress Center in the next two days, the convention had to be abruptly concluded a day before its scheduled ending.

As important as the protests in Prague was the debate held on September 23 at Prague Castle between representatives of civil society organizations (CSOs) and the leadership of the World Bank and the IMF, an event orchestrated by Czech President Vaclav Havel. Instead of bridging the gap between the two sides, the debate widened it. In response to concrete demands, World Bank president James Wolfensohn and IMF managing director Horst Koehler were not prepared to go beyond platitudes and generalities, as if worried that they might overstep the bounds set by their Group of Seven (G-7) masters. George Soros, who defended the Bank and the Fund at the debate, said it all when he admitted that Wolfensohn and Koehler had "performed terribly" and had blown their most important encounter with the CSOs.

After Seattle, much talk about reforming the global economic system to bring on board those "being left behind" by globalization was emitted by establishment personalities like Bill Gates, Bill Clinton, Tony Blair, Kofi Annan, and Nike CEO Phil Knight. The Davos Forum, in fact, placed the question of reform at the top of the agenda of the meetings it held for the global elite.

More than a year after the Seattle ministerial, however, there has been precious little in the way of concrete action. The most prominent reform initiative, the Group of Seven's plan to lessen the servicing of the external debt of the 41 highly indebted poor countries (HIPC) has actually delivered a debt reduction of only $1 billion since it began in 1996—or a reduction of their debt servicing by only three percent in the past four and a half years. Talk about reforming the decision-making process at the WTO has vanished, with the director general Mike Moore saying that the non-transparent, undemocratic "consensus/green room" system that triggered the developing country revolt in Seattle is "non-negotiable."

When it comes to the question of the international financial architecture, serious discussion of controls on speculative capital like the Tobin tax has been avoided. An unreformed IMF continues to be at the center of the "firefighting system." A preemptive, pre-crisis credit line at the Fund (which no country wants to avail of) and a toothless Financial Stability Forum—where there is little developing country participation—appear to be the only "innovations" to emerge from the Asian, Russian, and Brazilian financial crises of the last three years.

At the IMF and the World Bank there is no longer any talk about diluting the voting shares of the US and European Union in favor of greater voting power for the Third World countries, much less of doing away with the feudal practices of always having a European head the Fund and an American to lead the Bank. The much-vaunted consultative process in the preparation of "poverty reduction strategy papers" (PRSP) by governments applying for loans is turning out to be nothing more than an effort to add a veneer of public participation to the same technocratic process that is churning out development strategies with the same old emphasis on growth via deregulation and liberalization of trade, with maybe a safety net here and there. At the Bank, strong resistance to innovations that would put the priority on social reforms led to the resignation of two reformers: Joseph Stiglitz, the chief economist, and Ravi Kanbur, the head of the World Development Report task force.

DEBACLE IN THE HAGUE

The protests throughout the year 2000 had a strong anti-transnational corporation (TNC) strain, with the World bank, IMF, and WTO regarded as servitors of the corporations. A strong distrust of TNCs had developed even in the United States, where over 70 percent of the people surveyed felt corporations had too much power over their lives. Distrust and opposition to TNCs could only be deepened by the collapse in December 2000 of the Hague conference on climate change, owing to American industry's unwillingness to significantly cut back on its emission of greenhouse gases. At a time that most indicators are showing an acceleration of global warming trends, Washington's move reinforced the conviction of the anti-globalization movement that the US economic elite is determined to grab all the benefits of globalization while sticking the costs on the rest of the world.

Assessing the post-Seattle situation, C. Fred Bergsten, a prominent advocate of globalization, told a Trilateral Commission meeting in Tokyo in April 2000 that "the anti-globalization forces are now in the ascendancy." That description is even more accurate now. With the global elite itself having lost confidence in them, a classic crisis of legitimacy has overtaken the key institutions of global economic governance. If legitimacy is not regained, it is only a matter of time before structures collapse, no matter how seemingly solid they are, since legitimacy is the foundation of power structures. The process of de-legitimizing is difficult to reverse once it takes hold. The "withdrawal of consent" is likely to spread to the core institutions and practices of global capitalism, including the transnational corporation.

2001 promises to be an equally trying time for the globalist project.

19

WASHINGTON'S POLITICAL TRANSITION
THREATENS BRETTON WOODS TWINS

Focus on Trade, January 2001

The coming to power of the republicans in Washington, DC spells deep trouble for the International Monetary Fund (IMF) and the World Bank. The Bretton Woods institutions lost their liberal internationalist protectors like US Treasury secretary Larry Summers who believed in using the Fund and the Bank as central instruments to achieve US foreign economic policy objectives.

Coming in with President George Bush will be a set of conservative analysts and technocrats representing the thinking of the US Congress' Advisory Commission on International Financial Institutions. Also known as the "Meltzer Commission," after its chairman, conservative academic Alan Meltzer, the body issued a report in 2000 condemning the IMF for promoting global macroeconomic instability and portrayed the World Bank as irrelevant to the mission of promoting development and reducing global poverty.

Confronted with four years of republican hegemony, James Wolfensohn, president of the World Bank, is rumored to be contemplating resigning before the end of his second term in office.

THE IMF'S STALINGRAD

The Washington political transition catches the IMF and the World Bank at their most vulnerable state in years. If any event may be said to have contributed to undermining the Fund, it was the Asian financial crisis, whose legacy of collapsed financial systems, bankrupt corporations, and rising poverty and inequality continue to plague the region. One can say that the Asian financial crisis was the Stalingrad of the IMF. Bearing in mind the limits of metaphor, the IMF during the

Asian financial crisis acted like the German Sixth Army, making one wrong move after another on the way to disaster.

It was the IMF that helped trigger the massive flow of volatile speculative capital into the region by pressing the Asian governments for capital account liberalization prior to the crisis, egged on itself by the US Treasury Department. It was the IMF that confidently moved in after the panicky flight of speculative capital began, with a tight fiscal and monetary formula that, by drastically reducing government's capacity to act as counter-force to the downturn in private sector activity, converted the financial crisis into an economic collapse.

It was the IMF that assembled the high profile multibillion-dollar rescue packages that were meant to rescue foreign creditors even as local banks, finance companies, and corporations were told to bite the bullet by accepting bankruptcy. It was the IMF that imposed on the fallen economies a program of radical deregulation and financial and trade liberalization that was essentially Washington's pre-crisis agenda the tigers had been able to frustrate during their days of prosperity. And it was the IMF that, at the urging of the US Treasury Department, killed the proposal for an Asian Monetary Fund (AMF), which would have pooled together the reserves from the more financially sound economies to serve as a fund from which those subjected to speculative attack could draw to shore up their currencies. Among other things, this move contributed to widening the divergence in the policies toward the Asian region of the United States and Japan, the AMF's prime backer.

As the stricken economies registered negative growth rates and record unemployment rates in 1998, and over one million people in Thailand and 21 million in Indonesia fell below the poverty line, the IMF joined corrupt governments, banks, and George Soros as the villains of the piece in the view of millions of newly impoverished Koreans, Thais, and Indonesians.

But equally as consequential for its future as an institution was the fact that the IMF's actions brought the long simmering conflict over the role of the Fund within the US elite to a boil. The American right denounced the Fund for promoting moral hazard, with some personalities like former US Treasury secretary George Shultz calling for its abolition, while orthodox liberals like Jeffrey Sachs and Jagdish Bhagwati attacked the Fund for being a threat to global macroeconomic stability and prosperity. Late in 1998, a conservative-liberal alliance in the US Congress came within a hair's breath of denying the IMF a $14.5 billion increase in the US quota. The quota increase was salvaged, with arm-twisting on the part of the Clinton administration, but it was clear that the long-time internationalist consensus that had propped up the Fund for over five decades was unraveling.

ANOTHER DISASTER

The Fund's performance during the Asian financial crisis led to a widespread reappraisal of the Fund's role in the Third World in the 1980s and early 1990s, when structural adjustment programs were imposed over 90 developing and transition economies.

Judged by the extremely narrow criterion of promoting growth, structural adjustment programs were a failure, with a number of studies showing that adjustment had brought about a negative effect on growth. After over 15 years, it was hard to point to more than a handful as having brought about stable growth, among them the very questionable case of Pinochet's Chile. What structural adjustment had done instead was to institutionalize stagnation in Africa, Latin America, and other parts of the Third World. A study by the Center for Economic and Policy Research shows that 77 percent of countries for which data is available saw their per capita rate of growth fall significantly from the period 1960–1980 to the period 1980–2000, the structural adjustment period. In Latin America, income expanded by 75 percent during the 1960s and 1970s, when the region's economies were relatively closed, but grew by only six percent in the past two decades.

Structural adjustment was a blight on the Third World. Broadening the criteria of success to include reduction of inequality and bringing down poverty, the results were unquestionable. A study by Mattias Lundberg and Lyn Squire of the World Bank summed it up thus: "the poor are far more vulnerable to shifts in relative international prices, and this vulnerability is magnified by the country's openness to trade...(A)t least in the short term, globalization appears to increase both poverty and inequality."

As a consequence of greater public scrutiny following its disastrous policies in East Asia, the Fund could no longer pretend that adjustment had not been a massive failure in Africa, Latin America, and South Asia. During the World Bank-IMF meetings in September 1999, the Fund conceded failure by renaming the extended structural adjustment facility (ESAF) the "poverty reduction and growth facility" and promised to learn from the World Bank in making the elimination of poverty the "centerpiece" of its programs. But this was too little, too late, and too incredible. Support for the IMF in Washington was down to the US treasury. So starved of legitimacy and support was the Fund at the end of the twentieth century that US Treasury Secretary Larry Summers, who in an earlier incarnation as chief economist of the World Bank had been one of the chief backers of structural adjustment, found that he could only save it by damning it.

MELTZER REPORT ON THE BANK

Since assuming office in 1996, Australian-turned-American Jim Wolfensohn, by opening up channels of communication with the non-governmental organizations (NGOs) and with the help of a well-oiled public relations machine, tried to recast the Bank's image as an institution that was not only moving away from structural adjustment but was also making poverty-elimination its central mission, promoting good governance, and supporting environmentally-sensitive lending. The best defense, in short, was to expand the agency's agenda.

The report of the Meltzer Commission found its mark in February 2000. Exhaustively examining documents and interviewing all kinds of experts, the Commission came up with a number of devastating findings that bear being pointed out: 70 percent of the Bank's non-grant lending is concentrated in 11 countries, with 145 other member countries left to scramble for the remaining 30 percent; 80 percent of the Bank's resources are devoted not to the poorest developing countries but to the better off ones that have positive credit ratings and, according to the Commission, can therefore raise their funds in international capital markets; the failure rate of bank projects is 65–70 percent in the poorest countries and 55–60 percent in all developing countries. In short, the World Bank was irrelevant to the achievement of its avowed mission of global poverty alleviation.

And what to do with the Bank? The Commission urged that most of the Bank's lending activities be devolved to the regional developing banks. It does not take much for readers of the report to realize that, as one of the Commission's members revealed, it "essentially wants to abolish the International Monetary Fund and the World bank," a goal that had significant pockets of support...in our Congress."

Much to the chagrin of Wolfensohn, few people came to the defense of the Bank. Instead, the realities of the Bank's expanded mission were exposed in the months leading up to the World Bank-IMF meeting in Prague in September 2000. The claim that the Bank was concerned about "good governance" was contradicted by the exposure of its profound involvement with the Suharto regime in Indonesia, to which it funneled over $30 billion in 30 years. According to several reports, including a World Bank internal report that came out in 1999, the Bank tolerated corruption, accorded false status to false government statistics, legitimized the dictatorship by passing it off as a model for other countries, and was complacent about the state of human rights and the monopolistic control of the economy. That this close embrace of the Suharto regime continued well into the Wolfensohn era was particularly damning.

The image of a new, environmentally sensitive Bank under Wolfensohn also evaporated in the avalanche of criticism that came after the Meltzer report. The Bank was a staunch backer of the controversial Chad-Cameroon Pipeline, which would seriously damage ecologically sensitive areas like Cameroon's Atlantic Littoral Forest. Bank management was caught violating its own rules on environment and resettlement when it tried to push through the China Western Poverty Project that would have transformed an arid ecosystem supporting minority Tibetan and Mongolian sheepherders into land for settled agriculture for people from other parts of China.

A look at the bank's loan portfolio revealed the reality behind the rhetoric: loans for the environment as a percentage of the Bank's total loan portfolio declined from 3.6 percent in fiscal year 1994 to 1.02 percent in 1998; funds allocated to environmental projects declined by 32.7 percent between 1998 and 1999; and more than half of all lending by the World bank's private sector divisions in 1998 was for environmentally harmful projects like dams, roads, and power. So marginalized was the Bank's environmental staff within the bureaucracy that Herman Daly, the distinguished ecological economist, left the Bank staff because he felt that he and other in-house environmentalists were having no impact at all on agency policy.

Confronted with a list of thoroughly documented charges from civil society groups during the now famous Prague Castle debate sponsored by Czech president Vaclav Havel during the tumultuous IMF-World Bank meeting on September 23, 2000, Wolfensohn was reduced to giving the memorable answer, "I and my colleagues feel good about going to work everyday." It was an answer that underlined the depth of the Bretton Woods system crisis of legitimacy, and was matched only by IMF managing director Horst Koehler's famous line at that same event: "I also have a heart, but I have to use my head in making decisions."

All this makes for interesting politics in the next few years. The motivation of the incoming republicans in criticizing the IMF and the World Bank lies in their belief in free market solutions to development and growth. This may not coincide with that of progressives, who see the IMF and World Bank as a tool of US hegemony. But the two sides can united behind one agenda at this point: the radical downsizing, if not dismantling, of the Bretton Woods twins.

20

WHEN DAVOS MEETS PORTO ALEGRE:
A MEMOIR

Published as "The Superrich at Davos are the Voice of the Past,"
International Herald Tribune, February 9, 2001

"Ernest Hemingway said that the rich are different from you and me. How can anyone expect the people of Davos to understand the crisis that globalization has visited on the lives of people like those of us here in Porto Alegre?" That was going to be my opening line.

When I arrived at the university studio for the televised transatlantic debate with George Soros, the financier, and other representatives of the global elite gathered in Davos, Switzerland, a visibly shaken Florain Rochat of the Swiss delegation was waiting for me. Swiss are known for being impassive, but Florain was visibly shaken. "They are arresting protestors in Davos and other places in Switzerland," he told me. "They're killing democracy in our country. Our friends there are asking you to support them in calling for the shutting down of the World Economic Forum."

That request drove out any lingering desire to be "nice" in the coming exchange, which had been billed by its producers as a "dialogue between Davos and Porto Alegre." The ambitious million dollar-plus production involved four satellite hookups, and aimed to explore if there was a common ground between the annual elite gathering in Davos and the newly-launched World Social Forum (WSF) in the southern Brazilian city. Millions of people globally were waiting for this transmission.

Since I had been in Davos in 1999, the producers requested that I make the opening statement of Porto Alegre side. I obliged with the following: "We would like to begin by condemning the arrests of peaceful demonstrators to shield the global elite at Davos from protests. We would also like to register our consternation that while we in Porto Alegre have painstakingly come up with a diverse panel of speakers, you in Davos have come up with four white males to face us. But perhaps you are trying to make a political statement."

"I was in Davos last year, and believe me, Davos is not worth a second visit. I am here in Porto Alegre this year, and let me say that Porto Alegre is the future while Davos is the past. Hemingway wrote that the rich are different from you and me, and indeed, we live on two different planets: Davos, the planet of the super rich, Porto Alegre, the planet of the poor, the marginalized, the concerned. Here in Porto Alegre, we are discussing how to save the planet. There in Davos, the global elite is discussing how to maintain its hegemony over the rest of us."

The press termed the next 90 minutes not as a debate, but as an emotional exchange that, as *The Financial Times* put it, "sometimes degenerated into personal insults." But I and other panelists—among them, Oded Grajew of Brazil's Instituto Ethos, Bernard Cassen of *Le Monde Diplomatique*, Dianne Matte of Women's Global March, Njoki Njehu of 50 Years is Enough, Rafael Alegria of Via Campesina, Aminata Traole, former minister of culture of Mali, Fred Azcarte of Jobs with Justice, Trevor Ngbane of South Africa, Francois Houtart of Belgium, and Hebe de Bonafini of the Mothers of the Plaza de Mayo—were simply reflecting the non-conciliatory mood towards the Davos crowd of most of the 12,000 who flocked to Porto Alegre.

For this constituency, a significant number of whom watched the debate at a huge auditorium at the Catholic University, globalization is a deadly business. Many undoubtedly shared the feelings of Hebe de Bonafini when she screamed at Soros across the Atlantic divide, "Mr Soros, you are a hypocrite. How many children's deaths have you been responsible for?" That Soros in the course of the debate made some utterances regarding the need to control the negative impacts of globalization hardly endeared him to this crowd, who saw him mainly as a finance speculator who had made billions of dollars at the expense of Third World economies.

The holding of the week-long World Social Forum was nothing short of a miracle. Proposed by the Workers' Party of Brazil (PT) and a coalition of Brazilian civil society organizations, supported with significant funding by donors such as Netherlands Organization for International Development Cooperation (NOVIB), and provided with strong international support by the French monthly *Le Monde Diplomatique*, and Association for the Taxation of Financial Transactions for the Aid of Citizens (ATTAC), the European anti-globalization alliance, the event was put together in less than eight months time. The idea of holding an alternative to the annual retreat of the global corporate elite in Davos simply took off. While there were some glitches here and there, the event was resoundingly successful, despite the massive challenge of coordinating 16 plenary sessions, over 400 workshops, and numerous side events.

A major reason for the WSF's success is that it had the organizational support of the government of the city of Porto Alegre and the government of the state of Rio Grande do Sul, both of which are controlled by the PT. Porto Alegre has achieved the reputation of being a city that is run both efficiently and with sensitivity to social and environmental considerations. The city is said to be at the top of the quality of life index for Brazil.

The sharing in Porto Algre focused not only on drawing up strategies of resistance to globalization but also on elaborating alternative paradigms of economic, ecological, and social development. Militant action was not absent, with Jose Bove, the celebrated French anti-McDonald's activist, and the Brazilian Movement of the Landless (MST), leading the destruction of two hectares of land planted with transgenic soybean crops by the biotechnological firm Monsanto.

Porto Alegre achieved its goal of being a counterpoint to Davos. The combination of celebration, hard discussion, and militant solidarity that flowed from it contrasted with the negative images coming out of Davos. The Swiss town was the center of Switzerland's biggest security operation since WW II. The Swiss police pulled out all the stops to prevent protestors from reaching the Alpine resort, and fired water cannons and tear gas on demonstrators in Zurich, arresting many of them. Even conservative Swiss newspapers condemned the police operation as a threat to political liberties in Switzerland.

Perhaps the outcome of the duel between Davos and Porto Alegre was best summed up by George Soros. "The excessive precautions were a victory for those who wanted to disrupt Davos. It was an overreaction. It helped to radicalize the situation."

On his performance in the televised debate with Porto Alegre, Soros commented: "it showed it is not easy to dialogue… I don't particularly like to be abused. My masochism has its limits." Observed *The Financial Times*: "Such uncomfortable experiences seem temporarily to have scrambled his ability to deliver pithy sound bites."

But Soros was not alone in flubbing his lines. Soon after my opening statement, Bernard Cassen of *Le Monde Diplomatique* leaned over and told me: "Walden, it wasn't Hemingway who said the rich are different from you and me. It was F. Scott Fitzgerald."

A

Afghanistan, 184, 185

AFL-CIO, 177, 181, 182, 187, 192

Africa. *See also individual countries*
  cattle growers in, 23
  structural adjustment programs,
    xiii, 11–12

African Development Bank, 63

Agreement Governing Activities of
  States on the Moon and
  Other Celestial Bodies, 9

Agreement on Agriculture (AOA),
  22–28
  history of, 22–24
  key provisions of, 24
  negative effects of, on Third
    World countries, 43, 213
  supposed benefits of, 41–42, 43

Agreement on Textiles and
  Clothing, 41, 42

agriculture. *See also* Agreement on
  Agriculture; food
  in European Union, 23–28
  under GATT, 22–23, 37
  in Southeast Asia, 27
  subsidies for, 23, 25, 43
  tariffs and, 24–25
  in Thailand, 21, 27
  TRIPs and, 21–22
  in United States, 22–28, 37
  Uruguay Round and, 23

Aguinaldo, Emilio, 197

aircraft industry, 14, 15, 111, 112

airline industry, 166

Aiwa, 89

Alegria, Rafael, 244

Algiers Declaration, 8–9

Allen, Paul, 167, 211

Altbach, Eric, 113

American Paddy and Rice Industry
  League, 85–86

America Online, 165

AMF. *See* Asian Monetary Fund

Amnesty International, 182

Amoco, 166

Amsden, Alice, 83

Annan, Kofi, 218, 219, 235

Antarctica, 9

AOA. *See* Agreement on Agriculture

APEC. *See* Asia-Pacific Economic
  Cooperation

Aquino, Corazon, 52–53, 198–99,
  203, 204

arbitrage, 127, 129, 168

Arco, 166

Argentina, 204

Asia. *See also* Asian financial crisis;
  East Asia; Southeast Asia;
  individual countries
  investment advisors on, 72–73
  technocrats in, 68
  tiger economies, 2, 13, 74–75, 104
  US economic expansion's effects
    on, 167–69
  US economic policy toward, 2,
    12–15, 84–88, 169

Asian Development Bank (ADB), xvii, 55, 63, 134, 233
Asian financial crisis
  academic world and, 74–75
  business press and, 71–73
  causes of, viii–ix, xiii, 66–76, 100–109, 123–25, 138–43, 160
  consequences of, 76–77, 109–10, 117–21, 157–58
  crony capitalism and, 67–69, 75
  IMF and, xii–xiv, 14–15, 54, 57, 98–100, 102, 123, 210, 237–40
  Japan's reaction to, 66, 113–14
  speculative capital and, 69–71, 75–76, 138–43, 168, 210
  US response to, xii–xiii, 110–13, 169
Asian Monetary Fund (AMF), 66, 113–14, 146, 238
Asia-Pacific Economic Cooperation (APEC), 72, 80, 86–88, 94, 109, 111, 172
Asiaweek, 71
Association for the Taxation of Financial Transactions for the Aid of Citizens (ATTAC), 245
Association of Southeast Asian Nations (ASEAN), 47, 87
Australia, 87
auto industry, 14, 15, 19, 81, 89, 109, 111, 112, 129, 165
Azcarte, Fred, 244

B
Baker, James, 88
Bangkok Land Company, 103

Bangladesh, 206
Baring Brothers, 72
Barraclough, Solon, 200
Barshefky, Charlene, 27, 35, 44, 45, 99, 111, 112, 173, 214
Basle committee, 144
beef, 23
Belgrade, 16
Bergsten, C. Fred, xv, 28, 31, 38, 86–87, 216, 217, 236
Berliner, Meir, x
Bhagwati, Jagdish, 130, 157, 239
Biggs, Barton, 134
Bin Mohamad, Mahathir, 9
biopiracy, 22
Black, Eugene R., 5
Blair, Tony, 216, 217, 235
Blair House Accord, 23
Block, John, 37
Boeing, 15, 112
Bolivia, 200
Bove, Jose, 245
Bowring, Philip, 72
BP, 166, 218
Brazil. See also Porto Alegre
  economy of, 69
  financial crisis, 124, 135
  foreign investment in, 8
  land reform in, 200
  politics of, xvii, 204
Brazilian Movement of the Landless (MST), 245
Brenner, Robert, 165, 166
Bretton Woods institutions. See International Monetary Fund; World Bank
Brown, Lester, 177, 181

Brunei, 186
Buchanan, Pat, 184, 191
Buffet, Warren, 167, 211
Buira, Ariel, 137
Burma, 205
Bush (George H.) administration,
  12, 130, 203
Bush (George W.) administration,
  237
business publications, 71–73
Byers, Stephen, 35, 214, 232

C
Camdessus, Michel, xiii, 49, 56, 113,
  211, 232
Cameroon, 241
Canada, 28, 87, 157
capital
  changing flows of, 130–35
  controls on, 117–18, 125, 145–49,
    156, 158, 160
  crises due to movement of,
    135–43
  increased mobility of, 11, 69, 124,
    125–26, 129
  speculative, 69–71, 75–76, 100,
    118, 124
capitalism
  crony, 67–69, 75, 123, 125, 160
  state-assisted, 12, 31, 80, 82–83,
    91–94, 114–17
capital punishment, 186
carbon emissions, 180
Cartagena, 16
Carten, Jeff, 112
Cassen, Bernard, 244, 246

Castro, Fidel, 200, 201
cement industry, 166
CEPAL (United Economic
  Commission for Latin America), 2
Cetes, 137
Chad, 206
Chad-Cameroon Pipeline, 241
chaebol, 104, 105, 107–8, 116
Chang, Ha-Joon, 116
Chavez, Hugo, 206
Chiang Kai-Shek, 194
Chiang Mai protests, xvii, 233
Chile, 87, 118, 146, 148, 160, 200,
  204, 239
China, 177–92
  Asian financial crisis and, 148
  campaign against trade relations
    with, 184–88, 191–92
  democracy and, 183–84
  development model of, 179–80
  differences between other
    countries and, 178–79
  in EAEG, 87
  environmental destruction in,
    180–81
  excess manufacturing capacity
    of, 129
  human rights in, 182–83
  joining WTO, 173, 177, 184–85
  land reform in, 201
  markets in, 110
  Taiwanese exports to, 88
  US posture toward, xvi, 172
  Western Poverty Project, 241
  workers' rights in, 181–82, 187
  World Bank and, 179–80
Chino, Tadao, 233

chlorofluorocarbons (CFCs), 176
Christopher, Warren, 203
Chrysler, 129, 166
Chuan Leekpai, 114
civil society organizations (CSOs),
    218, 219, 227–30, 234
Clinton, Bill, 216, 235
Clinton administration, xvii, 14, 15,
    51, 112, 130, 145, 203, 205, 239
clothing, 41, 42
CNBC, 71
CNN, 71
cocoa, 27
coconut oil, 27
coffee, 27
Cohen, Bernice, 134
Cold War, 2, 4, 13, 186
Cologne program, 161
Colombia, 200, 206
commodities, price stabilization of,
    7, 16, 18
Common Agricultural Policy
    (CAP), 23
Compensatory Financing Facility
    (CFF), 7
Comprehensive Agrarian Reform
    Program, 199
comprehensive development frame-
    work, 50–51
computer industry, 8, 20, 166
corn, 27
corporations, transnational (TNCs).
    See also individual corporations
    behavior of, 222
    as beneficiaries of economic
        globalization, xii–xiii
    crisis of, xiv–xv
    disabling, 221–22
    Global Compact and, 218
    popular distrust of, xv, 236
    TRIMs and, 37
    UN Center on, 16
Costa Rica, 52
crony capitalism, 67–69, 75, 123, 125,
    160
Cuba, 184, 200, 201
currency
    devaluation, 11, 103–4, 137–38, 141
    speculation, ix, 104, 124, 141, 168

D

Daimler Benz, 129, 166
dairy products, 22
Daly, Herman, 242
Davidson, Kenneth, 91
Davos, vii, viii, xv, 216–20, 233–34,
    235, 243–46
de Bonafini, Hebe, 244
debt
    cancellation/relief, 16, 158, 235
    crisis of early 1980s, 10, 49–50,
        132, 135, 138
    structural adjustment and, 11,
        52–53
de-colonization, 2–3
deflation, 128
de-globalization, 148, 149–51, 223–25
democracy
    China and, 183–84
    in crisis, xvii–xviii, 206–8
    CSOs and, 229
    movement toward, 204
    US policy toward, 203–7

derivatives, 127
developing countries. *See also
individual countries*
  alliances of, 30–31
  attitude of, toward WTO, 1
  debt cancellation/relief for, 16,
    158, 235
  difficulties from WTO for, 17–18,
    38–39
  farmers in, 26
  under GATT, 40, 46
  special measures for, in WTO,
    41–43
  as spectators at Uruguay
    Round, 39
  strategies for, 29–32, 46–47,
    93–96, 149–51
  under UNCTAD, 40
  wage levels in, 187
development
  oriented toward domestic
    market, 119, 149–50
  sustainable, 91–94, 120, 150
Diamond, Larry, 206, 207–8
dolphins. *See* tuna-dolphin
  controversy
Dornbusch, Rudiger, 51
Dow Jones, 71

E
East Asia. *See also* Asian financial
  crisis
  "crony capitalism" in, 68
  development strategy for, 93–96,
    117–21
  economic growth of, 79–83

  economic models of, 83–84,
    114–17
  future of, 109–10
  industrialization of, 46
  Japan and, 13, 88–91
  state-assisted capitalism in, 12, 31,
    80
  US policy toward, 13, 17, 110–13
East Asia Economic Group (EAEG),
  87–88, 90, 94
The East Asian Miracle (World
  Bank), 75, 84
Eastern Europe, 50, 157
eco-labeling, 174–75
Economic Development
  Corporation (EDCOR), 197
The Economist, 156, 158
Ecuador, 200
The Edge of Chaos (Cohen), 134
Elliot, Dorinda, 72
Elliot, Larry, 165
El Salvador, 200
emerging markets
  financial crises in, 129
  fund managers, 134, 142–43
  mutual funds, 133–35
environmental issues, 92, 120, 150,
  170–76, 180–81, 229, 241–42
EPG (eminent persons' group), 80,
  86–87
ERM (exchange rate mechanism)
  crisis, 135
ESAF. *See* extended structural
  adjustment facility
Estrada, Joseph, 67, 160, 199, 208
European Union (EU)
  agriculture in, 23–28, 43

output gap of, 129
position of, on global financial
    reform, 145
role of, in WTO, 28, 36
trade rivalries with US, 17
Export Enhancement Program, 23
extended structural adjustment facil-
    ity (ESAF), xii, 52, 211–12, 240
Exxon, 166

F
Falklands War, 204
Fallows, James, 74
Far Eastern Economic Review, 71
The Financial Times, 156
Firestone, xv
Fischer, Stanley, 56, 70, 100, 113, 123,
    124
Fischler, Franz, 27
food
    consumption per country, 181
    dumping, 42
    imports, 41, 42
Food First, 61
Ford, xv, 129
foreign aid, 3, 5, 6
foreign investment. *See* capital
Forum of the Poor, 120–21, 233
Fox, Justin, 133
France, 145, 201
freedom, concept of, 212
Freedom from Debt Coalition, 53
Freedom House, 204
Friedman, Thomas, 160, 183
Fujimori, Alberto, 206
Fukuyama, Francis, 212
Fulbright, J. William, 186

G
Garten, Jeff, 15, 169
Gates, Bill, 167, 211, 216, 235
GATS (General Agreement on
    Trade in Services), 18
GATT (General Agreement on
    Trade and Tariffs). *See also*
    Uruguay Round
    agriculture under, 22–23, 37
    decision making in, 28, 43–44
    developing countries under, 40,
        46
    expansion of, 17
    trade expansion under, 36
    transition to WTO from, 17, 36
    tuna-dolphin controversy, 170,
        171
genetically modified organisms,
    xv, 227
Geneva WTO ministerial, 29
George, Susan, 61
Germany, 19, 145, 161
global warming, 180, 236
Goldman Sachs, 127, 130
Grajew, Oded, 244
Gray, John, 222, 225
Great Britain, 19, 126
Great Depression, 130, 131
Green, Duncan, 132
green protectionism, 174–75
Greenspan, Alan, 117, 130
Group of Seven (G-7), 50, 54, 57,
    60, 132, 144–45, 161, 212, 234, 235
Group of 77, 3, 6, 7
GSP (General System of
    Preferences), 40, 85, 107
Guatemala, 200

H

Hague protests, 236
Haiti, 205
Hardie, Robert, 197
Havel, Vaclav, 234, 242
hedge funds, 62, 69, 72, 127, 141–42,
    144, 145, 161, 168
Heritage Foundation, 9
high tech industry, 20
Hino, 109
Hoffa, James, 191
Hong Kong, 71, 80, 85, 101, 134, 138
Houtart, Francois, 244
Huntington, Samuel, 74
Hyundai, 105

I

IBM, 8, 106
IBRD. *See* International Bank for
    Reconstruction and Development
IDA. *See* International Development
    Association
IMF. *See* International Monetary
    Fund
income distribution, 92, 150, 166,
    167, 189, 211
Independent Commission on
    Global Governance, 17
India
    agriculture in, 21
    Asian financial crisis and, 148
    at Davos, viii
    labor costs in, 187
    leather tanning in, 174, 175
    at Seattle WTO ministerial,
        44–45

Indonesia
    aircraft industry in, 14, 15, 111, 112
    currency devaluation in, 104
    debt of, 158
    democratic transition in, 206
    destruction of communities in,
        93
    economic growth of, 80–81
    foreign investment in, 140
    poverty in, 238
    product specialization in, 89
    recent IMF program for, 14–15,
        55, 56–57, 98, 112, 114
    rice farmers in, 27
    on Special 301 watch list, 85
    structural adjustment and, 13, 54
industrialization, 18–20, 46
Information Technology Agreement
    (ITA), 173
Institute of International
    Economics, 38, 86, 216
Institute of International
    Finance, 140
Integrated Program for
    Commodities (IPC), 7, 16, 37
Intel, 20
Inter-American Development
    Bank, 12, 63
International Bank for
    Reconstruction and Development
    (IBRD), 4, 5
International Development
    Association (IDA), 5
International Finance Corporation
    (IFC), 133
International Labor
    Organization, 47

International Monetary Fund (IMF)
accountability of, 56
AMF and, 113
Asian financial crisis and, xii–xiv,
14–15, 54, 69, 98–100, 102, 109,
111–12, 114, 123, 210, 237–40
capital account liberalization
and, 133
Compensatory Financing Facility
and, 7
corporate-owned media's
presentation of, viii
crisis of legitimacy for, 45–46, 54,
190, 210–12, 237–40, 242
decision making in, 44, 235
decommissioning, 57–58, 64–65,
147–48, 190, 220–21
domination of, by rich
countries, 28
evolution of mission of, 4
as guardian of new economic
order, xi–xii
managing director of, xiii, 49
Meltzer Report on, 59–65, 237
origins of, 4
overloading, 30
poverty reduction and,
49, 55, 240
proposed expansion of
powers of, 145
protests against, xvii, 233, 234
recent actions of, 55–57
reforming, 57–58, 64–65, 146–47,
190, 220–21
structural adjustment programs,
xiii, 10–12, 14–15, 49–51, 62, 80,
83, 111, 132, 136, 210–12, 239–40
US role in, xii, 15
as watchdog of Third World's
economies, 2
International Trade Organization
(ITO), 17, 37
Internet stocks, overvaluation of,
164
investment advisors, 72–73
investment banks, 127
IPC. See Integrated Program for
Commodities
Iran, 186, 204
Iraq, 185
Isuzu, 109

J
Japan
Asian financial crisis and, 66, 101,
113–14, 146
EAEG and, 87–88, 90
East and Southeast Asia and, 13,
88–91, 138
economic growth of, 80
excluding from Asian economic
bloc, 95
industrialization of, 19
land reform in, 195
Ministry of Industry (MITT), 83
output gap of, 129
Plaza Accord and, 88, 101, 138
position of, on global financial
reform, 144–45, 161–62
regionalization of economy of,
88–91
relationship with US, 17, 84, 111,
161, 172
role of, in WTO, 28, 36

Jensen, Derrick, viii
Johnson, Chalmers, xii, 183

K
Kanbur, Ravi, 236
Kantor, Mickey, 31, 173
Kayotha, Bamrung 233
Kessler, Timothy, 133
Keynes, John Maynard, 4, 147
Kim Dae-jung, 114
Kirkpatrick, Jeane, 204
Knight, Phil, 216, 235
Koehler, Horst, 234, 242
Kosovo, vii, 185
Kroszner, Randall, 129
Krugman, Paul, 156
Kuhn, Thomas, 64
Kuwait, 8

L
labor. *See also* AFL-CIO
    attitudes toward, by country,
        181–82
    structural adjustment and, 11
    unrestricted flow of, 210
Lafontaine, Oskar, 145, 161
Lake, Anthony, 203
land reform, 119, 150, 194–202
Landsdale, Edward, 197

A Language Older Than Words
    (Jensen), viii
Laos, 184

Latin America. *See also individual
    countries*
    capital flows into, 131, 133,
        134, 168
    financial crises, 135
    import substitution in, 31
    land reform in, 200
    Mercosur in, 47
    structural adjustment in, xiii, 12
Law of the Sea Treaty, 9
Lazare, Daniel, 182
least developed countries
    (LDCs), 167
leather tanning, 174, 175
Leeson, Nick, 72
Le Monde Diplomatique, 244,
    245, 246
leveraged buyouts, 128
LG Electronics, 105
life forms, patenting, 21–22, 213
Lindsay, Charles, 52
Lindsey, Lawrence, 162
Lissakers, Karin, 131
Long-Term Capital Management,
    69, 70, 144
Lundberg, Mattias, 239
Luxemburg, Rosa, xviii

M
MacArthur, Douglas, 195, 197
Madagascar, 22
Magsaysay, Ramon, 197
Mahathir, Mohamad, 67, 76, 88, 95,
    117, 146, 156
MAI. *See* Multilateral Agreement on
    Investment

Malaysia
  capital controls in, 148, 156, 160
  car project of, 14, 15, 19, 81, 111
  currency devaluation in, 104
  destruction of communities
    in, 93
  economic growth of, 80–81
  foreign investment in, 140
  industrialization of, 19
  palm-oil plantations in, 27
  product specialization in, 89
  rice farmers in, 27
  shrimp industry in, 171
  2020 plan and, 87
  unions in, 181
Marcos, Ferdinand, 52, 72, 198,
  203, 204
Marrakech accord, 31, 39, 41, 42, 184
mass actions. *See* protests
Matsushita, 89
Matte, Dianne, 244
McNamara, Robert, 6, 10, 198
medicines, 8, 21–22
Melbourne protests, xvii, 233–34
Meltzer, Alan, xiv, 60, 237
Meltzer Commission, xiv, 60–65,
  215–16, 237, 240–42
Merck, 22
Mercosur, 47
mergers and acquisitions, 165, 166
Merrill Lynch, 127
Merriwether, John, 70
Mexico
  financial crisis, 103, 135–38
  foreign investment in, 8, 133, 168
  labor in, 186
  NAFTA and, 157

structural adjustment and, 136
  2020 plan and, 87
  unions in, 181
Microsoft, xv, 20, 165, 211
military
  power, US, xvi
  regimes, 207
Milken, Michael, 128
Mitsubishi, xv, 19, 81, 89, 109, 221
Miyazawa, Kiichi, 161
Miyazawa Plan, 55, 66, 161
Mobil, 166
Monsanto, xv, 21, 213, 221, 245
Montreal Protocol, 176
Moon Treaty, 9
Moore, Michael, 28, 45, 235
Morgan Stanley, 134
"most favored nation" status, 18
multifiber agreement (MFA), 42
Multilateral Agreement on
  Investment (MAI), 31
Murdoch, Rupert, 71

N
Nader, Ralph, xiv, 213, 214
NAFTA (North American Free Trade
  Agreement), 86, 157
Naiman, Robert, 232
Nairobi, 7, 16
National Endowment for
  Democracy (NED), 205
National Power Corporation
  (Philippines), 55, 161
"national treatment" principle, 18
natural resources, 9
Neiss, Hubert, 56

Netherlands Organization for
   International Development
   Cooperation (NOVIB), 245
Netscape, 165
New International Economic Order
   (NIEO), 3, 6, 9, 16, 29, 39
Newly Industrializing Countries
   (NICs), 12–16
   economic models of, 83–84
   free market explanation of, 80
   under GATT, 46
   increasing stresses on, 74
   state-assisted capitalism and,
      82–83, 91–94
   trade regulations of, 19, 31
New Zealand, 87
Ngbane, Trevor, 244
NGOs. *See* non-governmental
   organizations
Nicaragua, 200
NICs. *See* Newly Industrializing
   Countries
NIEO. *See* New International
   Economic Order
Niger, 206
Nigeria, 186, 221
Nike, xv, 216, 218, 235
Nissan, 89, 166
Nixon, Richard, 4, 125
Njehu, Njoki, 244
Non-Aligned Movement, 3, 8–9, 29
non-governmental organizations
   (NGOs), 30, 31, 35, 211, 216, 219,
   227–30, 240
North American Free Trade
   Agreement. *See* NAFTA
North Korea, 184
Novartis, xv, 213, 218, 221

O
OECD (Organization for Economic
   Cooperation and Development),
   26, 31, 43, 136
oil industry, xv, 8, 166. *See also*
   OPEC
Okazaki, Hisahiko, 90
OPEC (Organization of Petroleum
   Exporting Countries), 3, 6–7, 8–9,
   126, 131, 132
Opus Dei, 227
Organization for Economic Co-
   operation and Development. *See*
   OECD
Organization of Petroleum
   Exporting Countries. *See* OPEC
output gap, 129
over-capacity, 129, 166–67

P
packaging laws, 174
Pakistan, xvii, 171, 186, 204, 206
palm oil, 27
parachute journalism, 72
Paschke, Karl Theodor, 17
patents
   duration of, 20
   on life forms, 21–22
Payer, Cheryl, 61
pension funds, 127, 128
permanent normal trading relations
   (PNTR), 177, 184
Peru, 200, 206, 208
Pfaff, William, 207
pharmaceutical industry, 8, 9, 21–22
Philippines
   currency devaluation in, 104

destruction of communities
  in, 93
foreign investment in, 140, 160
land reform in, 196–99, 202
medicinal plants in, 22
political system of, xvii, 204, 207,
  208
product specialization in, 89
recent IMF program for, 55
shrimp industry, 171
structural adjustment and, 52–54
Plaza Accord, 88, 101, 138
political action committees
  (PACs), 68
polyarchy, 205–7
Porto Alegre, vii, 243–46
poverty
  ADB and, 55
  IMF and, 49, 55
  number of people living in, 167,
    211
  World Bank's program for, 6, 63,
    64–65
Prague protests, xvii, 209, 234
Prebisch, Raul, 2–3
product defects, xv
Prosterman, Roy, 198
protests, 231–36, 243–46. See also
  individual locations
Proton Saga, 14, 81, 111

Q
Quantum Fund, 104

R
Ramos, Fidel, 53, 199
Reagan administration, 10–12, 130,
  180, 203, 204
Renault, 166
rice, 27, 85–86
Rich, Bruce, 61
Rio Tinto, 218, 221
Robinson, William, 206
Rochat, Florain, 243
Rodrik, Dani, 147, 149
Roth, Stanley, 203
Roxas, Manuel, 197
rubber, 7
Rubin, Robert, xiii, 67, 69, 124, 130,
  161
Ruggiero, Renato, 28
Russia, 50, 68–69, 124, 135, 144, 157,
  201. See also Soviet Union

S
Sachs, Jeffrey, 50, 57, 58, 98–99, 136,
  157, 239
Sakakibara, Eisuke, 113
Saker, Neil, 73
Samsung, 105
SAPs. See structural adjustment
  programs
Saudi Arabia, 8, 186
savings and loan debacle (US), 135
Schultz, George, 238
Schwab, Klaus, 216
Seattle WTO ministerial, vii, xiv,
  xvii, 31, 35, 43, 212–14, 231–32
securitization, 127
Serbia-Montenegro, 184

Shell, xv, 218, 221
Shilling, Gary, 166
shock therapy, 50
shrimp-turtle controversy, 170–76
Singapore, 80, 85, 89, 92, 181, 186, 187
Singapore WTO ministerial, 29, 44, 173
Singson, Gabriel, 156
Smith, Adam, 143, 209, 222
Solarz, Stephen, 203
Soros, George, 70, 104, 158, 168, 234, 238, 243, 244, 245–46
South Africa, 23, 181, 205
South Asian Association for Regional Development (SAARC), 47
Southeast Asia. *See also* Asian financial crisis
  agriculture in, 27
  ASEAN, 47, 87
  future of, 109–10
  industrialization of, 46
  Japan and, 13, 88–91
  as market for South Korea, 88
  state-assisted capitalism in, 12, 31
  trade liberalization in, 13–14
Southern Africa Development Coordination Conference (SADCC), 47
Southern Cone financial crisis, 135
South Korea
  democracy movement in, 204
  in EAEG, 87
  economic growth of, 104–5
  financial crisis in, 105–9
  foreign investment in, 140

income distribution in, 92
industrialization of, 19, 20, 83
Japan and, 101, 105–6, 138
land reform in, 194, 195–96
recent IMF program for, 57, 99–100, 109, 112, 114
structural adjustment and, 13, 15, 54
US economic policy toward, 84–85, 106–8, 111, 172
wage levels in, 187
Soviet Union, 4, 8. *See also* Russia
soybeans, 56
special and differential treatment (SDT), 40–41
Special 301 sanctions, 85, 107, 172, 173
Special UN Fund for Economic Development. *See* SUNFED
Squire, Lyn, 239
Sri Lanka, 206
stagflation, 126
Star Television, 71
state-assisted capitalism, 12, 31, 80, 82–83, 91–94, 114–17
State Law and Order Restoration Council (SLORC), 205
Stiglitz, Joseph, 55, 236
structural adjustment program review initiative (SAPRI), 51, 211
structural adjustment programs (SAPs), 10–12, 49–54, 62, 80, 83, 111, 132, 136, 210–12, 239–40. *See also individual countries*
structuralism, 3
Sudan, 185
sugar, 7, 22, 27

Suharto, 114, 115, 117, 241
Summers, Larry, xii, 49, 54, 56,
    58, 123, 156, 157, 160, 161, 162,
    212, 237, 240
SUNFED (Special UN Fund for
    Economic Development), 5
Supachai Panitchpakdi, 1, 28
Super 301 sanctions, 85, 172, 173
sustainable development, 91–94,
    120, 150
Sweeney, John, 177
Switzerland. *See* Davos
Syngman, Rhee, 194

T
Taiwan, 82–83, 85, 88, 92, 101, 138,
    184, 187, 194–96
tariffication, 24
tariffs
    agricultural, 24–25
    lowering industrial, 18
    preferential, for developing
        countries, 3, 7, 40
taxes
    regressive vs. progressive, 118, 149
    Tobin, 118, 130, 145–46, 158, 235
technology
    diffusion of, 19–20, 95
    transfer, 175
"tequila effect," 135
Tesebonos, 137
Texas Instruments, 20
textiles, 41, 42, 85, 174
Thailand
    agriculture in, 21, 27, 85–86
    Chiang Mai protests, xvii, 233

currency devaluation in,
    103–4, 141–42
at Davos, viii
debt of, 158
destruction of communities
    in, 92–93
economic growth of, 80–82
economy of, in
    December 1996, 73
environmental issues and,
    92, 174, 175
finance companies in, 70
financial crisis in, 138–43
foreign investment in, 101–3,
    139–40
income distribution in, 92
land reform in, 200
poverty in, 238
product specialization in, 89
recent IMF program for, 14, 55,
    57, 98–99, 111–12, 114
shrimp industry in, 170–71
on Special 301 watch list, 85–86
structural adjustment and, 13, 54
2020 plan and, 87
Thatcher, Margaret, 126, 180
Tienanmen massacre, 182, 191
Time-Warner, 71, 165
tin, 7
TNCs. *See* corporations,
    transnational
Tobin tax, 118, 130, 145–46, 158, 235
Toyota, 89, 109
trade liberalization, 13–14, 56–57, 87,
    111, 126, 162
Traole, Aminata, 244

TRIMs (Trade Related Investment
Measures) agreement, 19, 37, 213
TRIPs (Trade Related Intellectual
Property Rights) agreement, 19–22,
37–38, 213
Truman administration, 17
tuna-dolphin controversy, 170, 171,
172
Turkey, 52, 206
turtles. *See* shrimp-turtle controversy
2020 plan, 87, 90

U
UNCTAD (UN Conference on
Trade and Development)
curtailing of scope of, 16–17, 39
establishment of, 6
global reform strategy of, 3, 29
international trade rules and,
7, 37
protest at tenth assembly of, 232
rise of OPEC and, 6–7
special consideration for
developing countries under,
40, 47
structuralism and, 3
Trade and Development Report,
30, 128
UNESCO, 9
unilateralism, 31, 84, 87–88, 111, 172,
173, 178, 185, 191–92
United Economic Commission for
Latin America. *See* CEPAL
United Fruit Company, 200

United Nations. *See also* UNCTAD
Center on Transnational
Corporations, 16
Commission for Africa, 11
Conference on Environment and
Development, 176
Development Program (UNDP),
3, 5, 16, 30
Economic and Social Council
(ECOSOC), 3, 16
Food and Agriculture
Organization (FAO), 181
General Assembly, 3, 6, 9, 16, 28
Global Compact, 218
Office of Internal Oversight
Services, 17
preserving legitimacy of, 29
right-wing criticism of, 9–10
Special Fund, 5
structuralism and, 3
SUNFED, 5
as vehicle for southern agenda,
9–10, 16–17, 29–30
United States
agriculture in, 22–28, 37, 43,
85–86
AMF and, 113
Asian economic policy of,
xii–xiii, 2, 12–15, 84–88, 106–8,
110–13, 169
China and, xvi, 177–92
during Cold War, 4
consumption levels in, 181
corporate power of, xi
economic expansion of, 164–65,
167–69

excluding from Asian economic
bloc, 95
expansion of GATT and, 17
greenhouse gas emissions by, 180,
236
ideological power of, xvii–xviii
income distribution in, 166
industrialization of, 19
land reform and, 194–98,
200, 201
moral record of, 186
NAFTA and, 157
OPEC's effect on, 8
policy of, toward
democratization, 203–7
popular distrust of corporations
in, xv, 236
position of, on global financial
reform, 144–45, 162
relationship with Japan, 17, 84,
111, 161
role of, in WTO, 28
in selection of WTO director
general, 1, 28–29
shrimp-turtle controversy, 170–76
strategic power of, xv–xvi
SUNFED resisted by, 5
technology diffusion and, 20
trade rivalries with Europe, 17
transnational corporations and,
xii–xiii
2020 plan and, 87
UN development system
dismantled by, 16–17
unilateral actions by, 13–14, 84,
87–88, 111, 172, 173, 178, 185

Uruguay Round
agriculture included in, 23
containment of developing
countries by, 1–2
GATS and, 18
role of developing countries
in, 39
transition from GATT to
WTO, 17
US role in, 37, 111
US Agency for International
Development (USAID), 198

V
Venezuela, 8, 200, 206, 208
Vietnam, 6, 125, 179, 184, 186
Volcker, Paul, 132
Volvo, 129

W
wage levels, 187
Walters, Maxine, 54, 212
Washington, protests in, xvii, 215,
233
Whalley, John, 42
wheat, 26–27, 56
White, Harry Dexter, 4
Williamson, John, 50
Winters, Jeffrey, 142–43
Wolf, Martin, 216, 227
Wolfensohn, James, xiv, 51, 55,
61, 211, 215, 219, 234, 237, 240,
241, 242
Workers' Party of Brazil, 244

World Bank
  in the 1950s, 2
  in the 1970s, 6
  in the 1980s and early 1990s,
    10–12
  abolishing, 64–65, 190, 220–21
  accountability of, 56
  Asian economies and, 75
  capital account liberalization
    and, 133
  China and, 179–80
  comprehensive development
    framework, 50–51
  crisis of legitimacy for, 190, 242
  decision making in, 44, 235
  domination of, by rich
    countries, 28
  evolution of mission of, 4
  failure rate of, 63, 240–41
  as guardian of new economic
    order, xii
  International Development
    Association and, 5
  land reform and, 198
  leadership of, xiv
  Meltzer Report on, xiv, 59–61,
    63–65, 215–16, 237, 240–42
  poverty reduction and, 63, 64–65
  protests against, xvii, 233, 234
  reforming, 64–65, 146–47, 190,
    220–21
  structural adjustment programs,
    10–12, 49–50, 80, 83, 111, 132,
    136
  US support of, xii
World Economic Forum, vii, xvii,
  216, 233–34, 243

world financial authority
  (WFA), 143, 147
World Resources Institute, 53
World Social Forum (WSF), vii, 243,
  244–45
World Trade Organization (WTO).
  See also Uruguay Round
  abolishing, 147–48, 190, 220–21
  birth of, xi, 36–38
  China joining, 173, 177, 184–85
  crisis of legitimacy for, 45–46,
    190, 232
  decision making within, 28–29,
    43–45, 213, 235
  developing countries' attitude
    toward, xiv, 1
  difficulties for developing
    countries from, 17–18, 38–39
  domination of, by a few
    countries, 28–29
  Geneva ministerial, 29
  industrialization in the South
    and, 17–20
  overloading, 30
  popular movements against,
    xiv, 231–32
  reforming, 29–32, 45–47, 146–47,
    190, 220–21
  Seattle ministerial, vii, xiv, xvii,
    31, 35, 43, 212–14, 231–32
  selection of director general of,
    1, 28–29
  shrimp-turtle controversy, 170
  Singapore ministerial, 29, 44, 173
  special measures for developing
    countries in, 41–43
  transition from GATT to, 17

transnational corporations
  benefiting from, xii
  UNCTAD rendered impotent by,
  17–18
  US support of and influence on,
  xii, 36–38, 173
World War II, 130
W.R. Grace, 21
Wriston, Walter, 131

Y
Yemen, 186

Z
Zambia, 57, 206
Zia, Muhammad, 204
Zimbabwe, 181

FOOD FIRST BOOKS OF RELATED INTEREST

Views from the South:
The Effects of Globalization and the WTO on Third World Countries
Foreword by Jerry Mander
Afterword by Anuradha Mittal
Edited by Sarah Anderson
   This rare collection of essays by Third World activists and scholars describes in pointed detail the effects of the WTO and other Bretton Woods institutions.   Paperback, $12.95

America Needs Human Rights
Edited by Anuradha Mittal and Peter Rosset
   This new anthology includes writings on understanding human rights, poverty in America, and welfare reform and human rights.
   Paperback, $13.95

The Paradox of Plenty: Hunger in a Bountiful World
Edited by Douglas H. Boucher
   Excerpts from Food First's best writings on world hunger and what we can do to change it.   Paperback, $18.95

A Siamese Tragedy: Development and Disintegration in Modern Thailand
Walden Bello, Shea Cunningham, and Li Kheng Poh
   Critiques the failing economic system that has propelled the Thai people down an unsustainable path.   Paperback, $19.95

Basta! Land and the Zapatista Rebellion in Chiapas
Revised edition
George A. Collier with Elizabeth Lowery Quaratiello
Foreword by Peter Rosset
   The classic on the Zapatista in a new revised edition, including a preface by Roldolfo Stavenhagen, a new epilogue about the present challenges to the indigenous movement in Chiapas, and an updated bibliography.   Paperback, $14.95

Benedita da Silva: An Afro-Brazilian Woman's Story of Politics and Love
As told to Medea Benjamin and Maisa Mendonça
Foreword by Jesse Jackson
   Afro-Brazilian Senator Benedita da Silva shares the inspiring story of her life as an advocate for the rights of women and the poor.
   Paperback, $15.95

Breakfast of Biodiversity: The Truth about Rain Forest Destruction
John Vandermeer and Ivette Perfecto
   Analyzes deforestation from both an environmental and social justice perspective.   Paperback, $16.95

Dark Victory: The U.S. and Global Poverty
Walden Bello, with Shea Cunningham and Bill Rau
Second edition, with a new epilogue by the author
   Offers an understanding of why poverty has deepened in many countries, and analyzes the impact of US economic policies.
   Paperback, $14.95

Dragons in Distress: Asia's Miracle Economies in Crisis
Walden Bello and Stephanie Rosenfeld
   After three decades of rapid growth, the economies of South Korea, Taiwan, and Singapore are in crisis. The authors offer policy recommendations to break these countries from their unhealthy dependence on Japan and the US.   Paperback, $12.95

Kerala: Radical Reform as Development in an Indian State
Revised edition
Richard W. Franke and Barbara H. Chasin
   In the last eighty years, the Indian state of Kerala has experimented in the use of radical reform that has brought it some of the Third World's highest levels of health, education, and social justice.
   Paperback, $10.95

Needless Hunger: Voices from a Bangladesh Village
James Boyce and Betsy Hartmann
     The global analysis of Food First is vividly captured here in a single village.   Paperback, $6.95

A Quiet Violence: View from a Bangladesh Village
Betsy Hartmann and James Boyce
     The root causes of hunger emerge through the stories of both village landowners and peasants who live at the margin of survival.
     Paperback, $17.95

Video: *The Greening of Cuba*
Directed by Jaime Kibben
     Cuba has combined time-tested traditional methods with cutting edge bio-technology, reminding us that developed and developing nations can choose a healthier environment and still feed their people.
     VHS videotape, $29.95.

Write or call our distributor to place book orders. All orders must be pre-paid. Please add $4.50 for the first book and $1.50 for each additional book for shipping and handling.

LPC Group
1436 West Randolph Street
Chicago, IL 60607
(800) 243-0138
www.coolbooks.com

ABOUT FOOD FIRST

(Institute for Food and Development Policy)

Food First, also known as the Institute for Food and Development Policy, is a nonprofit research and education-for-action center dedicated to investigating and exposing the root causes of hunger in a world of plenty. It was founded in 1975 by Frances Moore Lappé, author of the bestseller *Diet for a Small Planet*, and food policy analyst Dr. Joseph Collins. Food First research has revealed that hunger is created by concentrated economic and political power, not by scarcity. Resources and decision-making are in the hands of a wealthy few, depriving the majority of land, jobs, and therefore food.

Hailed by *The New York Times* as "one of the most established food think tanks in the country," Food First has grown to profoundly shape the debate about hunger and development.

But Food First is more than a think tank. Through books, reports, videos, media appearances, and speaking engagements, Food First experts not only reveal the often hidden roots of hunger, they show how individuals can get involved in bringing an end to the problem. Food First inspires action by bringing to light the courageous efforts of people around the world who are creating farming and food systems that truly meet people's needs.

HOW TO BECOME A MEMBER OR
INTERN OF FOOD FIRST

BECOME A MEMBER OF FOOD FIRST

Private contributions and membership gifts form the financial base of Food First/Institute for Food and Development Policy. The success of the Institute's programs depends not only on its dedicated volunteers and staff, but on financial activists as well. Each member strengthens Food First's efforts to change a hungry world. We invite you to join Food First. As a member you will receive a twenty percent discount on all Food First books. You will also receive our quarterly publication, *Food First News and Views*, and timely *Backgrounders* that provide information and suggestions for action on current food and hunger crises in the United States and around the world. If you want to subscribe to our internet newsletter, *Food Rights Watch*, send us an e-mail at foodfirst@foodfirst.org. All contributions are tax-deductible.

BECOME AN INTERN FOR FOOD FIRST

There are opportunities for interns in research, advocacy, campaigning, publishing, computers, media, and publicity at Food First. Our interns come from around the world. They are a vital part of our organization and make our work possible.

To become a member or apply to become an intern, just call, visit our web site, or clip and return the attached coupon to

Food First/Institute for Food and Development Policy
398 60th Street, Oakland, CA 94618, USA
Phone: (510) 654-4400 Fax: (510) 654-4551
E-mail: foodfirst@foodfirst.org
Web site: www.foodfirst.org

You are also invited to give a gift membership to others interested in the fight to end hunger.

JOINING FOOD FIRST

❑ I want to join Food First and receive a 20% discount on this and all subsequent orders. Enclosed is my tax-deductible contribution of:

❑ $35   ❑ $50   ❑ $100   ❑ $500   ❑ $1,000   ❑ OTHER

NAME _____

ADDRESS _____

CITY/STATE/ZIP _____

DAYTIME PHONE (_____) _____

E-MAIL _____

ORDERING FOOD FIRST MATERIALS

ITEM DESCRIPTION	QTY	UNIT COST	TOTAL

PAYMENT METHOD:

❑ CHECK

❑ MONEY ORDER

❑ MASTERCARD

❑ VISA

MEMBER DISCOUNT, 20% $ _____

CA RESIDENTS SALES TAX 8.25% $ _____

SUBTOTAL $ _____

POSTAGE: 15%   UPS: 20%   ($2 MIN.) $ _____

MEMBERSHIP(S) $ _____

ADDITIONAL CONTRIBUTION $ _____

TOTAL ENCLOSED $ _____

_____
NAME ON CARD

_____
CARD NUMBER   EXP. DATE

_____
SIGNATURE

MAKE CHECK OR MONEY ORDER PAYABLE TO:

Food First, 398 - 60th Street, Oakland, CA 94618